Lecture Notes in Computer Science   12165

More information about this series at http://www.springer.com/series/7408

Wolfgang Ahrendt · Heike Wehrheim (Eds.)

Tests and Proofs

14th International Conference, TAP 2020
Held as Part of STAF 2020
Bergen, Norway, June 22–23, 2020
Proceedings

 Springer

Editors
Wolfgang Ahrendt (ID)
Chalmers University of Technology
Gothenburg, Sweden

Heike Wehrheim (ID)
Paderborn University
Paderborn, Germany

ISSN 0302-9743   ISSN 1611-3349   (electronic)
Lecture Notes in Computer Science
ISBN 978-3-030-50994-1   ISBN 978-3-030-50995-8   (eBook)
https://doi.org/10.1007/978-3-030-50995-8

LNCS Sublibrary: SL2 – Programming and Software Engineering

This Springer imprint is published by the registered company Springer Nature Switzerland AG
The registered company address is: Gewerbestrasse 11, 6330 Cham, Switzerland

Preface

This volume contains the papers accepted for the 14 International Conference on Tests and Proofs (TAP 2020), originally to be held during June 22–23, 2020, in Bergen, Norway, as part of Software Technologies: Applications and Foundations (STAF), a federation of some of Europe's leading conferences on software technologies. Due to the outbreak of the corona virus pandemic, STAF and TAP had to be postponed and will be held 2021. The TAP conference promotes research in verification and formal methods that targets the interplay of proofs and testing: the advancement of techniques of each kind and their combination, with the ultimate goal of improving software and system dependability. Research in verification has recently seen a steady convergence of heterogeneous techniques and a synergy between the traditionally distinct areas of testing (and dynamic analysis) and of proving (and static analysis). Formal techniques for counter-example generation based on, for example, symbolic execution, SAT/SMT-solving, or model checking, furnish evidence for the potential of a combination of test and proof. The combination of predicate abstraction with testing-like techniques based on exhaustive enumeration opens the perspective for novel techniques of proving correctness. On the practical side, testing offers cost-effective debugging techniques of specifications or crucial parts of program proofs (such as invariants). Last but not least, testing is indispensable when it comes to the validation of the underlying assumptions of complex system models involving hardware or system environments. Over the years, there is growing acceptance in research communities that testing and proving are complementary rather than mutually exclusive techniques. TAP takes this insight one step further, and puts the spotlight on combinations (understood in a broad sense) of the complementary techniques.

TAP 2020 received 20 submissions out of which we accepted 10 papers after reviewing and discussion with the Program Committee (PC) members, with 2 tool papers and 1 short paper. The submissions came from the following countries (in alphabetical order): Austria, Canada, Czech Republic, France, Germany, Italy, Japan, The Netherlands, Portugal, Russia, Singapore, Spain, Sudan, Sweden, Tunisia, the UK, and the USA. We thank the PC members and reviewers for doing an excellent job!

For the second time, TAP featured an artifact evaluation (AE) and three papers were awarded with AE badges. We thank the AE chairs Daniel Dietsch (University of Freiburg, Germany) and Marie-Christine Jakobs (TU Darmstadt, Germany) for organizing artifact submission and evaluation, and the AE Committee members for thoroughly evaluating all artifacts.

This volume also contains two short abstracts: an abstract of the talk of our invited speaker Mohammad Mousavi (University of Leicester, UK) on "Conformance Testing of Cyber-Physical Systems: From Formal Foundations to Automotive Applications," and an abstract of our invited tutorial on Runtime Verification by Martin Leucker (University of Lübeck, Germany). Both invited talk and invited tutorial are planned to be given next year. We thank the organizing team of STAF in Bergen, in particular

Adrian Rutle who had to deal with a very difficult situation. We also thank Alfred Hofmann and his publication team at Springer for their support.

We hope that you will enjoy reading the volume.

May 2020

Wolfgang Ahrendt
Heike Wehrheim

Organization

Program Committee

Wolfgang Ahrendt (PC Chair)	Chalmers University of Technology, Sweden
Heike Wehrheim (PC Chair)	University of Paderborn, Germany
Bernhard Beckert	Karlsruhe Institute of Technology, Germany
Dirk Beyer	LMU Munich, Germany
Jasmin Blanchette	Vrije Universiteit Amsterdam, The Netherlands
Koen Claessen	Chalmers University of Technology, Sweden
Brijesh Dongol	University of Surrey, UK
Catherine Dubois	ENSIIE, France
Gordon Fraser	University of Passau, Germany
Chantal Keller	LRI, Université Paris-Sud, France
Nikolai Kosmatov	CEA, France
Martin Leucker	University of Lübeck, Germany
Karl Meinke	KTH Royal Institute of Technology, Sweden
Stephan Merz	Inria Nancy, France
Corina Pasareanu	CMU/NASA, USA
François Pessaux	ENSTA ParisTech, France
Alexandre Petrenko	CRIM, Canada
Jan Tretmans	TNO - Embedded Systems Innovation, The Netherlands

Artifact Evaluation Committee (AEC)

Daniel Dietsch (AEC Chair)	University of Freiburg, Germany
Marie-Christine Jakobs (AEC Chair)	TU Darmstadt, Germany
Sadegh Dalvandi	University of Surrey, UK
Simon Dierl	TU Dortmund, Germany
Mathias Fleury	Johannes Kepler University Linz, Austria
Ákos Hajdu	Budapest University of Technology and Economics, Hungary
Marcel Hark	RWTH Aachen University, Germany
Sven Linker	The University of Liverpool, UK
Marco Muñiz	Aalborg University, Denmark
Kostiantyn Potomkin	The Australian National University, Australia
Virgile Robles	CEA, France
Martin Sachenbacher	University of Lübeck, Germany
Christian Schilling	IST Austria, Austria

Steering Committee

Bernhardt K. Aichernig	TU Graz, Austria
Achim D. Brucker	University of Sheffield, UK
Catherine Dubois (Chair)	ENSIIE, France
Martin Gogolla	University of Bremen, Germany
Nikolai Kosmatov	CEA, France
Burkhart Wolff	LRI, France

Additional Reviewers

Avellaneda, Florent
Blanchard, Allan
Khosrowjerdi, Hojat
Nair, Aravind
Nguena Timo, Omer
Papadakis, Mike
Pessaux, François
Soulat, Romain

Abstracts of Invited Events

Conformance Testing of Cyber-Physical Systems: From Formal Foundations to Automotive Applications: Invited Talk TAP 2020

Mohammad Reza Mousavi

University of Leicester, School of Informatics, Leicester, UK

Conformance testing is a structured and model-based approach to testing. It aims to establish conformance between a model and a black-box implementation by running several test cases. Cyber-physical systems feature a tight integration of discrete computations, continuous dynamics, and (asynchronous) communications in cyber-physical systems; hence, applying conformance testing to them involves models that allow for specifying the integration and interaction of these phenomena.

In this talk, we review a few notions of conformance relations that are suitable for the purpose of testing cyber-physical systems. We present intensional representations of these notions of conformance, in terms of mathematical relations on hybrid systems trajectories, as well as a logical characterisation using Metric Temporal Logic.

Subsequently, we present a test-case generation algorithm and its implementation, in terms of an open-source Matlab toolbox for conformance testing cyber-physical systems. We present a number of case-studies we have conducted in the automotive domain, including a case-study on platooning and another one on doping detection concerning diesel car emissions.

The work presented in this talk are the result of my collaboration with several people including: Arend Aerts, Hugo Araujo, Sebastian Biewer, Gustavo Carvalho, Rayna Dimitrova, Maciej Gazda, Holger Hermanns, Morteza Mohaqeqi, Bruno Oliveira, Michel A. Reniers, Augusto Sampaio, Masoumeh Taromirad, and Bryan Tong Minh.

Testing, Runtime Verification and Automata Learning: Invited Tutorial TAP 2020

Martin Leucker

University of Lübeck, Institute for Software Engineering and Programming
Languages, Lübeck, Germany

Testing and *runtime verification* are both verification techniques for checking whether a system is correct. The essential artefacts for checking whether the system is correct are actual executions of the system, formally *words*. Such a set of words should be representative for the systems behavior.

In the field of *automata learning* (or grammatical inference) a formal model of a system is derived based on exemplifying behavior. In other words, the question is addressed what model fits to a given set of words.

In testing, typically, the system under test is examined on a finite set of *test cases*, formally words, which may be derived manually or automatically. *Oracle-based testing* is a form of testing in which an *oracle*, typically a manually developed piece of code, is attached to the system under test and employed for checking whether a given set of test cases passes or fails.

In runtime verification, typically, a formal specification of the correct behavior is given from which a so-called *monitor* is synthesised and used for examining whether the behavior of the system under test, or generally the system to monitor, adheres to such a specification. In a sense, the monitor acts as a test oracle, when employed in testing.

From the discussion above we see that testing, runtime verification, and learning automata share similarities but also differences. The main artefacts used for the different methods are formal specifications, models like automata, but especially sets of words, on which the different system descriptions are compared, to eventually obtain a verdict whether the system under test is correct or not.

In this tutorial we recall the basic ideas of testing, oracle-based testing, model-based testing, conformance testing, automata learning and runtime verification and elaborate on a coherent picture with the above mentioned artefacts as ingredients. We mostly refrain from technical details but concentrate on the big picture of those verification techniques.

Contents

Regular Research Papers

Benchmarking Combinations of Learning and Testing Algorithms for Active Automata Learning

Bernhard K. Aichernig[1], Martin Tappler[1,2(✉)], and Felix Wallner[1]

[1] Institute of Software Technology, Graz University of Technology, Graz, Austria
{aichernig,martin.tappler}@ist.tugraz.at, felix.wallner@student.tugraz.at
[2] Schaffhausen Institute of Technology, Schaffhausen, Switzerland
mt@sit.org

Abstract. Active automata learning comprises techniques for learning automata models of black-box systems by testing such systems. While this form of learning enables model-based analysis and verification, it may also require a substantial amount of interactions with considered systems to learn adequate models, which capture the systems' behaviour.

The test cases executed during learning can be divided into two categories: (1) test cases to gain knowledge about a system and (2) test cases to falsify a learned hypothesis automaton. The former are selected by learning algorithms, whereas the latter are selected by conformance-testing algorithms. There exist various options for both types of algorithms and there are dependencies between them. In this paper, we investigate the performance of combinations of four different learning algorithms and seven different testing algorithms. For this purpose, we perform learning experiments using 39 benchmark models. Based on experimental results, we discuss insights regarding the performance of different configurations for various types of systems. These insights may serve as guidance for future users of active automata learning.

Keywords: Active automata learning · Conformance testing · Model-based testing · Model learning · LearnLib

1 Introduction

Using active automata learning it is possible to automatically generate automata models of black-box systems through testing those systems. This enables the application of model-based verification techniques, such as model checking [10] and model-based regression testing [3]. Successful applications range from communication protocols [10,11,23,29], through embedded systems [2,25], to cyber-physical systems [1,18].

Generally, active automata learning repeatedly alternates between two phases of learning involving two types of queries. *Membership queries* are test cases that are executed to gain knowledge about the system under learning (SUL) to build

© Springer Nature Switzerland AG 2020
W. Ahrendt and H. Wehrheim (Eds.): TAP 2020, LNCS 12165, pp. 3–22, 2020.
https://doi.org/10.1007/978-3-030-50995-8_1

hypothesis automata, while *equivalence queries* check whether a hypothesis conforms to the SUL. The former are selected by the used learning algorithm, while the latter are usually implemented through conformance testing. The selection of test cases for both types of queries affects the learning runtime. Since the dominant factor in active automata learning is usually the test execution time [23,29], it is paramount to minimise the number and length of tests.

Various approaches have been suggested for minimising the number of tests required for membership queries [15,22] and for equivalence queries [4,14]. In this paper, we empirically analyse the interaction between these approaches. We examine the learning performance of combinations of various learning algorithms and conformance-testing algorithms implementing equivalence queries. Our goal is to provide data on the relative performance of different learning setups by determining the testing budget required for correct learning. Such data may support practitioners in choosing a particular learning setup. Our analysis focuses on communication protocols and is based on 39 benchmark models[1] from the field of active automata learning [20]. These models have between three and 58 states, which is sufficient to model systems, such as transmission control protocol (TCP) servers [10]. Parts of this paper have been included in the doctoral thesis of one of the authors [28]. The presented experiments have been performed as part of the Bachelor's thesis project of one of the authors [32].

Structure. The rest of this paper is structured as follows. In Sect. 2, we discuss related work. In Sect. 3, we discuss active automata learning in more detail. Section 4 introduces the experimental setup and briefly discusses the examined learning and conformance-testing techniques. Section 5 presents the results of our performance measurements. We provide a summary in Sect. 6 and conclude with a discussion of our findings in Sect. 7.

2   Related Work

The Zulu challenge [9] addressed the problem of implementing automata learning without equivalence queries and a limited number of membership queries. Put differently, it called for solutions to test-based automata learning, where equivalence queries need to be implemented via conformance testing with a limited testing budget. Howar et al. reviewed their experience gained in this challenge and noted that it is necessary to find counterexamples to equivalence with only few tests for automata learning to be practically applicable [14]. Here, we apply existing learning and conformance-testing algorithms and compare those combinations with respect to the required testing budget. In previous work, we presented a fault-based approach to conformance testing in automata learning [4]. We performed similar measurements to evaluate this approach, but considered only four testing algorithms and a single learning algorithm.

Berg et al. [6] performed early work on the practical evaluation of the performance of L^*-based learning. The authors studied the impact of various system

---

[1] Available online at http://automata.cs.ru.nl/, accessed: February 2, 2020.

properties on the learning performance, including the alphabet size, the number of states, and prefix-closedness of the target language. Smetsers et al. [26] presented an efficient method for finding counterexamples in active automata learning that applies mutation-based fuzzing. In their evaluation, they compared four learning configurations with respect to learning performance, measured in terms of the size of learned models and the required number of queries. They considered combinations of the L^* algorithm [5] and the TTT algorithm [15] with their proposed method and the W-method [8,31].

Groz, Brémond and Simão applied concepts from finite-state-machine-based testing to implement an efficient algorithm for active learning of Mealy machines without resets [7,13]. The authors evaluated various active learning configurations, including L^*-based configurations with and without resets.

3 Preliminaries

In this section, we define Mealy machines, provide an overview of active learning of Mealy-machine models of black-box systems and discuss test-case selection for this kind of learning.

3.1 Mealy Machines

We use Mealy machines as modelling formalism, as they have successfully been used in contexts combining learning and verification [10,19,23,29]. Additionally, the Java-library LearnLib [16] provides algorithms for both learning and conformance testing of Mealy machines.

Mealy machines are finite-state machines with inputs and outputs. Their execution starts in an initial state and they change their state by executing inputs. During execution, they produce exactly one output in response to each input. Formally, Mealy machines can be defined as follows.

Definition 1 (Mealy Machines). *A Mealy machine $\mathcal{M}$ is a 6-tuple $\mathcal{M} = \langle Q, q_0, I, O, \delta, \lambda \rangle$ where*

- *Q is a finite set of states,*
- *q_0 is the initial state,*
- *I and O are finite sets of input and output symbols,*
- *$\delta : Q \times I \to Q$ is the state transition function, and*
- *$\lambda : Q \times I \to O$ is the output function.*

We require Mealy machines to be input enabled and deterministic. This means that outputs and successor states must be defined for all inputs in all states. A Mealy machine is deterministic if their is at most one output and one successor state for every pair of input and source state.

We extend λ to sequences of inputs in the standard way. For $s \in I^*$ and $q \in Q$, the output function $\lambda(q, s) = t \in O^*$ returns the outputs produced in response to s executed in state q and we define $\lambda(s) = \lambda(q_0, s)$. We say that

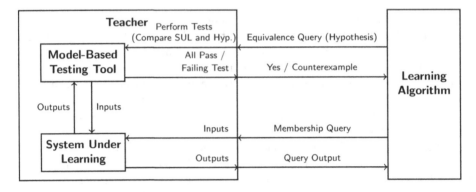

Fig. 1. The interaction between a learner and a teacher communicating with a SUL to learn a Mealy machine [30]

two Mealy machines over the same alphabets are equivalent if they produce the same outputs in response to all possible inputs. Let $\mathcal{M}_1$ and $\mathcal{M}_2$ be two Mealy machine with output functions λ_1 and λ_2, respectively. They are equivalent, denoted $\mathcal{M}_1 \equiv \mathcal{M}_2$, iff

$$\forall s \in I^* : \lambda_1(s) = \lambda_2(s). \tag{1}$$

3.2 Active Automata Learning

We apply learning algorithms in the minimally adequate teacher (MAT) framework introduced by Angluin for the L^* algorithm [5]. While L^* has originally been proposed for deterministic finite automata (DFA), it has been extended to other types of automata, such as Mealy machines [19,21,24]. For the following discussion of learning, we assume that we interact with a MAT to learn a Mealy machine producing the same outputs as a black-box SUL. In this context, the MAT basically wraps the SUL, which is assumed to behave like a Mealy machine.

A MAT is usually required to answer two types of queries that are posed learning algorithms. These queries are commonly called *membership queries* and *equivalence queries*; see Fig. 1 for a schematic depiction of the interaction between a learning algorithm, also called learner, and a MAT, also called teacher.

In membership queries (also called output queries [24]), the learner provides a sequence of inputs and asks for the corresponding outputs. The teacher usually implements this by performing a single test on the SUL, while recording the observed outputs. In equivalence queries, the learner provides a learned hypothesis automaton and asks whether this automaton is correct, i.e., if it is equivalent to the SUL. This is commonly implemented through conformance testing, i.e., the teacher generates a test suite from the hypothesis and executes it on the SUL. If a test case reveals a difference between SUL and hypothesis, it is returned as a counterexample to equivalence. Otherwise, the teacher returns *yes*, signalling that SUL and hypothesis are considered to be equivalent. Put differently, conformance testing approximates equivalence checking between the hypothesis and the Mealy machine underlying the SUL. It basically checks Eq. (1) while sampling only a finite set of input sequences from I^*.

Active automata learning operates in rounds by performing the two types queries in alternation. In every round, the learner performs some membership queries until there is sufficient information to build a hypothesis. After that, the learner issues an equivalence query, asking whether the hypothesis is correct and learning can stop. If the teacher returns a counterexample, the learner integrates it into its knowledge and starts a new round of learning. Otherwise, learning stops with the correctly learned hypothesis as output.

Test-Case Selection for Learning. There are several factors influencing the test-case selection in the learning process outlined above. First, learning algorithms differ in the amount of membership queries required for creating hypotheses. This largely depends on the used internal data structures, such as observation tables used in L^* [5]. Tree-based learners often require fewer membership queries per round [15, 17]. The second factor concerns counterexample processing, which may also require testing. There are different ways to extract information from counterexamples, affecting the content stored in data structures and consequently future membership queries. Third, the test-case selection for conformance testing depends on the applied testing technique. Since test cases revealing differences serve as counterexamples, conformance testing affects subsequent counterexample processing and selection of membership queries. Therefore, we investigate which combinations of learners and testing techniques are the most efficient overall, i.e., which combinations require the lowest testing budget for learning.

4 Experimental Setup

We evaluate the performance of combinations of four learning algorithms and seven conformance-testing algorithms. For this purpose, we determine the lowest conformance-testing budget for learning to be successful, i.e., for learning correct models. In order to determine whether a given testing budget is sufficient to learn correctly, we "re-learn" known models of network protocols, which are part of a benchmark suite for learning and testing [20]. We treat these models as black boxes during learning by simulating them to generate outputs in response to input sequences. Once learning terminates, we compare the learned to the true model. We deem learning successful, if the correct model has been learned once with a configuration involving deterministic testing. In experiments involving randomised testing, we repeat learning runs ten times and deem learning successful if all runs produce the correct model. To ensure reproducibility, we use fixed seed values for random number generators.

The setup for the learning experiments and the measurement results from these experiments can be found in the supplementary material [33]. The results include all relevant data, such as system resets (executions of test cases) and test steps (executions of test inputs) for equivalence and membership queries. Here, we present statistics computed from these data. In our target application

Table 1. Evaluated learning and testing algorithms

Learning algorithm	Testing algorithm
L^* [5,24]	W-method [8,31]
RS [22]	partial W-method [12]
KV [17]	random words
TTT [15]	random walks
	mutation [4]
	transition coverage [4]
	random Wp-method

of network protocols, we consider test steps to be the most relevant performance measure, as resets often can be implemented efficiently by simply reconnecting. Since we are interested in the overall performance of learning, we generally consider the combined number of test steps required for equivalence queries and membership queries.

Selection of Algorithms. The evaluated learning algorithms are listed in the first column of Table 1 and the testing techniques are listed in the second column of Table 1. These lists include various popular algorithms available in LearnLib [16]. Hence, our evaluation, e.g., considers the performance of L^* [5] combined with the partial W-method [12].

In the following, we provide a brief discussion of the most important features of the applied algorithms. Generally, we apply the implementations of these algorithms available in LearnLib 0.14 [16]. In some cases, we slightly adapted the testing techniques to be able to control the number of test cases executed during equivalence queries.

L^* and RS. Angluin established the basis for active automata learning by introducing the L^* algorithm and the MAT framework [5]. L^* stores information in so-called observation tables and processes counterexamples by adding all prefixes of a counterexample to the table. Rivest and Schapire improved L^* by maintaining smaller observation tables [22]. This is achieved through advanced counterexample processing that extracts a distinguishing suffix from a counterexample. Such a suffix distinguishes two SUL states corresponding to a single state in the current hypothesis. We refer to this improved version as RS algorithm.

The advanced counterexample processing of RS affects the membership query complexity. Angluin's L^* requires $O(kmn^2)$ membership queries [22], where k is the (input) alphabet size, m is the length of the longest counterexample and n is the size of the learned automaton, while RS requires $O(kn^2 + n\log(m))$ membership queries. Hence, the number of test cases performed for membership queries depends only logarithmically on the counterexample length.

KV and TTT. Kearns and Vazirani presented an active automata learning algorithm that stores queried data in trees [17]. We refer to this algorithm as KV algorithm. Without going into details, the original KV algorithm required one round of learning for each state of the final hypothesis, thus conformance testing needs to be performed more often. However, we have observed that each round requires fewer membership queries. The TTT algorithm [15] also stores information in trees, but improves upon KV in various ways. It, e.g., also processes counterexamples by extracting distinguishing suffixes. Additionally, counterexample prefixes are processed as well.

Analogously to L^*, the number of membership queries performed by KV depends linearly on the counterexample length [17]. TTT in contrast has the same worst-case membership query complexity as RS [15]. We can expect TTT and RS to perform better than KV and L^* in the presence of long counterexamples.

Random Testing. Random-words-based testing and random-walks-based testing generate random sequences of inputs. Both select inputs completely randomly and differ only in the distribution of the test-case length. The length of random words is uniformly distribution within some range, whereas random walks have a geometrically distributed length.

Variations of the W-Method. The W-method [8,31] is a deterministic conformance testing technique, which requires a bound m on the number of SUL states. Given such an m, it can prove equivalence between hypothesis and SUL up to m. Hence, if all generated test cases pass, then we know that either SUL and hypothesis are equivalent, or the SUL has strictly more than m states. LearnLib [16] uses a depth parameter to define m, which specifies the difference between the number of hypothesis states and m. The partial W-method [12], also called Wp-method, improves upon the W-method by requiring fewer test cases, while providing the same guarantees. However, the number of test cases generated by both techniques is exponential in the bound m, thus it usually does not scale to large systems. The random Wp-method, as implemented in LearnLib [16], uses the partial W-method as basis, but executes only a random subset of all generated test cases, therefore it does not prove equivalence.

Since the W-method generally creates larger test suites than the partial W-method, individual equivalence queries using the partial W-method are more efficient. However, the partial W-method and the W-method may find different counterexamples leading to different intermediate hypotheses. For this reason, we included both testing algorithms in our evaluation.

Mutation and Transition Coverage. In our previous work, we developed two conformance testing techniques for active automata learning, which work similarly. Both techniques start by generating a large set of test cases through random walks on the hypothesis. The random walks alternate between completely random sequences and paths to randomly chosen transitions. Afterwards a subset of the generated test cases is selected and executed. The mutation-based technique selects test cases based on mutation coverage, where mutants model potential successor hypotheses. The transition-coverage-based technique selects test cases with the goal covering all hypothesis transitions.

Configuration of Testing Techniques. We apply the same configuration of every testing technique for all considered models. The configurations have been chosen to enable learning of system with up to approximately 50 states. For instance, we configured random-words-based testing such that all generated test cases have a length between 10 and 50. The parameter configurations are as follows.

- *random words:* minimum length: 10 and maximum length: 50.
- *random walks:* test stop probability: $\frac{1}{30}$. This setting ensures that the expected length of random walks is the same as of random words.
- *random Wp-method:* we set the minimal length of the middle sequences in test cases to 0 and the expected length to 4.
- *transition coverage:* maximum test-case length: 50, maximum length of random sequences: 4, retry and stop probability for test-case generation: $\frac{29}{30}$ and $p_{\text{stop}} = \frac{1}{30}$, respectively. For more information on the parameters, we refer to our previous work [4].
- *mutation:* we used the same test-case generation settings as for transition coverage. For test-case selection, we generated mutants with distinguishing sequences of length two and applied mutation sampling such that at most 10,000 mutants are considered.

The only parameter of the deterministic algorithms, the *W-method* and the *partial W-method*, is the depth parameter. In the remainder of this paper, we write testing techniques in italics.

Search for Required Testing Budget. While learning with deterministic conformance testing, we increase the *depth* parameter linearly until learning correctly. In case of randomised testing techniques, we control the number of test cases that are executed during each individual equivalence query to find a counterexamples to equivalence. We apply a binary search to find the minimum number of test cases to reliably learn correct models, i.e., to learn correctly in ten repeated learning runs.

In our analysis, we consider the testing budget in terms of test steps. This quantity is more difficult to control uniformly across the different testing techniques, but it is clearly correlated with the number of test cases. For this reason, we deem the search appropriate. The exact relation between the number of test cases and test steps depends on the applied test-case generation algorithm.

Benchmark Models. We consider a subset of the benchmark models from the automata-learning benchmark models collected at the Radboud University Nijmegen [20][2]. In particular, we use all six TCP models, including both server and client models of the TCP stacks of Ubuntu, Windows, and BSD, learned by Fiterău-Broştean et al. [10]. We consider all 32 Message Queuing Telemetry Transport (MQTT) models, created in our previous work on learning-based testing of MQTT [29]. Finally, we also consider a simple coffee machine that is similar to a model used by Steffen et al. [27]. We have chosen this selection to cover system models of different categories, which are defined below.

---

[2] Available online at http://automata.cs.ru.nl/, accessed: February 2, 2020.

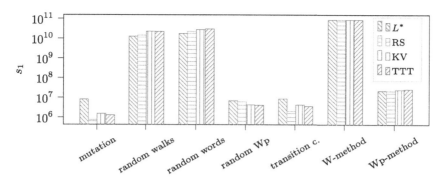

Fig. 2. The score s_1 computed over all experiments for all learner-tester combinations, grouped by testing technique

Categories. Certain behavioural aspects of communication-protocol models may favour a particular learner-tester combination, while other aspects may favour different combinations. For this reason, we grouped the benchmark models into categories based on the following properties:

– *small:* a model is *small* if it has less than or equal to 15 states
– *large:* a model is *large* if it has more than 15 states
– *sink-state:* a model satisfies the property *sink-state* if there exists a (sink) state q such that all outgoing transitions from q reach q
– *strongly-connected:* a model satisfies the property *strongly-connected* if its underlying directed graph is strongly connected, i.e., for each ordered pair of nodes exists a directed path between these nodes.

The above categories have been chosen with common application scenarios in mind. Given a concrete application scenario, learned models can often be expected to have certain properties. For instance, we may want to learn a behavioural model capturing a single session of an application protocol. In this case, learned models are likely to have a sink state that is reached after closing a session. On the contrary, if restarting of sessions is allowed during learning, learned models can be expected to be strongly connected. The size of models depends on the abstraction. Harsh abstraction leads to small models and is often applied when testing is expensive. Hence, such assumptions on model categories are reasonable and do not require sacrificing our black-box view of systems. Therefore, we have, for instance, examined which learner-tester combinations perform best for small models that have a sink state.

5   Experimental Results

Altogether we performed 39 learning experiments with each of the 28 learner-tester combinations. We present selected results from these experiments in the following, focusing on the number of test steps required for both equivalence

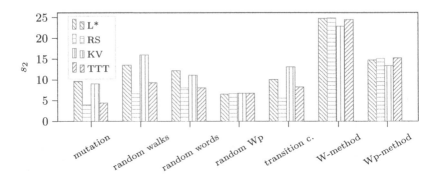

Fig. 3. The score s_2 computed over all experiments for all learner-tester combinations, grouped by testing technique

queries and membership queries. In particular, we consider the maximum and mean number of test steps required to learn reliably. Due to the large amount of learning experiments, we present aggregated results for learner-tester combinations in (1) cactus plots and (2) bar plots. Additional information and the complete results can be found in the accompanying supplementary material [33].

The cactus plots show how many experiments can be finished successfully, such that learning is reliable, given a maximum number of test steps. The bar plots show two different scores, s_1 and s_2, computed for the learner-tester combinations lt. The actual scores are not important, but they allow for comparisons, where a lower value means better performance. The scores are given by

$$s_1(lt) = \sum_{b \in B} meanSteps(lt, b) \text{ and } s_2(lt) = \sum_{b \in B} \frac{meanSteps(lt, b)}{\max_{lt' \in LT} meanSteps(lt', b)},$$

where B is the set of considered benchmark models, LT is the set of all learner-tester combinations, and $meanSteps(lt, b)$ returns the mean number of steps to reliably learn models of the benchmark b with the combination lt. The first score $s_1(lt)$ simply sums up the average number of test steps required in all experiments, whereas $s_2(lt)$ is normalised, through dividing by the worst-performing combination of each benchmark. Hence, s_1 allows to analyse which combinations perform best, when learning all 39 models consecutively and under the assumption that test steps require the same amount of time in every benchmark experiment. The normalised score s_2 accounts for the large variation in terms of model complexity across the different benchmarks. Normalisation ensures that individual performance outliers do not severely affect the overall score of a learner-tester combination. As information about outliers is useful, it is represented in the cactus plots.

5.1 Overview

First, we want to provide a rough overview. Figure 2 shows the score $s_1(lt)$ for each learner-tester combinations computed over all experiments. Due to large

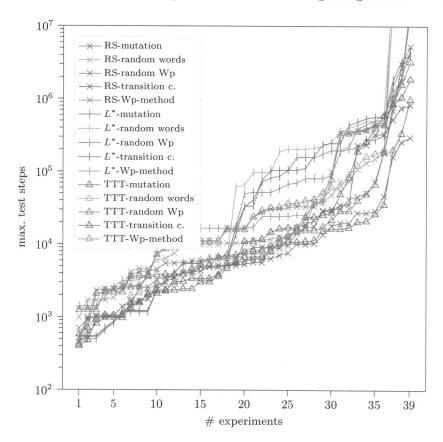

Fig. 4. A cactus plot showing how many learning experiments can be completed successfully with a limited number of test steps

variations in the required test steps, it uses logarithmic scale. Figure 3 shows the normalised score $s_2(lt)$. Similar to observations in previous work [4], we see that *mutation, transition coverage,* and *random Wp* perform well in comparison to other techniques. In Fig. 2, we can observe that the relative gap between *mutation* and the worst-performing techniques is very large. This is caused by a few outliers. In particular, the TCP server models required a very large number of test steps for *random walks* and *random words* to learn reliably. For this reason, we see a smaller gap between those test techniques and *mutation* in Fig. 3, because s_2 is less affected by outliers.

Furthermore, we see that the *W-method* indeed generally performs worse than the *partial W-method. Random words* and *random walks* perform similarly well. Figure 3 shows that, using the same testing algorithm, KV and L^* perform similarly efficient. For these reasons and to ease readability, we will ignore certain combinations in the following. In the remainder of this section, we will

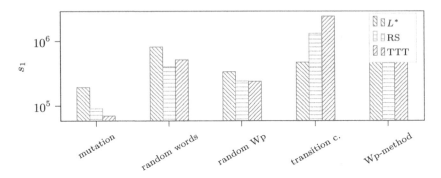

Fig. 5. The score s_1 computed for experiments involving small models with a sink state

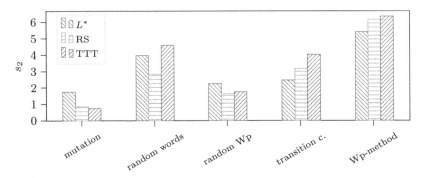

Fig. 6. The score s_2 computed for experiments involving small models with a sink state

not show performance plots for combinations involving the *W-method*, random-walks-based testing, or the KV algorithm.

Figure 4 shows a cactus plot describing how many learning experiments can reliably be completed with a limited number of test steps. For instance, with RS-*mutation* we are able to learn about 28 models with at most approximately 10,000 test steps, whereas L^*-*mutation* requires about 100,000 test steps to learn only 25 models. We see a steep increase in the required test steps for random-words-based testing to learn three of the 39 models. This explains the discrepancy between the s_1-score and the s_2-score of random-words-based testing. It is interesting to note that L^* combinations require a very low number of test steps to learn eight of the models. In general, L^* combinations perform worst, though.

5.2   Selected Findings

Next, we discuss a few selected findings related to features of the examined techniques and benchmark categories.

Counterexample Processing. In Figs. 2 and 3, we see that *mutation* combined with RS and *mutation* combined with TTT perform best overall. In contrast to

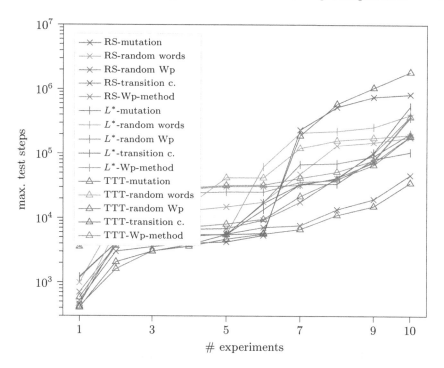

Fig. 7. A cactus plot showing how many learning experiments involving small models with a sink state can be completed successfully with limited test steps

that, *mutation* combined with KV and *mutation* combined with L^* perform substantially worse, whereas *random Wp* shows uniform performance across different combinations with learning algorithms. Similar observations as for *mutation* can be made for *transition coverage*.

This can be explained by considering the counterexample-processing techniques of different learning algorithms. RS processes counterexamples by extracting distinguishing suffixes [22], like TTT which also performs additional processing steps [15]. This reduces the length and number of sequences that are added to the learning data structures. L^* and KV do not apply such techniques, therefore the performance of these learning algorithms suffers from long counterexamples. We have chosen the parameters for *mutation* conservatively to create long test cases, which leads to long counterexamples, explaining our observations. In contrast to this, *random Wp* generates much shorter test cases. Therefore, we see uniform performance in combination with different learning algorithms. Hence, *mutation* and *transition coverage* should be combined with either RS or TTT. In such combinations, mutation-based testing performs efficient equivalence queries, while sophisticated counterexample processing ensures that a low number of short membership queries is performed. Comparing RS and TTT combined with *mutation*, there is no clear winner; both combinations performed similarly well in our experiments.

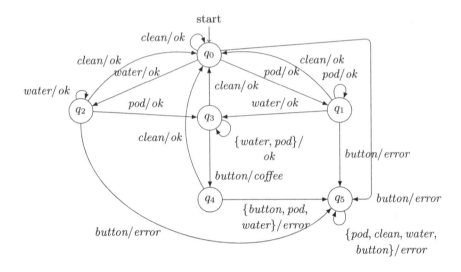

Fig. 8. A Mealy-machine model of a coffee machine [27]

Small Models with Sink State. We evaluated the learner-tester combinations on ten small models that have a sink state. Small models may result from harsh abstraction. Sink states may be created if learning focuses on individual sessions in a communication protocol, where the sink state is reached upon session termination. Hence, this is an important class of systems that we can identify prior to learning. Therefore, it makes sense to analyse which active automata learning configurations work well in such scenarios.

Figure 5 and Fig. 6 show scores computed for this kind of models. The non-normalised score s_1 shows that transition-coverage-based testing may be very inefficient for such models. In particular, the combinations with RS and TTT are the two worst-performing with respect to s_1. However, the normalised score s_2 is in a similar range as the s_2 score of random-words-based testing. This suggests that the s_1 score is affected by a few experiments for which *transition coverage* performs very poorly. The cactus plot shown in Fig. 7 demonstrates that this is indeed the case. There is a steep increase in the test steps required to reliably learn in seven or more experiments. Thus, four benchmark models seem to be difficult to learn with *transition coverage*.

We analysed one of these models in more detail to determine the reason for the poor performance of *transition coverage*. It is a coffee-machine model similar to the model used as an illustrative example by Steffen et al. [27]. Figure 8 shows the corresponding Mealy machine. Two properties of the coffee machine cause the poor performance of transition-coverage-based testing. First, many input sequences reach the sink state q_5 that only produces error outputs. Second, other states require very specific input sequences. In experiments, we observed that learning frequently produced incorrect models with 5 states that did not include q_1 or q_2. The transition-coverage heuristic does not help to detect these states.

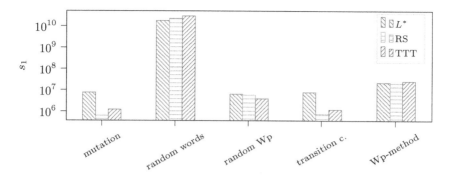

Fig. 9. The score s_1 computed for experiments involving large models

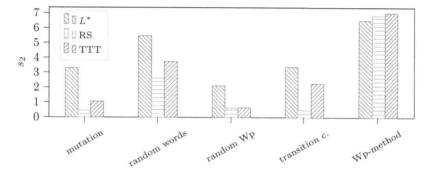

Fig. 10. The score s_2 computed for experiments involving large models

In fact, it is even detrimental. To reach q_1 or q_2, we need to reach the initial state q_0 first. Consequently, covering any known hypothesis transition other than the *water (pod)* transition in q_0 leads away from reaching and detecting q_2 (q_1). Random testing from q_0 is necessarily more effective. Moreover, the transition-coverage heuristic generates very long test cases. For this reason, most suffixes of these test cases merely execute the self-loop transitions in q_5, because the probability of reaching q_5 is high. This worsens the performance of *transition coverage* even more.

It is interesting to note that mutation-based conformance testing performs well on the coffee machine, although it applies the same test-case generation strategy as transition coverage. In contrast to transition coverage, *mutation* applies mutation-coverage-based test-case selection. Hence, this form of test-case selection is able to drastically improve performance, as can be seen in Fig. 7. This can be explained by considering the same situation as outlined above. Suppose that an intermediate hypothesis with five states has been learned. In this scenario, the true model is a mutant of the hypothesis that can be generated through the used split-state mutation [4]. By covering that mutant, it is possible to detect the last remaining state and learn the true model.

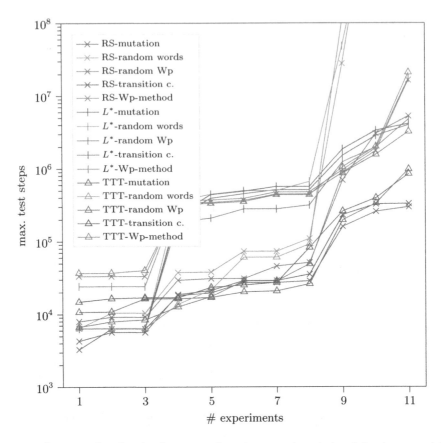

Fig. 11. A cactus plot showing how many learning experiments involving large models can be completed successfully with a limited number of test steps

Large Models. Finally, we examine the learning performance on large models. In our classification, models are large if they have more than 15 states. Our benchmark set includes 11 such models. Figure 9 and Fig. 10 show scores computed for learning these models. Figure 11 shows the corresponding cactus plots.

We can observe that both *random words* and the *Wp-method* show poor performance. Their detailed performance characteristics is different, though. On the one hand, we see in Fig. 11 that the *Wp-method* combined with any learning algorithm performs bad over the whole range of experiments. On the other hand, *random words* is able to efficiently learn eight of 11 models, but it requires a very large amount of test steps for the remaining three models. These are the TCP-server models, which are much larger than the other considered models. Hence, random-words-based testing is only feasible for moderately large models. We can also observe that the combinations RS-*mutation* and RS-*transition coverage* perform very well for large models. This is in line with findings from our previous work on the mutation-based testing technique [4].

6   Summary

We examined the performance of 28 combinations of learning and conformance testing algorithms in the context of learning Mealy machines of black-box systems. After an initial analysis, we identified 15 representative combinations that we analysed in more detail. Since the learning runtime in practical applications is usually dominated by the time required for interacting with systems, we generally quantify learning performance in terms of required test steps for correct learning. The performed experimental evaluation is based on 39 benchmark models including models of implementations of TCP and MQTT. It focuses on learning and testing techniques available in LearnLib [16] and also includes two testing algorithms developed in our previous work. We presented measurement results and discussed selected insights with respect to overall learning performance and specific properties of systems. The results and insights may serve as guidance for practitioners seeking to apply active automata learning.

7   Conclusion

Our results regarding the performance of learning algorithms are in line with their asymptotic query complexity. The TTT algorithm [15] and L^* extended with improvements by Rivest and Schapire [22] have the same membership query complexity and they performed similarly well. It is interesting to note that the TTT algorithms generally performs more equivalence queries, but requires a similar amount of test steps overall.

Our measurements demonstrate that neither deterministic conformance testing nor pure random testing scales. Deterministic conformance testing showed especially poor performance for large models. Random-words-based testing also cannot reliably learn large models with a limited number of test steps. Hence, it is not efficient to guarantee conformance up to some bound and it is not efficient to test completely blind. *Transition coverage* showed weaknesses for small models with sink states, an important class of system models. However, *transition coverage* combined with RS performed very well for large models. In general, we have observed that the counterexample processing implemented by RS and TTT may have a large impact on efficiency. This is especially true if test cases are long, as is the case in transition-coverage-based testing.

The random Wp-method and mutation-based testing [4] performed well for all types of benchmarks. Both techniques benefit from learned hypotheses and add variability through randomisation. While *random Wp* showed uniform performance for different learners, *mutation* combined with RS performed best overall. Mutation-based testing requires a low number of test cases for equivalence queries, while the counterexample processing by RS keeps the number and length of membership queries low. In conclusion, *mutation* or *random Wp* combined with RS or TTT should be chosen to efficiently learn automata.

References

1. Aichernig, B.K., et al.: Learning a behavior model of hybrid systems through combining model-based testing and machine learning. In: Gaston, C., Kosmatov, N., Le Gall, P. (eds.) ICTSS 2019. LNCS, vol. 11812, pp. 3–21. Springer, Cham (2019). https://doi.org/10.1007/978-3-030-31280-0_1
2. Aichernig, B.K., Bloem, R., Ebrahimi, M., Tappler, M., Winter, J.: Automata learning for symbolic execution. In: Bjørner, N., Gurfinkel, A. (eds.) 2018 Formal Methods in Computer Aided Design, FMCAD 2018, Austin, TX, USA, October 30–November 2, 2018, pp. 1–9. IEEE (2018). https://doi.org/10.23919/FMCAD.2018.8602991
3. Aichernig, B.K., Mostowski, W., Mousavi, M.R., Tappler, M., Taromirad, M.: Model learning and model-based testing. In: Bennaceur, A., Hähnle, R., Meinke, K. (eds.) Machine Learning for Dynamic Software Analysis: Potentials and Limits. LNCS, vol. 11026, pp. 74–100. Springer, Cham (2018). https://doi.org/10.1007/978-3-319-96562-8_3
4. Aichernig, B.K., Tappler, M.: Efficient active automata learning via mutation testing. J. Autom. Reason. **63**(4), 1103–1134 (2019). https://doi.org/10.1007/s10817-018-9486-0
5. Angluin, D.: Learning regular sets from queries and counter examples. Inf. Comput. **75**(2), 87–106 (1987). https://doi.org/10.1016/0890-5401(87)90052-6
6. Berg, T., Jonsson, B., Leucker, M., Saksena, M.: Insights to Angluin's learning. Electron. Notes Theor. Comput. Sci. **118**, 3–18 (2005). https://doi.org/10.1016/j.entcs.2004.12.015
7. Brémond, N., Groz, R.: Case studies in learning models and testing without reset. In: 2019 IEEE International Conference on Software Testing, Verification and Validation Workshops, ICST Workshops 2019, Xi'an, China, April 22–23, 2019, pp. 40–45. IEEE (2019). https://doi.org/10.1109/ICSTW.2019.00030
8. Chow, T.S.: Testing software design modeled by finite-state machines. IEEE Trans. Softw. Eng. **4**(3), 178–187 (1978). https://doi.org/10.1109/TSE.1978.231496
9. Combe, D., de la Higuera, C., Janodet, J.-C.: Zulu: an interactive learning competition. In: Yli-Jyrä, A., Kornai, A., Sakarovitch, J., Watson, B. (eds.) FSMNLP 2009. LNCS (LNAI), vol. 6062, pp. 139–146. Springer, Heidelberg (2010). https://doi.org/10.1007/978-3-642-14684-8_15
10. Fiterău-Broştean, P., Janssen, R., Vaandrager, F.: Combining model learning and model checking to analyze TCP implementations. In: Chaudhuri, S., Farzan, A. (eds.) CAV 2016. LNCS, vol. 9780, pp. 454–471. Springer, Cham (2016). https://doi.org/10.1007/978-3-319-41540-6_25
11. Fiterău-Broştean, P., Lenaerts, T., Poll, E., de Ruiter, J., Vaandrager, F.W., Verleg, P.: Model learning and model checking of SSH implementations. In: Erdogmus, H., Havelund, K. (eds.) Proceedings of the 24th ACM SIGSOFT International SPIN Symposium on Model Checking of Software, Santa Barbara, CA, USA, July 10–14, 2017, pp. 142–151. ACM (2017). https://doi.org/10.1145/3092282.3092289
12. Fujiwara, S., von Bochmann, G., Khendek, F., Amalou, M., Ghedamsi, A.: Test selection based on finite state models. IEEE Trans. Softw. Eng. **17**(6), 591–603 (1991). https://doi.org/10.1109/32.87284
13. Groz, R., Brémond, N., Simão, A.: Using adaptive sequences for learning non-resettable FSMs. In: Unold, O., Dyrka, W., Wieczorek, W. (eds.) Proceedings of the 14th International Conference on Grammatical Inference, ICGI 2018, Wrocław, Poland, September 5–7, 2018. Proceedings of Machine Learning Research, vol. 93, pp. 30–43. PMLR (2018). http://proceedings.mlr.press/v93/groz19a.html

14. Howar, F., Steffen, B., Merten, M.: From ZULU to RERS. In: Margaria, T., Steffen, B. (eds.) ISoLA 2010. LNCS, vol. 6415, pp. 687–704. Springer, Heidelberg (2010). https://doi.org/10.1007/978-3-642-16558-0_55

15. Isberner, M., Howar, F., Steffen, B.: The TTT algorithm: a redundancy-free approach to active automata learning. In: Bonakdarpour, B., Smolka, S.A. (eds.) RV 2014. LNCS, vol. 8734, pp. 307–322. Springer, Cham (2014). https://doi.org/10.1007/978-3-319-11164-3_26

16. Isberner, M., Howar, F., Steffen, B.: The open-source LearnLib - a framework for active automata learning. In: Kroening, D., Păsăreanu, C.S. (eds.) CAV 2015. LNCS, vol. 9206, pp. 487–495. Springer, Cham (2015). https://doi.org/10.1007/978-3-319-21690-4_32

17. Kearns, M.J., Vazirani, U.V.: An Introduction to Computational Learning Theory. MIT Press, Cambridge (1994). https://mitpress.mit.edu/books/introduction-computational-learning-theory

18. Khosrowjerdi, H., Meinke, K.: Learning-based testing for autonomous systems using spatial and temporal requirements. In: Perrouin, G., Acher, M., Cordy, M., Devroey, X. (eds.) Proceedings of the 1st International Workshop on Machine Learning and Software Engineering in Symbiosis, MASES@ASE 2018, Montpellier, France, September 3, 2018, pp. 6–15. ACM (2018). https://doi.org/10.1145/3243127.3243129

19. Margaria, T., Niese, O., Raffelt, H., Steffen, B.: Efficient test-based model generation for legacy reactive systems. In: Ninth IEEE International High-Level Design Validation and Test Workshop 2004, Sonoma Valley, CA, USA, November 10–12, 2004, pp. 95–100. IEEE Computer Society (2004). https://doi.org/10.1109/HLDVT.2004.1431246

20. Neider, D., Smetsers, R., Vaandrager, F., Kuppens, H.: Benchmarks for automata learning and conformance testing. In: Margaria, T., Graf, S., Larsen, K.G. (eds.) Models, Mindsets, Meta: The What, the How, and the Why Not?. LNCS, vol. 11200, pp. 390–416. Springer, Cham (2019). https://doi.org/10.1007/978-3-030-22348-9_23

21. Niese, O.: An integrated approach to testing complex systems. Ph.D. thesis, Dortmund University of Technology (2003). https://d-nb.info/969717474/34

22. Rivest, R.L., Schapire, R.E.: Inference of finite automata using homing sequences. Inf. Comput. 103(2), 299–347 (1993). https://doi.org/10.1006/inco.1993.1021

23. de Ruiter, J., Poll, E.: Protocol state fuzzing of TLS implementations. In: Jung, J., Holz, T. (eds.) 24th USENIX Security Symposium, USENIX Security 15, Washington, D.C., USA, August 12–14, 2015, pp. 193–206. USENIX Association (2015). https://www.usenix.org/conference/usenixsecurity15/technical-sessions/presentation/de-ruiter

24. Shahbaz, M., Groz, R.: Inferring Mealy machines. In: Cavalcanti, A., Dams, D.R. (eds.) FM 2009. LNCS, vol. 5850, pp. 207–222. Springer, Heidelberg (2009). https://doi.org/10.1007/978-3-642-05089-3_14

25. Smeenk, W., Moerman, J., Vaandrager, F., Jansen, D.N.: Applying automata learning to embedded control software. In: Butler, M., Conchon, S., Zaïdi, F. (eds.) ICFEM 2015. LNCS, vol. 9407, pp. 67–83. Springer, Cham (2015). https://doi.org/10.1007/978-3-319-25423-4_5

26. Smetsers, R., Moerman, J., Janssen, M., Verwer, S.: Complementing model learning with mutation-based fuzzing. CoRR abs/1611.02429 (2016). http://arxiv.org/abs/1611.02429

27. Steffen, B., Howar, F., Merten, M.: Introduction to active automata learning from a practical perspective. In: Bernardo, M., Issarny, V. (eds.) SFM 2011. LNCS, vol. 6659, pp. 256–296. Springer, Heidelberg (2011). https://doi.org/10.1007/978-3-642-21455-4_8

28. Tappler, M.: Learning-based testing in networked environments in the presence of timed and stochastic behaviour. Ph.D. thesis, Graz University of Technology (2019)

29. Tappler, M., Aichernig, B.K., Bloem, R.: Model-based testing IoT communication via active automata learning. In: 2017 IEEE International Conference on Software Testing, Verification and Validation, ICST 2017, Tokyo, Japan, March 13–17, 2017, pp. 276–287. IEEE Computer Society (2017). https://doi.org/10.1109/ICST.2017.32

30. Vaandrager, F.W.: Model learning. Commun. ACM **60**(2), 86–95 (2017). https://doi.org/10.1145/2967606

31. Vasilevskii, M.P.: Failure diagnosis of automata. Cybernetics **9**(4), 653–665 (1973). https://doi.org/10.1007/BF01068590

32. Wallner, F.: Benchmarking active automata learning configurations. Bachelor's thesis, Graz University of Technology (2019)

33. Wallner, F.: Learn-combinations: evaluation framework for combinations of learning and testing algorithms (2019). https://gitlab.com/felixwallner/learn-combinations. Accessed 2 Feb 2020

Mutation Testing of Smart Contracts at Scale

Pieter Hartel[1,2]([⊠])(iD) and Richard Schumi[3](iD)

[1] Singapore University of Technology and Design, Singapore, Singapore
[2] Delft University of Technology, Delft, The Netherlands
`pieter.hartel@tudelft.nl`
[3] Singapore Management University, Singapore, Singapore
`rschumi@smu.edu.sg`

Abstract. It is crucial that smart contracts are tested thoroughly due to their immutable nature. Even small bugs in smart contracts can lead to huge monetary losses. However, testing is not enough; it is also important to ensure the quality and completeness of the tests. There are already several approaches that tackle this challenge with mutation testing, but their effectiveness is questionable since they only considered small contract samples. Hence, we evaluate the quality of smart contract mutation testing at scale. We choose the most promising of the existing (smart contract specific) mutation operators, analyse their effectiveness in terms of killability and highlight severe vulnerabilities that can be injected with the mutations. Moreover, we improve the existing mutation methods by introducing a novel killing condition that is able to detect a deviation in the gas consumption, i.e., in the monetary value that is required to perform transactions.

Keywords: Mutation testing · Ethereum · Smart contracts · Solidity · Gas limit as a killing criterion · Vulnerability injection · Modifier issues

1 Introduction

Smart contracts are programs designed to express business logic for managing the data or assets on a blockchain system. Although smart contracts already exist for some years, they still suffer from security vulnerabilities, which can lead to huge monetary losses [2]. Hence, it is crucial to make sure that smart contracts do not contain such vulnerabilities. The most important method for finding both vulnerabilities and semantic errors is testing. Testing smart contracts is even more essential than testing regular programs, since their source is often publicly available, which makes them an easy target, and updating them is cumbersome due to their immutable nature. Moreover, it is critical to ensure the quality of the tests. There are a few quality metrics, like code coverage, i.e., the percentage of the source code that is executed by a test, but code coverage is not able to measure the error detection capability of tests and it is rarely a good indicator

© Springer Nature Switzerland AG 2020
W. Ahrendt and H. Wehrheim (Eds.): TAP 2020, LNCS 12165, pp. 23–42, 2020.
https://doi.org/10.1007/978-3-030-50995-8_2

for the number of faults in a software [28]. A technique that can perform such measurements is mutation testing, which injects faults into a program to check if the tests can detect these faults. A program with an injected fault is called a mutant, and detcting a fault is called killing the mutant.

There have already been a number of publication that showed mutation approaches for Solidity[1] smart contracts [1,3,4,6,8,12,25,29,30,32]. Solidity is a JavaScript like language[2] with several special features to interact with the underlying Ethereum blockchain. The blockchain stores code and data, and it is managed by the owners of the Ethereum peer-to-peer network. Many of the related mutation testing approaches introduced interesting smart contract specific mutations, but they only performed small evaluations with a few contracts. We selected the most promising mutation operators of the related work, generalized them, and performed a large scale evaluation with about a thousand contracts for a meaningful quality assessment of the operators. There is no generally accepted benchmark of smart contracts. Hence we use replay tests downloaded from Truffle-tests-for-free [10] that are automatically produced from historic transaction data on the blockchain. The achieved mutation score can serve as a baseline for testing other, more sophisticated testing methods.

We are particularly interested in smart contract specific mutations that simulate common mistakes made by smart contract developers. An example is a forgotten or wrong function modifier [12]. A modifier can express conditions that have to be fulfilled for the execution of a function, e.g., that the caller of the function is the owner of the contract. Since modifiers are often concerned with access control, omitting a modifier can have catastrophic effects. For example management functions of a smart contract can become publicly available.

Another smart contract specific aspect is the gas consumption of transactions. Everything on Ethereum costs some units of gas [31]. For example, executing an ADD bytecode costs 3 gas. Storing a byte costs 4 or 68 gas, depending on the value of the byte (zero or non-zero). The price of gas in Ether varies widely[3], and the market determines the exchange rate of Ether. The cost of a transaction can be anything from less than a cent to several US$. Executing smart contracts is therefore not just a matter of executing the code with the right semantics but also of cost control. Therefore, all transactions have a gas limit to make sure that the cost is managed. Executing smart contracts with a gas limit is comparable to executing code on a real time system with a deadline [19]. This opens up new possibilities for killing mutants, over and above the standard killing conditions. Similar to detecting mutants on real-time systems with a different timing behaviour, we measure the gas consumption of tested transactions to find deviations to reference executions of these transactions. This allows us to kill mutants that consume a significantly greater amount of gas.

---

[1] Solidity documentation https://solidity.readthedocs.io.

[2] On the differences between Solidity and Javascript https://vomtom.at/whats-the-difference-between-javascript-solidity-and-ethereum.

[3] Gas price tracking https://etherscan.io/chart/gasprice.

Our major contributions are: (1) We propose a set of mutation operators on the basis of related work and evaluate these operators at scale. (2) To further improve the mutation score, we introduce a novel killing condition based gas limits for smart contract transactions.

2 Background

Mutation testing [15,23,24] is an evaluation technique for assessing the quality of a set of test cases (i.e., a test suite). It works by introducing faults into a system via source code mutation and by analysing the ability of the test suite to detect these faults. The idea is that the mutation should simulate common mistakes by developers. Hence, when a test suite is able to find such artificial faults, it should also find real faults that can occur through programming mistakes.

Developers are likely to make mistakes with standard language features, but because Ethereum is relatively young, they are more likely to confuse Solidity specific features. For example, Solidity offers two different types of assertions: `require(.)` is used to check external consistency, and `assert(.)` is used to check internal consistency. Both terminate the contract but with a different status.

Developers also have trouble with the qualifiers that Solidity offers, for example `external` is for functions that can be called from other contracts and via transactions, but not internally, and `public` is for functions that can either be called internally or via transactions.

Finally, the addresses of contracts and externally owned accounts play such an important role in smart contracts that there are several ways of specifying addresses that may confuse the developer. For example `msg.sender` is the address of the sender of a message, and `tx.origin` is the address of the externally owned account that sent a transaction. They are the same for a short call chain but not for a longer call chain.

Mutation testing is an old technique, but it has still open challenges, like the equivalent mutant problem, which occurs when a mutation does not change the original program, e.g., when a fault is injected in dead code. There are methods to detect equivalent mutants [9,11,21,22], but it is still not possible to remove all equivalent mutants. Hence, this limits the usability of mutation testing, since a high manual effort is required to identify equivalent mutants.

There are 11 related papers that propose mutation testing operators for Solidity. The number of introduced mutation operators in these publications varies widely, since it is up to the tester to choose the scope or specificity of the operators. Some authors prefer to introduce a specific operator for every singular change, others choose to group together similar changes into one operator, which is more common and was also done by us.

Bond[4] implements just one mutation operator from the Mothra set and does not provide an evaluation. Burgrara [3] does not mutate Solidity, but manually mutates lower level EVM code, ABI encodings and public key operations.

---

[4] There is no paper available on eth-mutants, but there is a GitHub page https:// github.com/federicobond/eth-mutants.

Chapman [4] proposes 61 mutation operators for Solidity and evaluates them on a set of six DApps. Fu et al. [6] propose mutation testing for the implementation of the Ethereum Virtual Machine (EVM), but not for smart contracts. Groce et al. [8] describe a generic mutation tool with a set of specific operators for Solidity, but without an evaluation. Peng et al. [25] describe five mutation operators and evaluate them on a set of 51 smart contracts. Wang et al. [30] use some unspecified mutations from the Mothra set to study test coverage. Wang et al. [29] do not mutate Solidity but transactions sequences.

Three papers are closely related to ours and served us as a basis for our mutation operators: Andesta et al. [1] propose 57 mutation operators for Solidity and evaluate them by investigating how the mutation operators are able to recreate known attacks, such as the DAO attack [18]. The authors do not provide mutation scores, and they only evaluate to what extent they can reproduce known vulnerabilities in a few contracts. Hence, they show no evaluation for most of their operators. Honig et al. [12] describe two Solidity specific operators and adopt four existing operators. They evaluate the operators on two popular DApps that have extensive test suites with high code coverage. These test suites allow them to achieve high mutation scores, but the scope of their mutations is limited. Wu et al. [32] propose 15 Solidity specific operators, which were also supported by their tool called MuSC[5], and tested the operators on four DApps. They evaluate their approach by comparing the effectiveness of a test suite that was optimised based on the mutation score to one that was optimised based on code coverage. Moreover, they point out vulnerabilities that can be simulated with their operators. In contrast to our work, they have fewer operators concerning access control and hence they cannot reproduce some severe vulnerabilities regarding unauthorized access. There are other smart contract languages, like Vyper[6], Pact[7], Simplicity [20], which would require their own mutation operators. In principle, our novel killing condition would also work for these languages, but we focus on Solidity since it is the most popular smart contract language.

With our generalised mutation operators we are able to inject nearly all the changes from related work, with a few minor exceptions. For example, we do not mutate data types because it causes too many compilation errors. The evaluation of related work is limited to just a few DApps, and the results vary. The research question that follows from the analysis above is: *How efficient are the standard mutation operators as compared to Solidity specific operators?*

To break this question down into its more manageable sub questions we present a case study in mutation testing of a sample smart contract first, and then list the sub questions.

---

[5] There was a tool demo at ASE 2019 without a paper, but there is a GitHub page https://github.com/belikout/MuSC-Tool-Demo-repo.

[6] Vyper language documentation https://vyper.readthedocs.io.

[7] Pact white paper https://www.kadena.io/kadena-pactwhitepaper.

2.1   A Case Study in Mutation: Vitaluck

As a case study we use a lottery contract called Vitaluck [5]. The source of the contract can be browsed on Etherscan[8]. The contract contains a main method called Play and a number of management methods; Play contains the core of the business logic of the lottery. Each call to Play draws a random number in the range 1 to 1000 using the time stamp of the current block as a source of entropy. If the random number is greater than 900, the player wins the jackpot, and a percentage of each bet is paid to the owner of the contract.

Vitaluck is a relatively short contract (139 lines of source code excluding comments). It has not been used extensively; there are only 27 historic transactions that can also be browsed on Etherscan. The first transaction deploys the contract, and the remaining historic transactions are all calls to the Play method. None of management methods of the contract are ever called by the historic transactions on the blockchain. However, the Play method occupies the majority of the code and provides ample opportunities for using standard and Solidity specific operators. We give a number of examples of mutations below.

Each example is labelled with the mutation operator and a brief description of the operator. We indicate common known vulnerabilities, as described in the smart contract weakness classification (SWC) registry [27], which can be simulated with the mutation operators. Table 1 summarises the operators.

LR_I - Literal Integer replacement Since Vitaluck is a lottery, any mutation to the code that manages the jackpot has a high likelihood of causing a fault in the contract. The first sample mutation (line 149) changes 900 to 1 This is shown below, using an output format inspired by the Unix diff command. The range of _finalRandomNumber is 1 to 1000. If the condition in the if statement is true, the jackpot will be paid out, which in the original code happens on average 10% $(1-900/1000=0.1)$ of the time. After the mutation, the jackpot will be paid out 99.9% $(1-1/1000=0.999)$ of the time, which completely breaks the contract.

```
< if(_finalRandomNumber >= 900) {
> if(_finalRandomNumber >=  1 ) {
```

To determine if a replay test kills a mutant, we compare the output of the original contract to the output of the mutant. The output of a contract consists of the status and the emitted events of the transactions, and the outputs of the pure functions called by the test. The mutant above does not affect the status of any of the transactions of the test (they all succeed), but it does cause the event NewPlay(address player, uint number, bool won); to be emitted 17 times more with won=true than the original contract. Similarly, the mutant causes the pure function GetWinningAddress() to return a different address than the original contract. Both these differences are easy to detect from the output of the replay test, thus supporting the conclusion that this particular mutant is killed. For the remaining examples, we will not discuss the outputs.

MORD* - Modifier Replacement or Deletion The sample mutation below (line 257) deletes the modifier onlyCeo from the method that installs the address of a

---

[8] Vitaluck on Etherscan https://etherscan.io/address/0xef7c7254c290df3d1671823 56255cdfd8d3b400b.

new CEO. This allows anyone to set the payout address to his own, rather than just the CEO. This behaviour also corresponds to the vulnerability SWC-105, which can occur when the access control for functions is insufficient. The operator can further cause vulnerabilities, like the SWC-106 Unprotected SELFDESTRUCT Instruction, or SWC-123 Requirement Violation. Note that adequate tests for such faults would try to call these functions with unauthorized users in order to check if the expected error message occurs.

```
< function modifyCeo(address _newCeo) public onlyCeo {
> function modifyCeo(address _newCeo) public {
```

BOR - Boolean Operator Replacement The last sample mutation (line 93) replaces the Boolean operator = in the second statement of the function Play.

```
< if(totalTickets  = 0) {  ... return; }
> if(totalTickets != 0) {  ... return; }
```

Most smart contracts use the constructor to initialise the state of the contract. For some unknown reason, Vitaluck does not have a constructor. Instead, the contract relies on the first call to Play to initialise the state, including the jackpot. This is poor coding style, and it may be a security problem too. The mutant above allows us to discover the problem as follows. The first Play transaction executes the then branch, for which it needs 62347 gas out of a gas limit of 93520. However, the mutant skips the then branch and executes the rest of the Play method. This takes 272097 gas, which is about 3 times the gas limit. This suggests that using the gas limit to kill mutants might be of interest.

2.2   Sub Questions

Based on the Vitaluck case study we formulate subsidiary research questions.

Discarding Stillborn Mutants. We created a simple tool (ContractMut) that makes maximum use of existing state-of-the-art tools, such as the Truffle framework[9] and the Solidity compiler. In particular, the tool relies heavily on the Solidity compiler to read the source file and to generate the abstract syntax tree (AST). It would also be possible to mutate at the bytecode-level, but this would make it more difficult to understand what a mutant is doing. The AST approach has the advantages that the amount of bespoke tooling to be built is limited. The disadvantage is that the compiler has more information than it exposes via the AST. Our mutation tool does not have semantic information about the original code or the mutant as it works on the AST generated by the Solidity compiler. This means that some mutants are generated that do not compile. For example, when replacing * by - in an expression such as 1 * 9 / 10000000000000000000, an error occurs because a rational constant cannot be subtracted from an integer. This raises the sub question: *To what extent does the tool generate stillborn mutants?*

Discarding Duplicate and Equivalent Mutants. Duplicate and equivalent mutants distort the mutation score. The next sub question is therefore: *How to detect duplicate and equivalent mutants?*

---

[9] Truffle framework documentation https://www.trufflesuite.com.

Mutation Score. The purpose of generating mutants is to assess the quality of a test. If too few mutants are killed by a test, the usual course of action is to develop more tests, which is labour-intensive. However, for a smart contract like Vitaluck that has already been deployed on the blockchain, all historic transactions are available and can be decompiled into a test. A test then consists of replaying the sequence of historic transactions. We can control the size of the test by varying the number of transactions executed by the mutant. As the size of the test increases, we expect the mutation score to increase. Unfortunately, most historic transactions execute the same method calls, so the increase in mutation score should tail off rapidly. The sub question then is: *What is the relation between the mutation score and the length of the test?*

Efficiency of the Mutation Operators. We follow the competent programmer hypothesis [34] by mutating a subtle variant of a program fragment that could have been created by mistake. The sub question is: *What is the relative success of standard mutation operators as compared Solidity specific operators?*

Using Outputs in a Mutant Killing Condition. To determine whether a mutant is killed, a test compares the output of the original to the output of the mutant and kills the mutant if there are difference. The next sub question is: *Which observable outputs can be used in the killing condition?*

Using Gas in a Mutant Killing Condition. A tight limit on the amount of gas reduces the risk of having to pay too much for a transaction. However, if the limit is too tight, some method calls may fail unexpectedly. Deciding on the gas limit is therefore a non-trivial problem. This raises the following sub question: *To what extent is killing mutants based on exceeding the gas limit efficient?*

Table 1. Mutation operators for Solidity programs. Operators marked with an asterisk are Solidity specific.

Mothra operator	Our operator	Description	SWC ID
AOR/LCE/ROR	AOR	Assignment Operator Replacement	129
AOR/LCR/ROR	BOR	Binary Operator Replacement	129
SDL	ESD	Expression Statement Deletion	
SVR	ITSCR	Identifier with same Type, Scope, and Constancy Replacement	105,106
RSR	JSRD	Jump Statement Replacement/Deletion	
-	LR_A*	Literal Address Replacement	115
CRP/CSR/SCR/SRC	LR_{B,I,S}	Boolean, Int, String Replacement	
-	MORD*	Modifier Replacement/Deletion	105,106,123
-	QRD*	Qualifier for storage local or state mutability Replacement/Deletion	100,108
-	RAR*	R-Value Address Replacement	115
AOR/LCR/ROR	UORD	Unary Operator Replacement/Deletion	129
SVR	VDTSCS	Variable Declaration with same Type Scope and Constancy Swap	

3   Method

We describe an experiment in mutation testing of smart contracts on Ethereum. The experiments have been conducted on a uniform random sample of 1,120 smart contracts with tests from Truffle-tests-for-free that can also be downloaded from the replication package of this paper. We removed 157 contracts from the set because either they were non-deterministic or they did not have a test with 50 transactions. These 963 contracts are representative for the entire collection of 50,000+ verified smart contracts on Etherscan [10], and the sample is relatively large [24]. The tests are replay tests and relatively short, with an average bytecode coverage of 51.4% [10]. Our results are therefore a baseline.

A test for a contract begins by compiling and re-deploying the contract on a pristine blockchain. We use the Truffle framework for this with the exact same time stamps and transaction parameters as the historic deployment on the public Ethereum blockchain. All mainnet addresses are replaced by testnet addresses and all externally owned accounts have a generous balance. After re-deployment, the first 50 historic transactions are re-played, also with the historic time stamps and transaction parameters [10]. After each transaction all pure methods of a contract are called, with fuzzed parameters. This is intended to simulate any actions by a Distributed Application (DApp) built on top of the contract.

To detect whether a mutant is killed, we compare the outputs of a transaction generated by the original contract to the outputs of the corresponding transaction generated by the mutant contract. We compare only observable outputs of a transaction, which means that we consider only strong mutants that propagate faults to the outputs.

Discarding Stillborn Mutants. ContractMut uses the Solidity compiler to compile all the mutants it generates. If the compilation fails, the mutant is discarded. Smart contracts are usually relatively small, hence the time wasted on failed compilations is limited.

Discarding Duplicate and Equivalent Mutants. ContractMut implements the trivially equivalent mutant detection method [17] to discarded duplicate and equivalent mutants. Each new mutant is compiled and the bytecode of the new mutant is compared to the bytecode of the original and the bytecode of all previously generated mutants. If there is a match, the new mutant is discarded.

Mutation Score. Since the tests are machine generated, they are consistent in the sense that all sample contracts are tested by making 50 transactions. The advantage of using machine-generated tests is that this scales well to large numbers of contracts. The disadvantage is that the tests are not necessarily representative for handcrafted tests. For example, the bytecode coverage of the tests varies considerably, from 6% to 98% [10].

Efficiency of the Mutation Operators. ContractMut implements the core of the Mothra set [16], which is considered the minimum standard for mutation testing [24], as well as the essence of recently proposed Solidity specific operators. Table 1 lists the operators in alphabetical order. The first column of the table indicates the correspondence with the Mothra operators, and operators marked with an asterisk are Solidity specific. The next two columns give the name of the operator, and a description. The last column shows the relation of the operators to known vulnerabilities based on the smart contract weakness classification (SWC) registry [27].

We have implemented 84.8% of all 191 mutation operators from related work as a manageable set of 14 operators. We have not implemented object oriented operators (5.2%), and leave this for future work. Signed integers are rare in contracts; hence we have not implemented related operators (1.6%). We did not insert mutations at random locations in the code (6.8%), or type level mutations (1.0%), because these would generate mostly stillborn mutants. Our BOR operator covers 30.4% of the operators from related work, followed by QRD (18.3%), and ITSCR (11.0%). The replication package of this paper provides a table (`comparison.xslx`) mapping the operators from related work onto ours.

Mutants are created as follows. Each node in the AST represents a program fragment that could in principle be mutated. Therefore, all relevant AST nodes are collected in a candidate list. This includes simple statements, literals, identifiers, function parameters, and operators. Compound statements, methods, and even entire contracts are not in the candidate list, because mutations to such large program fragments are not consistent with the competent programmer hypothesis. Once the candidate list has been built, the tool repeatedly selects a mutation candidate uniformly at random from the list [33] and applies the appropriate mutation operator from Table 1.

Table 2. Gas used by the historic transaction as a percentage of the historic gas limit versus gas used by the replayed transaction as a percentage of the calculated gas limit.

% gas used of limit	Historic		Replay	
	(count)	(%)	(count)	(%)
$\geq$ 0% & < 20%	5062	11.3%	4292	12.3%
$\geq$ 20% & < 40%	6893	15.4%	5439	15.6%
$\geq$ 40% & < 60%	6405	14.3%	4314	12.4%
$\geq$ 60% & < 80%	9847	21.9%	7522	21.6%
$\geq$ 80% & < 100%	9564	21.3%	9119	26.2%
= 100%	7127	15.9%	4171	12.0%
Tx success	44898	100.0%	34857	100.0%
Tx failed	6032		16073	
Total Tx	50930		50930	
Minimum gas limit	21000		21000	
Maximum gas limit	8000029		15279099	
Mean gas limit	397212		416350	
Std. deviation gas limit	1002691		1071615	

Using Outputs in a Mutant Killing Condition. To determine whether a mutant is killed the outputs of the original contract are compared to the outputs of the mutant while executing each transaction of the test. *TxEvMeth* indicates a comparison of all observable outputs of a transaction as follows. *Tx* compares the transaction status (i.e., success, failure, or out of gas). *Ev* compares all outputs of all events emitted by a transaction. *Meth* compares all outputs of all pure methods called by the DApp simulation after each transaction. The combination *TxEvMeth* is the standard mutant killing condition.

Using Gas in a Mutant Killing Condition. To assess how tight the gas limits on historic transactions are, we have analysed the statistics of all $N = 50,930$ historic transactions downloaded from Truffle-tests-for-free. Columns two and three of Table 2 show that 15.9% of the sample use exactly the gas limit, and 11.3% use less than 20% of the gas limit. The minimum gas limit is 21,000 and the maximum is 8,000,029, which represents a large range. The standard deviation is also relatively large (1,002,691). Hence, there is considerable variance in how developers estimate the limit on transactions.

There are two reasons why the gas limit is often loose. Firstly, the standard tool `estimateGas` (from `web3.eth`) has to work out which EVM instructions a transaction will execute. Since each instruction costs a known amount of gas [31], the total gas cost of the transaction can then be calculated. However, for any non-trivial transaction the exact list of EVM instructions depends on the data in storage, and the data passed as parameters etc. This makes the estimates unreliable. [10]

Secondly, since gas costs real money, ultimately the developer has to decide on the basis of the gas estimate what the gas limit of the transaction should be. For example, setting the gas limit lower than the estimate reduces the risk of losing money via gas-based attacks, but also increases the risk of failing transactions.

For every transaction of a mutant, we could have called `estimateGas` to obtain an up-to-date gas estimate. However, we cannot go back to the developer and ask him to decide whether to increase or decrease the gas limit. In general, we do not even know who the developer might be. Therefore, we have developed a heuristic that transfers the developers decision on the gas limit of the historic transaction to the gas limit of the mutant transaction.

Assume that the limit as provided by a historic transaction, *glh*, is a hard limit on the amount of gas that the developer is prepared to use. Then, in principle we can use this limit to kill all mutants executing the same transaction that exceed the limit. However, since we are replaying each historic transaction on the Truffle framework, the amount of gas used by replaying the transaction may be slightly different. To compensate for this, we propose to calculate the gas limit on replaying a transaction, *glr*, as the maximum of the gas limit of the historic transaction, and the scaled gas limit of the historic transaction. The scaling applied is the ratio of *gur*, the gas used by the replay, and *guh*, the gas used by the historic transaction:

$$glr = max(glh, \frac{gur}{guh} glh)$$

---

[10] What are the limitations to estimateGas and when would its estimate be considerably wrong? https://ethereum.stackexchange.com/questions/266.

Here glh, and guh are both obtained from historic transaction on the blockchain. gur is obtained by replaying the historic (i.e. not mutated) transaction on the Truffle framework, with the maximum gas limit.

With this heuristic the last sample mutant of Sect. 2 will be killed. If we had used `web3.eth.estimateGas` instead of the heuristic, the mutation would not have been killed. However, this would go against the intention of the developer, who had anticipated that the first call of the `Play` method should just initialise the contract, thus never taking a large amount of gas.

The last two columns of Table 2 show the statistics of glr calculated according to the formula above. The distribution is similar to that of the gas used by the historic transaction, but there is more variance. The max operation in particular makes the limit on the gas used by the replay less tight than the gas limit on the historic transaction. In the next section, we will investigate to what extent glr is efficient as a killing condition. We will call this the *Limit* condition, and apply it on its own, and in combination with the other two conditions.

4   Results

This section describes the results of our experiment in mutation testing of smart contracts on Ethereum. For each smart contract with a test we tried to generate exactly 50 non-equivalent mutants. Since each attempt requires a call to the Solidity compiler, we set an upper limit of 1,000 on the number of attempts to generate a mutant. For 18 smart contracts fewer than 50 trivially non-equivalent mutants were generated, but for the remaining 98.3% of the contracts we obtained 50 non-equivalent mutants. In total, we generated 71,314 mutants, of which 47,870 were compilable and not trivial equivalent [17] or duplicate. For each contract we then executed the tests against all trivially non-equivalent mutants on the Truffle framework. We ran $47,870 \times 50 = 2,393,500$ transactions, which took over a week to run on 14 Linux virtual machines (Xeon dual core, 2.4 GHZ, with 16 GB RAM).

Discarding Stillborn Mutants. Of the generated 71,314 mutants, 11,252 (15.8%) could not be compiled. As expected the QRD^* operator generates the most stillborn mutants: 63.3% of the mutants with this operator did not compile. We take this as an indication that using the limited amount of semantic information available in the Solidity AST is an acceptable approach towards building a baseline mutation tool. The percentage of stillborn mutants can be reduced to zero if the full power of various semantics analyses of the compiler could be leveraged, but the cost of building such a mutation tool just to reduce a relatively small percentage of failed compilations alone would not be justifiable.

Discarding Duplicate and Equivalent Mutants. Of the 71,314 generated mutants, 12,192 (17.1%) were trivially equivalent to the original or a duplicate of another mutant. The trivial equivalent detection method [17] that we used is therefore reasonably effective, especially since often about 40–45% of the mutants can be equivalent [9,26].

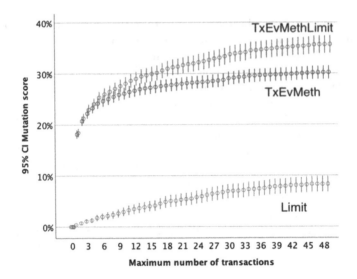

Fig. 1. Percentage of non-equivalent mutants killed as a function of the length of the test. The error bars correspond to a confidence interval of 95%.

Mutation Score. Fig. 1 shows how the mutation score increases with the test size. The error bars for a 95% confidence interval are small. The standard mutant killing condition *TxEvMeth* has most success early on, whereas the success of the *Limit* condition increases more gradually. This difference can be explained as follows. All tests execute the constructor method in transaction 0 and one regular method in transaction 1. A large fraction of the tests only execute these two methods, hence most of the opportunity for killing a mutant on regular outputs occurs during transactions 0 and 1.

Since in general size matters [13], we fixed the size of the tests to 50 transactions. However, we could not fix the size of the smart contracts. To study the influence of contract size we have calculated the rank correlation of the size of the bytecode and the mutation score. For the combined killing condition *TxEvMeth-Limit*, we found Kendall's $\tau = -0.11$ ($p = 0.01$, 2-tailed). This means that the mutation score is not correlated with the size of the test. We also calculated the correlation between the mutation score and the fraction of bytecodes that was executed by the test and found the correlation to be moderate: Kendall's $\tau = 0.45$ ($p = 0.01$, 2-tailed). The literature reports similar figures [7].

Efficiency of the Mutation Operators. Table 3 shows to what extent the mutation operators from Table 1 have been successful. The first column gives the name of the mutation operator. The next two columns indicate how many mutants were not killed, and how many were killed. The fourth column gives the total number of trivially non-equivalent mutants. The last two columns give the percentages related to the numbers in columns two and three.

Table 3. Contingency table of the mutation operators against the mutation score with the *TxEvMethLimit* mutant killing condition.

Mutation operator	Non-equivalent mutants			Percentage	
	Not killed	Killed	Total	Not killed	Killed
AOR	2178	1039	3217	67.7%	32.3%
BOR	3549	2245	5794	61.3%	38.7%
ESD	5246	2595	7841	66.9%	33.1%
ITSCR	7796	4085	11881	65.6%	34.4%
JSRD	1866	1090	2956	63.1%	36.9%
LR_A*	46	58	104	44.2%	55.8%
LR_B	973	225	1198	81.2%	18.8%
LR_I	1526	1089	2615	58.4%	41.6%
LR_S	158	329	487	32.4%	67.6%
MORD*	921	143	1064	86.6%	13.4%
QRD*	1041	1761	2802	37.2%	62.8%
RAR*	3002	1158	4160	72.2%	27.8%
UORD	297	189	486	61.1%	38.9%
VDTSCS	2215	1050	3265	67.8%	32.2%
Total	30814	17056	47870	64.4%	35.6%

$\chi^2 = 1759.6, df = 13, p < 0.001$

Table 4. Comparison of the effectiveness of all mutants versus the manually analysed mutant after test bootstrapping.

Mutation operator	All mutants		Stratified sample			
	Killed	Total	Killed	Total	Equivalent	Killable
Mothra	35.1%	39740	41.3%	223	3.1%	96.9%
Solidity	38.4%	8130	48.1%	27	3.7%	92.6%
Total	35.6%	47870	42.0%	250	3.2%	96.4%

$\chi^2 = 32.2, df = 1, p < 0.001$ $\chi^2 = 8.3, df = 2, p = 0.016$

Table 3 shows that of the four Solidity specific operators (marked with an asterisk) *QRD** is the most efficient when it comes to being easily killed. This is because subtle changes to the qualifiers, such as removing the `payable` attribute from a method completely breaks the contract. The standard *LR_S* operator is the most efficient operator overall, because strings in Solidity are typically used for communication with the DApp built on top of a smart contract. This means that even the smallest change to a string will be detected by comparing event parameters or method results. The *MORD** operator has the lowest efficiency (13.4%), because relatively few historic transactions try to violate the access control implemented by the modifiers. The *RAR** operator also has a low efficiency, for the same reason: few historic transactions try to exploit bugs in address checking.

Table 5. Comparison of coverage and mutation scores with related work.

Related work	Average mutation score	Average statement coverage	DApps or smart contracts
[12]	96.0%	99.5%	Aragon OS, Openzeppelin-Solidity
[32]	43.9%	68.9%	Skincoin, SmartIdentity, AirSwap, Cryptofin
[4]	40.3%	95.4%	MetaCoin, MultiSigWallet, Alice
This	35.5%	47.6%*	963 Verified smart contracts
bootstr.	96.4%		DBToken, MultiSigWallet, NumberBoard, casinoProxy, mall

* Average bytecode coverage

To assess the effect of using a replay test suite on the mutation score, we have analysed by hand all 250 mutants generated for 5 carefully selected smart contracts. The analysis meant that for each mutant we looked at whether the test could be extended in such a way that the output could kill the test. We call this *test bootstrapping*: a method that uses the replay tests to systematically create proper tests. Each contract took us about one day to analyse, hence we had to limit the number of contracts to a small number like 5.

We used a stratified sampling method, taking one contract for the top 5% contracts by mutation score, one contract from the bottom 5%, and one contract each from $25 \pm 2.5\%$, $50 \pm 2.5\%$ and $75 \pm 2.5\%$. In selecting the contracts from the five ranges, we tried to avoid analysing the same type of contract more than once. We analysed: DBToken[11], MultiSigWallet[12], the auction NumberBoard[13], the game casinoProxy[14], and the asset manager mall[15].

Table 4 shows that the key statistics of the 250 manually analysed mutants and all 47,870 mutants are comparable, which suggests that the results we obtain for the 250 mutants are representative for all mutants. The left and right half of Table 4 show a contingency table for the mutation operator types versus the status of the different mutation results. The Mothra operators generate more semantically equivalent mutants than the solidity operators, but overall the per-

---

[11] DBToken on Etherscan https://etherscan.io/address/0x42a952Ac23d020610355 Cf425d0dfa58295287BE.

[12] MultiSigWallet on Etherscan https://etherscan.io/address/0xa723606e907bf842 15d5785ea7f6cd93a0fbd121.

[13] NumberBoard on Etherscan https://etherscan.io/address/0x9249133819102b2 ed31680468c8c67F6Fe9E7505.

[14] casinoProxy on Etherscan https://etherscan.io/address/0x23a3db04432123ccdf 4459684329cc7c0b022.

[15] mall on Etherscan https://etherscan.io/address/0x3304a44aa16ec40fb53a5b8f086 f230c237f683d.

centage of semantically equivalent mutants in the stratified sample is only 3.2%. This indicates that semantically equivalent mutants do not inflate the base line statistics by more than a few per cent points. The second conclusion that can be drawn from Table 4 is that almost 100% mutation scores are possible with bootstrapped versions the replay tests. A mutation score of 100% is not achievable with the current implementation because it cannot detect the success or failure of an internal transaction.

Of the 3,304,002 bytecode instructions of all original contracts together, the replay tests execute 1,574,239 instructions, giving an average bytecode coverage of 47.6%. This makes achieving a high mutation score more difficult, as a mutation to code that is not executed will never be killed. Our results are thus a baseline, and to explore how far removed the base line is from results with hand-crafted tests we compare our results to related work in Table 5. The first column lists the citation to all related work that we aware of that report mutation scores for smart contracts. The next two columns give the average mutation score, and the statement (bytecode) coverage. The last column lists the DApps tested.

High statement coverage does not necessarily lead to a high mutation score, because the effect of the mutant may not be visible in the outputs. Honig et al. [12] propose a small set of highly efficient mutants. Chapman [4] has about the same code coverage as Honig et al. but he proposes a large set of mutants; this reduces his mutation score. Our main result is comparable to that of Wu et al. [32], but we have also shown that by taking the replay tests as a basis and improving them by test bootstrapping leads to the same high mutation scores that others have found.

Using Outputs in a Mutant Killing Condition. The mutation score for *TxEvMethLimit* reaches 35.6%, for *TxEvMeth* 30.2%, and for *Limit* 8.3%. These mutation scores are low compared to state-of-the-art approaches [24]. However, this figure is useful as a baseline for other approaches that use realistic tests instead of replay tests, and our aim was not to achieve a high mutation score, but to evaluate the applicability of mutation operators for a high number of contracts. Moreover, even such a small score is helpful to show what kind of tests are missing and what has to be done to improve the tests.

Using Gas in a Mutant Killing Condition. The contribution of the gas limit as killing condition is 35.6%−30.2%= 5.4%, which seems rather small, but since it can require a huge manual effort to analyse the surviving mutant, even such a small fraction can save hours or days of manual work.

5   Discussion and Limitations

We put the results in a broader context and answer the research question.

Discarding Stillborn Mutants We believe that the percentage of the generated mutants that do not compile was relatively small and that it was acceptable in the exploratory context. A production tool would have to implement more sophisticated mutations and would therefore have more knowledge of the semantics of smart contracts.

Discarding Duplicate and Equivalent Mutants. A simple but state-of-the-art approach has been used to address the equivalent mutant problem. What we have not investigated is to what extent gas usage can be leveraged to discard more equivalent mutants; we suggest this as a topic for future work.

Mutation Score. By leveraging the historic data available on the Ethereum blockchain we have been able to generate tests that can be truncated to explore the relationship between test strength and the mutation score. As expected, the efficiency of the mutation operators tails off quickly.

Efficiency of the Mutation Operators. One of the Solidity specific mutation operators was found to be more effective in producing mutants that have a high chance of being killed than most of the standard mutation operators. We take this as an indication that further research is needed to develop more sophisticated Solidity specific mutation operators. Another, important aspect of mutation operators is to which extent they can introduce common or severe bugs. To assess this quality, we inspected the ability of our operators to introduce known vulnerabilities that can have severe consequences. The associated vulnerabilities as (specified by the SWC) are shown in Table 1. It should be noted that we are able to simulate most vulnerabilities, which are related to simple mistakes in the source code. Additionally, it can be seen that the specific operators are concerned with more vulnerabilities and that they are more severe compared to the standard operators. For example, $MORD^*$ can trigger three different kinds of access control related vulnerabilities, which would not be possible with the standard operators. This allowed us to discover a vulnerability in one of the contracts, which we have reported to the owners by way of responsible disclosure: the modifier `onlyOwner` is missing on one of the methods.

Our mutation score is lower than the scores reported by related work but this is not due to the choice of mutation operators but caused by the use of replay tests. Bootstrapped replay tests are comparable to hand crafted tests.

Using Outputs in a Mutant Killing Condition. Comparing the observable outputs of a transaction of mutant and original is an efficient killing condition.

Using Gas in a Mutant Killing Condition. We have shown that using the gas consumption as a killing condition can improve the mutation score and hence the effectiveness of the mutation approach in general. The contribution of the gas limit as a killing condition is small because gas limits are usually not tight. We suggest as future work an exploration of alternative heuristics to determine a tighter gas limit.

We are now able to answer the main research question: Our Solidity specific mutation operators are more efficient than the standard operators, and they also are able to introduce more and more severe vulnerabilities. Table 4 shows that the difference in efficiency is 3.3% point, which is modest, but also statistically significant at $(p < 0.001)$.

5.1   Limitations and Threats to Validity

A threat to the validity of our evaluation might be that we only consider a replay test suite that is less powerful than other testing techniques, which might obtain a higher mutation score. Although there are better testing techniques, the focus of this work was not to find them, but to build a mutation-based test quality assurance method that can also serve as a baseline for other testing techniques.

Another argument regarding the validity of our method might be that it is not wise to kill a mutant only based on a different gas usage since it could still be semantically equal. However, we believe that a different gas usage is still a valid reason to kill a mutant, because it represents a change in the monetary cost of a transaction. Moreover, there are other comparable cost factors, like energy [14] or execution time [19] that have been used as killing condition in the past.

The replication package of this paper presents the recently proposed checklist [24] for research on mutation testing to analyse our work.

6   Conclusions and Future Work

From almost 200 mutation operators from related work, we have generalized a compact set of 14 operators and tested them on a large scale. Our Solidity specific operators were able to produce nearly all the mutations that were proposed in the related work, with only a few minor exceptions.

To achieve scale, we used replay tests that were automatically generated from the Ethereum blockchain. To the best of our knowledge there is no related work that performs mutation testing for smart contracts at scale.

The average mutation scores that we achieved with our replay tests were not as good as the scores from the best handwritten tests, but also various studies with manual tests have comparable scores. It should be pointed out that the score can depend strongly on the choice of the mutation operators, and manual tests often undergo many iterations to improve the score. We have also shown that the replay tests can be improved manually, such that a score close to 100% can be reached.

Using our novel killing condition based on the gas limit allowed us to improve the mutation score by a maximum of 5.5%. This does not sound like much, but it can save a lot of manual effort for the analysis of surviving mutants.

Four of the 14 operators have been specifically developed for Solidity and the others originate form the core of the Mothra set. The Solidity-specific operators are on average more efficient than the standard Mothra operators. We have shown that serious vulnerabilities can be detected with the help of specific operators; this shows that tailor-made mutation operators are useful.

It would be interesting to study errors made by Solidity developers at scale to validate the mutation operators. Another area of future work would be to use the gas limit on transactions to detect equivalent mutants.

Acknowledgments. This work was supported in part by the National Research Foundation (NRF), Prime Minister's Office, Singapore, under its National Cybersecurity

R&D Programme (Award No. NRF2016NCR-NCR002-028) and administered by the National Cybersecurity R&D Directorate.

We thank Maarten Everts, Joran Honig, Sun Jun, and the anonymous reviewers for their comments on our work.

The replication package for the experiments can be found at https://doi.org/10.5281/zenodo.3726691.

References

1. Andesta, E., Faghih, F., Fooladgar, M.: Testing smart contracts gets smarter. Technical report, Department of Electrical and Computer Engineering University of Tehran, December 2019. https://arxiv.org/abs/1912.04780
2. Atzei, N., Bartoletti, M., Cimoli, T.: A survey of attacks on ethereum smart contracts (SoK). In: Maffei, M., Ryan, M. (eds.) POST 2017. LNCS, vol. 10204, pp. 164–186. Springer, Heidelberg (2017). https://doi.org/10.1007/978-3-662-54455-6_8
3. Bugrara, S.: User experience with language-independent formal verification. Technical report, ConsenSys, December 2019. https://arxiv.org/abs/1912.02951
4. Chapman, P.: Deviant: a mutation testing tool for Solidity smart contracts. Master thesis 1593, Boise State University, August 2019. https://doi.org/10.18122/td/1593/boisestate
5. Chia, V., et al.: Rethinking blockchain security: position paper. In: Atiquzzaman, M., Li, J., Meng, W. (eds.) Confs on Internet of Things, Green Computing and Communications, Cyber, Physical and Social Computing, Smart Data, Blockchain, Computer and Information Technology, Congress on Cybermatics, pp. 1273–1280. IEEE, Halifax, Canada, July 2018. https://doi.org/10.1109/Cybermatics_2018.2018.00222
6. Fu, Y., Ren, M., Ma, F., Jiang, Y., Shi, H., Sun, J.: Evmfuzz: differential fuzz testing of Ethereum virtual machine. Technical report, Tsinghua University, China, April 2019. https://arxiv.org/abs/1903.08483
7. Gopinath, R., Jensen, C., Groce, A.: Code coverage for suite evaluation by developers. In: 36th International Conference on Software Engineering (ICSE), pp. 72–82. ACM, New York, Hyderabad, India, May 2014. https://doi.org/10.1145/2568225.2568278
8. Groce, A., Holmes, J., Marinov, D., Shi, A., Zhang, L.: An extensible, regular-expression-based tool for multi-language mutant generation. In: 40th International Conference on Software Engineering: Companion Proceeedings (ICSE), pp. 25–28. ACM, New York, Gothenburg, Sweden, May 2018. https://doi.org/10.1145/3183440.3183485
9. Grün, B.J.M., Schuler, D., Zeller, A.: The impact of equivalent mutants. In: Second International Conference on Software Testing Verification and Validation, ICST 2009, Denver, Colorado, USA, 1–4 April 2009, Workshops Proceedings, pp. 192–199. IEEE Computer Society (2009). https://doi.org/10.1109/ICSTW.2009.37
10. Hartel, P., van Staalduinen, M.: Truffle tests for free - replaying Ethereum smart contracts for transparency. Technical report, Singapore University of Technology and Design, Singapore, July 2019. https://arxiv.org/abs/1907.09208
11. Hierons, R.M., Harman, M., Danicic, S.: Using program slicing to assist in the detection of equivalent mutants. Softw. Test. Verif. Reliab. **9**(4), 233–262 (1999). https://doi.org/10.1002/(sici)1099-1689(199912)9:4⟨233::aid-stvr191⟩3.0.co;2-3

12. Honig, J.J., Everts, M.H., Huisman, M.: Practical mutation testing for smart con-tracts. In: Pérez-Solà, C., Navarro-Arribas, G., Biryukov, A., Garcia-Alfaro, J. (eds.) DPM/CBT -2019. LNCS, vol. 11737, pp. 289–303. Springer, Cham (2019). https://doi.org/10.1007/978-3-030-31500-9_19

13. Inozemtseva, L., Holmes, R.: Coverage is not strongly correlated with test suite effectiveness. In: 36th International Conference on Software Engineering (ICSE), pp. 435–445. ACM, New York, Hyderabad (2014). https://doi.org/10.1145/2568225.2568271

14. Jabbarvand, R., Malek, S.: μdroid: an energy-aware mutation testing framework for android. In: Bodden, E., Schäfer, W., van Deursen, A., Zisman, A. (eds.) Pro-ceedings of the 2017 11th Joint Meeting on Foundations of Software Engineering, ESEC/FSE 2017, Paderborn, Germany, 4–8 September 2017. pp. 208–219. ACM (2017). https://doi.org/10.1145/3106237.3106244

15. Jia, Y., Harman, M.: An analysis and survey of the development of mutation testing. IEEE Trans. Softw. Eng. **37**(5), 649–678 (2011). https://doi.org/10.1109/TSE.2010.62

16. King, K.N., Offutt, A.J.: A fortran language system for mutation-ased software testing. Softw.-Pract. Experience **21**(7), 685–718 (1991). https://doi.org/10.1002/spe.4380210704

17. Kintis, M., Papadakis, M., Jia, Y., Malevris, N., Traon, Y.L., Harman, M.: Detect-ing trivial mutant equivalences via compiler optimisations. IEEE Trans. Softw. Eng. **44**(4), 308–333 (2018). https://doi.org/10.1109/TSE.2017.2684805

18. Mehar, M.I., et al.: Understanding a revolutionary and flawed grand experiment in blockchain: the dao attack. J. Cases Inf. Technol. **21**(1), 19–32 (2019). https://doi.org/10.4018/JCIT.2019010102

19. Nilsson, R., Offutt, J., Mellin, J.: Test case generation for mutation-based testing of timeliness. Electron. Notes Theor. Comput. Sci. **164**(4), 97–114 (2006). https://doi.org/10.1016/j.entcs.2006.10.010

20. O'Connor, R.: Simplicity: a new language for blockchains. In: Proceedings of the 2017 Workshop on Programming Languages and Analysis for Security, PLAS@CCS 2017, Dallas, TX, USA, 30 October 2017. pp. 107–120. ACM (2017). https://doi.org/10.1145/3139337.3139340

21. Offutt, A.J., Craft, W.M.: Using compiler optimization techniques to detect equiv-alent mutants. Softw. Test. Verif. Reliab. **4**(3), 131–154 (1994). https://doi.org/10.1002/stvr.4370040303

22. Offutt, A.J., Pan, J.: Automatically detecting equivalent mutants and infeasible paths. Softw. Test. Verif. Reliab. **7**(3), 165–192 (1997). https://doi.org/10.1002/(sici)1099-1689(199709)7:3⟨165::aid-stvr143⟩3.0.co;2-u

23. Offutt, A.J., Untch, R.H.: Mutation 2000: uniting the orthogonal. In: Wong, E.W. (ed.) Mutation Testing for the New Century, pp. 34–44. Springer, Boston (2001). https://doi.org/10.1007/978-1-4757-5939-6_7

24. Papadakis, M., Kintis, M., Zhang, J., Jia, Y., Traon, Y.L., Harman, M.: Muta-tion testing advances: an analysis and survey. Adv. Comput. **112**, 275–378 (2019). https://doi.org/10.1016/bs.adcom.2018.03.015. Elsevier

25. Peng, C., Rajan, A.: Sif: a framework for Solidity code instrumentation and anal-ysis. Technical report, University of Edinburgh, UK, May 2019. https://arxiv.org/abs/1905.01659

26. Schuler, D., Zeller, A.: (un-)covering equivalent mutants. In: Third International Conference on Software Testing, Verification and Validation, ICST 2010, Paris, France, 7–9 April 2010, pp. 45–54. IEEE Computer Society (2010). https://doi.org/10.1109/ICST.2010.30

27. SmartContractSecurity: Smart contract weakness classification registry (2019). https://github.com/SmartContractSecurity/SWC-registry/

28. Tengeri, D., et al.: Relating code coverage, mutation score and test suite reducibility to defect density. In: Ninth IEEE International Conference on Software Testing, Verification and Validation Workshops, ICST Workshops 2016, Chicago, IL, USA, 11–15 April 2016, pp. 174–179. IEEE Computer Society (2016). https://doi.org/10.1109/ICSTW.2016.25

29. Wang, H., Li, Y., Lin, S.W., Artho, C., Ma, L., Liu, Y.: Oracle-supported dynamic exploit generation for smart contracts. Technical report, Nanyang Technological University, Singapore, September 2019. https://arxiv.org/abs/1909.06605

30. Wang, X., Xie, Z., He, J., Zhao, G., Ruihua, N.: Basis path coverage criteria for smart contract application testing. Technical report, School of Computer Science, South China Normal University Guangzhou, China, Noveember 2019. https://arxiv.org/abs/1911.10471

31. Wood, G.: Ethereum: a secure decentralised generalised transaction ledger - EIP-150 revision. Technical report 759dccd, Ethcore.io, August 2017. https://ethereum.github.io/yellowpaper/paper.pdf

32. Wu, H., Wang, X., Xu, J., Zou, W., Zhang, L., Chen, Z.: Mutation testing for Ethereum smart contract. Technical report, Nanjing University, China, August 2019. https://arxiv.org/abs/1908.03707

33. Zhang, L., Hou, S.S., Hu, J.J., Xie, T., Mei, H.: Is operator-based mutant selection superior to random mutant selection? In: 32nd International Conference on Software Engineering (ICSE), pp. 435–444. ACM, New York, Cape Town, May 2010. https://doi.org/10.1145/1806799.1806863

34. Zhu, Q., Panichella, A., Zaidman, A.: A systematic literature review of how mutation testing supports quality assurance processes. J. Softw. Test. Verif. Reliab. **28**(6), e1675:1–e1675:39 (2018). https://doi.org/10.1002/stvr.1675

Deductive Binary Code Verification Against Source-Code-Level Specifications

Alexander Kamkin[1,2,3,4]($\boxtimes$), Alexey Khoroshilov[1,2,3,4], Artem Kotsynyak[1], and Pavel Putro[1,4]

[1] Ivannikov Institute for System Programming of the Russian Academy of Sciences, Moscow, Russia
{kamkin,khoroshilov,kotsynyak,pavel.putro}@ispras.ru
[2] Lomonosov Moscow State University, Moscow, Russia
[3] Moscow Institute of Physics and Technology, Moscow, Russia
[4] National Research University – Higher School of Economics, Moscow, Russia

Abstract. There is a high demand in practical methods and tools to ensure total correctness of critical software components. A usual assumption is that the machine code (or binary code) generated by a compiler follows the semantics of the programming language. Unfortunately, modern compilers such as GCC and LLVM are too complex to be thoroughly verified, and bugs in the generated code are not uncommon. As an alternative approach, we suggest proving that the generated machine code still satisfies the functional properties expressed at the source code level. The suggested approach takes an ACSL-annotated C function along with its binary code and checks that the binary code meets the ACSL annotations. The main steps are as follows: (1) disassembling the machine code and extracting its semantics; (2) adapting the annotations to the machine level and generating the verification conditions. The implementation utilizes MicroTESK, Frama-C, Why3, and other tools. To illustrate the solution, we use the RISC-V microprocessor architecture; however, the approach is relatively independent of the target platform as it is based on formal specifications of the instruction set. It is worth noting that the presented method can be exploited as a test oracle for compiler testing.

Keywords: Binary code analysis · Deductive verification · Equivalence checking · Formal instruction set specification · Compiler testing

1 Introduction

The role of software in safety- and security-critical infrastructure grows continuously and at an ever-increasing speed. As a result, there is a high demand in practical methods and tools to ensure correctness of the most important software components. There are a number of research projects in the area: some of them confine themselves to checking the absence of specific kinds of bugs (e.g. runtime errors), while the others try to prove *total correctness* of the software under analysis. The total correctness typically means that each possible execution of

© Springer Nature Switzerland AG 2020
W. Ahrendt and H. Wehrheim (Eds.): TAP 2020, LNCS 12165, pp. 43–58, 2020.
https://doi.org/10.1007/978-3-030-50995-8_3

the software component *terminates* and meets the *functional contract* expressed in the form of *pre-* and *postconditions* on the component's interfaces. To prove such kind of properties, *deductive verification methods* are usually applied.

While the first ideas of the methods appeared in the works of R.W. Floyd [1] and C.A.R. Hoare [2] at the end of 1960s (inductive assertions, axiomatic semantics, etc.), deductive verification of production software became realistic just recently [3–7]. All the examples of deductive verification tools for the imperative programming paradigm follow the similar approach:

– all statements of the programming language get *formal semantics*;
– functional requirements to the software component are formalized as *pre-* and *postconditions* of the functions (or methods) in a *specification language*;
– additional hints to a verification framework such as *loop invariants* and *variants, ghost code*, and *lemma functions* are provided by a user;
– *verification conditions* are generated by the framework and are discharged either automatically with a *solver* or with an *interactive proof assistant*;
– proof of all the verification conditions means that *all possible executions* of the software component satisfy the functional requirements under a set of *assumptions* on execution environment, development tools, etc.

A usual assumption is that the *machine code* (or *binary code*) generated by a *compiler* follows the formal semantics of the programming language defined by the verification framework. It would be reasonable if the compiler transformations were formally verified. Though there is ongoing research and development of such tools (a good example is CompCert [8]), the industry is still bound to high-end optimizing compilers, like GCC and Clang/LLVM. Unfortunately, they are too complex to be thoroughly verified, and bugs in the generated machine code are not uncommon [9].

As an alternative approach dismissing the unwarranted trust to a compiler, we propose to prove that the produced binary code still satisfies the functional properties expressed in the pre- and postconditions of the source code functions. The idea looks attractive because it should be much easier to check the correctness of one particular code transformation than to verify the entire compiler (in a sense, this is a test oracle that determines whether the compiler behavior is correct or not). Moreover, it makes it possible to enable aggressive optimizations that are unsafe in general but are acceptable for a given component and its functional contract. At the same time, there are a lot of difficulties to overcome:

– the target *instruction set architecture* (*ISA*) – the registers, the memory, the addressing modes, and the instructions – should be *formally specified* (there is no other way to reason about the machine code's semantics);
– the *source-code-level specifications* should be *adapted* to the binary code level (in particular, one needs to find a correspondence between the variables in the source code and the registers and memory locations in the machine code);
– the *verification hints*, including loop invariants and variants, ghost code, and, probably, lemma functions, should be *reused* at the binary code level or there should be an alternative way to provide them for the machine code.

Our contributions are as follows (references to the languages mentioned here will be given in Sect. 3):

- we have developed a tool to extract machine code's semantics based on the ISA specifications in nML: given a binary, the result is the control flow graph (CFG) whose basic blocks contain operations over bit vectors and bit-vector arrays representing the registers and the memory;
- we have proposed a technique for adapting functional contracts and verification hints to the binary code level (unless the code is optimized): given an ACSL-annotated C source and the generated binary, the result is a set of ISA-aware assertions and verification conditions in SMT-LIB;
- we have applied the suggested approach to a number of small C functions supplied with ACSL annotations and have automatically verified the total correctness of their non-optimized RISC-V code by proving the extracted verification conditions with an SMT solver.

The rest of this paper is organized as follows. Section 2 overviews the works addressing deductive verification of software components at the machine code level. Section 3 describes the proposed approach in details. Namely, the following steps are considered: formalizing the target ISA; disassembling the binary code and extracting the SMT-LIB implementation model; translating the ACSL annotations to the SMT-LIB specification model; adapting the specification model to the machine code and generating the verification conditions. All the steps are illustrated by the example of the memset library function being compiled to the RISC-V ISA. Section 4 contains experimental evaluation of the approach. Finally, Sect. 5 concludes the paper and outlines future work directions.

2   Related Work

In the Why3-AVR project [10], the deductive verification approach is applied to prove correctness of branch-free assembly programs for the AVR microcontrollers. The AVR ISA is formally specified in the WhyML language. A programmer is allowed to annotate assembly code with pre- and postconditions and check its correctness by using the Why3 platform [11] along with external solvers and proof assistants. The approach seems to be useful for low-level development as Why3 has rich capabilities for code analysis and transformation. Our goal is a bit different: we would like to reuse the source-code-level specifications at the binary code level. It is also unclear if the approach scales to more complex ISAs.

In [12], the HOL4 proof assistant [13] is used to verify machine-code programs for subsets of ARM, PowerPC, and x86 (IA-32). The mentioned ISAs were specified independently: the ARM and x86 models [14,15] were written in HOL4, while the PowerPC model [16] was written in Coq [17] (as a part of the CompCert project [8]) and then manually translated to HOL4. The author distinguishes four levels of abstraction. Machine code (level 1) is automatically decompiled into the low-level functional implementation (level 2). A user manually develops a high-level implementation (level 3) as well as a high-level specification (level 4). By proving the correspondence between those levels, he or she ensures that the machine code complies with the high-level specification. The advantage of the solution is that it allows reusing verification proofs between different ISAs. In our opinion, automation can be increased by using specialized ISA description languages such as nML [18].

An interesting approach aimed at verifying machine code against ACSL specifications [19] is presented in [20]. The workflow is as follows: first, the ACSL annotations are rewritten as an inline assembly code; second, the modified sources are compiled into the assembly language; third, the assembly code is translated into WhyML; finally, the Why platform generates the verification conditions and discharges them with an external solver. The approach looks similar to the proposed one; however, there are some distinctions. For example, there are separate primitives for loading and storing variables of different types (32- and 64-bit integers, single and double floating-point numbers, etc.), which leads to certain limitations in dealing with pointers. More importantly, verification at the assembly level does not allow abandoning the compiler correctness assumption as the assembly code is an intermediate form and needs further translation.

In [21], there have been demonstrated the possibility of reusing proofs of source code correctness for verifying the machine code. The approach is illustrated on the example of a Java-like source language and a bytecode target language for a stack-based abstract machine. The paper describes how to use such a technology in the context of proof-carrying code (PCC) and shows (in a particular setting) that non-optimizing compilation preserves proof obligations, i.e. source code proofs (built either automatically or interactively) can be transformed to the machine code proofs. Although the ideas of the approach may be useful, the problem we are solving is different. Moreover, one of our goals is to minimize dependence on the target architecture and the compiler, while that solution is tied to a specific platform.

3   Suggested Approach

This section describes our approach to deductive machine code verification against high-level specifications. The primary input is an *ACSL-annotated C function* [19]. It is assumed that the total correctness is formally proved by a verification tool, e.g. Frama-C/AstraVer [6,22]. The source code is compiled (without optimizations) for a given platform by a compiler, e.g. GCC [23]. The generated *object code* (usually in the ELF format [24]) serves as a secondary input. Provided that the target ISA is formalized, the approach does the following steps (see Fig. 1):

- disassembling the machine code (input 2):
    - extracting the CFG;
    - building the SMT-LIB [25] implementation model;
- translating the ACSL annotations (input 1):
    - building the SMT-LIB specification model;
- adapting the specification model:
    - binding the specification model to the machine code;
    - generating the verification conditions.

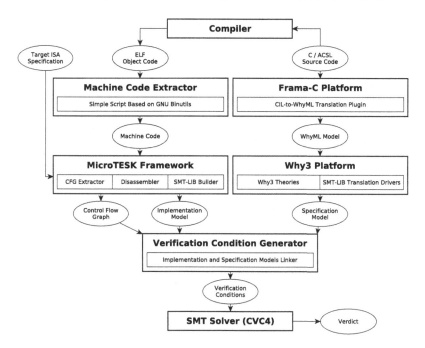

Fig. 1. The scheme of the suggested approach

To illustrate the proposed method, we will use the C library function memset, which fills a given block of memory with a specified byte value. The ACSL-annotated source code of memset is shown in Listing 1.1. Being a part of the VerKer project, the function has been formally verified by Frama-C/AstraVer [6]. As a target platform, we will use RISC-V, a free and open ISA based on the reduced instruction set computer (RISC) principles [26].

```
/*@ requires \typeof(s) <: \type(char*);
    requires \valid((char*)s + (0..count-1));
    assigns ((char*)s)[0..count-1];
    ensures \forall char *p;
      (char*)s <= p < (char*)s + count ==> *p == (char)c;
    ensures \result == s;
*/
void *memset(void *s, int c, size_t count) {
  char *xs = s;
  //@ ghost ocount = count;
  /*@ loop invariant \valid((char*)s + (0..ocount-1));
      loop invariant 0 <= count <= ocount;
      loop invariant (char*)s <= xs || xs <= (char*)s + ocount;
      loop invariant xs - s == ocount - count;
      loop invariant \forall char *p;
        (char *)s <= p < xs ==> *p == (char)c;
      loop assigns count, ((char*)s)[0..ocount-1];
      loop variant count;
  */
```

```
while(count--)
  *xs++ = (char)c;
return s;
}
```

Listing 1.1. The ACSL-annotated source code of memset

The remainder of this section begins with a description of how we formalize microprocessor ISAs (note that in this paper we deal only with the user-mode capabilities). Then the three method steps mentioned above are considered.

3.1 Formalizing Target Architecture

Reasoning about machine code as well as analysis of interaction between hardware and software implies deep knowledge of the target ISA. We use the nML language [18] to specify a microprocessor architecture: registers, memory, addressing modes, and operations (instructions and their parts). A specification serves as a configuration for the MicroTESK framework [27] responsible for disassembling machine code and capturing its semantics (see the next subsection).

Listing 1.2 below (a fragment of the RISC-V specification) shows the following definitions: a constant (XLEN), a type (XWORD), registers (XREG and PC), a temporary variable (prev_PC), an addressing mode (X), an operation (addi), a group of operations (Op), and the root operation (instruction). All necessary explanations are given directly in the code in the form of comments.

```
// Machine word size (configuration dependent)
let XLEN = 64
// Machine word type (unsigned integer of size XLEN)
type XWORD = card(XLEN)
// General-purpose registers (32 registers of type XWORD)
reg XREG[32, XWORD]
// Program counter (stores the current instruction address)
reg PC[XWORD]
// Temporary variable (used to track jumps)
var prev_PC[XWORD]

// Addressing mode for the XREG registers
mode X(i: card(5)) = XREG[i] // Semantics
  // Assembly syntax (mnemonics)
  syntax = format("%s", if i == 0 then "zero"
                         elif i == 1 then "ra"
                         elif i == 2 then "sp" ... endif)
  // Binary encoding
  image  = format("%5s", i)

// Adds a register's value with a signed 12-bit immediate
op addi(rd: X, rs1: X, imm: int(12))
  syntax = format("addi_%s,_%s,_%d",
                   rd.syntax, rs1.syntax, imm)
  image  = format("%12s%5s000%5s0010011",
                   imm, rs1.image, rd.image)
```

```
action = { // Semantics
  rd = rs1 + sign_extend(XWORD, imm);
}

op Op = ... | addi | ... // Group of operations

// Root operation (microprocessor instruction)
op instruction(operation: Op)
  syntax = operation.syntax
  image  = operation.image
  action = {
    XREG[0] = 0;             // Hardwire XREG[0] to zero
    prev_PC = PC;            // Save the previous PC value
    operation.action;       // Execute the operation action
    if PC == prev_PC then    // Update the program counter
      PC = PC + 4;
    endif;
  }
```

Listing 1.2. A fragment of the RISC-V specification in nML

More information on the RISC-V specification in nML can be found in [28]. Based on the specification, MicroTESK builds some useful tools: the *test program generator* (the primary purpose of the framework), the *instruction set simulator* (a part of the test program generator), the *disassembler*, and the *symbolic executor*. In this work, the last two are of importance.

3.2   Disassembling Machine Code

The initial step of the verification process is to disassemble the input ELF file. First, a script based on GNU Binutils [29] extracts the endian-independent machine code of the function. Then, MicroTESK's disassembler matches the machine code against the specified images and reconstructs the sequence of instruction calls. Each call is an instantiation tree (in other words, a ground term) describing how to construct the root instruction object from the specification primitives (operations, addressing modes, and immediates).

For example (see Table 1), the word 0xfc010113 is decoded to the instruction call instruction(addi(X(2),X(2),-64)), i.e. addi sp,sp,-64, where sp is an assembly mnemonics for X(2). Table 2 shows the machine code, the restored instruction calls (instruction is omitted for brevity), and the related assembly code of the memset function.

Table 1. Decoding 0xfc010113 to instruction(addi(X(2),X(2),-64))

111111000000	00010	000	00010	0010011
-64	X(2)	—	X(2)	addi
imm	rs1	—	rd	**op**

Table 2. The machine code, the instruction calls, and the assembly code of memset

Machine Code	Instruction Calls	Assembly Code
fc01 0113	addi(X(2),X(2),-64)	addi sp, sp, -64
0281 3c23	sd(X(8),X(2),56)	sd s0, 56(sp)
0401 0413	addi(X(8),X(2),64)	addi s0, sp, 64
fca4 3c23	sd(X(10),X(8),-40)	sd a0, -40(s0)
0005 8793	addi(X(15),X(11),0)	addi a5, a1, 0
fcc4 3423	sd(X(12),X(8),-56)	sd a2, -56(s0)
fcf4 2a23	sw(X(15),X(8),-44)	sw a5, -44(s0)
fd84 3783	ld(X(15),X(8),-40)	ld a5, -40(s0)
fef4 3423	sd(X(15),X(8),-24)	sd a5, -24(s0)
fc84 3783	ld(X(15),X(8),-56)	ld a5, -56(s0)
fef4 3023	sd(X(15),X(8),-32)	sd a5, -32(s0)
01c0 006f	jal(X(0),14))	jal zero, 14
fe84 3783	ld(X(15),X(8),-24)	ld a5, -24(s0)
0017 8713	addi(X(14),X(15),1)	addi a4, a5, 1
fee4 3423	sd(X(14),X(8),-24)	sd a4, -24(s0)
fd44 2703	lw(X(14),X(8),-44)	lw a4, -44(s0)
0ff7 7713	andi(X(14),X(14),255)	andi a4, a4, 255
00e7 8023	sb(X(14),X(15),0)	sb a4, 0(a5)
fc84 3783	ld(X(15),X(8),-56)	ld a5, -56(s0)
fff7 8713	addi(X(14),X(15),-1)	addi a4, a5, -1
fce4 3423	sd(X(14),X(8),-56)	sd a4, -56(s0)
fc07 9ee3	bne(X(15),X(0),-18)	bne a5, zero, -18
fd84 3783	ld(X(15),X(8),-40)	ld a5, -40(s0)
0007 8513	addi(X(10),X(15),0)	addi a0, a5, 0
0381 3403	ld(X(8),X(2),56)	ld s0, 56(sp)
0401 0113	addi(X(2),X(2),64)	addi sp, sp, 64
0000 8067	jalr(X(0),X(1),0)	jalr zero, ra, 0

The next task is to extract the machine code's CFG. MicroTESK searches for branch instructions, such as bne (branch if not equal), jal (jump [and link]), and jalr (jump [and link] register), and splits the sequence into the preliminary basic blocks: direct branches, e.g. bne a5, zero, -18, are resolved along the way, while indirect ones, e.g. jalr zero, ra, 0, require extra effort. The tool propagates constants and tries to derive the indirect targets; jumps into the middle of the basic blocks refine the code structure. Branches with unresolved targets and branches whose targets are out of the sequence range are considered to be external calls (or the function's returns). It is assumed that each external call returns and execution continues. Finally, the produced CFG is annotated with additional data gathered from the specification, e.g. the branch conditions. The extracted CFG for the given example is shown in Fig. 2.

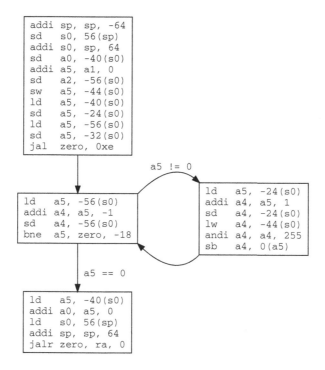

Fig. 2. The control flow graph of `memset`

Then, the CFG is translated to the SMT-LIB implementation model. For each basic block, MicroTESK constructs the internal representation (IR) by substituting each instruction call with the corresponding nML action. For example, the instruction call `instruction(addi(X(2),X(2),-64))` is replaced with the code shown in Listing 1.3 (note that the IR language differs from nML used in the example).

```
XREG[0] = 0;
prev_PC = PC;
XREG[2] = XREG[2] + sign_extend(XWORD, -64);
if PC == prev_PC then
   PC = PC + 4;
endif;
```

Listing 1.3. Inline expansion of `instruction(addi(X(2),X(2),-64))`

The IR is transformed to the gated single-assignment (GSA) form [30] with the conventional techniques [31]. Generally, GSA distinguishes three types of ϕ-functions (i.e. functions at CFG join points that merge the incoming variable versions to create new ones); namely, γ-functions (used in forward jumps) and μ- and η-functions (used in loops). Since nML does not support loops, only γ-functions, which serve as guarded ϕ-functions, are in use. During the transformation, IR optimizations, such as constant propagation and dead code elimination, are applied. Finally, the GSA is printed as an SMT-LIB formula.

The process is straightforward as every IR operation has its counterpart in SMT-LIB, while γ-functions are represented as if-then-else expressions. Listing 1.4 shows the SMT-LIB form of instruction(addi(X(2),X(2),-64)) preceded by the necessary declarations (x!n stands for the nth version of the variable x).

```
(declare-const XREG!1 (Array (_ BitVec 5) (_ BitVec 64)))
(declare-const XREG!2 (Array (_ BitVec 5) (_ BitVec 64)))
(declare-const XREG!3 (Array (_ BitVec 5) (_ BitVec 64)))
(declare-const PC!1 (_ BitVec 64))
(declare-const prev_PC!2 (_ BitVec 64))
(declare-const %1 (_ BitVec 64))
(declare-const %2 (_ BitVec 64))
(declare-const %3 (_ BitVec 64))

;; XREG[0] = 0
(assert (= XREG!2 (store XREG!1 #b00000 #x0000000000000000)))
;; prev_PC = PC
(assert (= prev_PC!2 PC!1))
;; XREG[2] = XREG[2] + sign_extend(XWORD, -64)
(assert (= %3 (select XREG!2 #b00010)))
(assert (= %2 (bvadd %3 #xffffffffffffffc0)))
(assert (= XREG!3 (store XREG!2 #b00010 %2)))
;; PC = PC + 4
(assert (= %1 (bvadd PC!1 #x0000000000000004)))
```

Listing 1.4. A fragment of the SMT-LIB implementation model of memset

The generated SMT-LIB formulae for the basic blocks are linked to the CFG along with the tables that map the microprocessor state elements (the registers and the memory locations) to the input and output versioned variables.

3.3   Translating ACSL Annotations

The second step of the verification process is to translate the input ACSL annotations to the SMT-LIB specification model. Our implementation is based on the Frama-C and Why3 platforms for program analysis and verification. Frama-C parses the ACSL-annotated C function and builds the C Intermediate Language (CIL) [32] representation, an abstract syntax tree (AST). Then, a Frama-C plugin developed by us as a part of the MicroVer project [33] translates the CIL AST into the WhyML language used in Why3. The latter converts the WhyML model into SMT-LIB. Listing 1.5 displays a part of the WhyML representation of memset's annotations. It contains selected clauses of the pre- and postconditions (usmemset_{pre,post}) and loop invariant (memset_inv_1).

```
(* The precondition: \valid( (char* )s + (0..count-1)) *)
predicate usmemset_pre mem r64 r32 r64
axiom usmemset_pre_axiom:
forall memory:mem,s:r64,c:r32,count:r64.
  usmemset_pre memory s c count <->
    valid memory s (sub count (of_int 1))

(* The postcondition: \result == s &&
 *   \forall char *p;
 *     (char* )s <= p < (char* )s + count ==> *p == (char)c *)
predicate usmemset_post mem mem r64 r32 r64 r64
axiom usmemset_post_axiom:
forall pmemory:mem,memory:mem,s:r64,c:r32,count:r64,result:r64.
  usmemset_post pmemory memory s c count result <->
    eq result s /\
      (forall p:r64. ule s p /\ ult p (add s count) ->
        eq1 (load8 pmemory p) (toSmall c))

(* The loop invariant: 0 <= count <= ocount *)
predicate memset_inv_1 (count:r64) (ocount:r64) =
  ule (of_uint 0) count /\ ule count ocount
```

Listing 1.5. A fragment of the WhyML specification model of memset

The same part of the SMT-LIB specification model is shown in Listing 1.6.

```
;; The precondition: \valid( (char* )s + (0..count-1))
(declare-fun usmemset_pre ((Array (_ BitVec 64) (_ BitVec 8))
  (_ BitVec 64) (_ BitVec 32) (_ BitVec 64)) Bool)
(assert
  (forall ((memory (Array (_ BitVec 64) (_ BitVec 8)))
           (s (_ BitVec 64))
           (c (_ BitVec 32))
           (count (_ BitVec 64)))
    (= (usmemset_pre memory s c count)
       (valid memory s (bvsub count (_ bv1 64))))))

;; The postcondition: \result == s &&
;;   \forall char *p;
;;     (char* )s <= p < (char* )s + count ==> *p == (char)c
(declare-fun usmemset_post ((Array (_ BitVec 64) (_ BitVec 8))
  (Array (_ BitVec 64) (_ BitVec 8)) (_ BitVec 64)
  (_ BitVec 32) (_ BitVec 64) (_ BitVec 64)) Bool)
(assert
  (forall ((pmemory (Array (_ BitVec 64) (_ BitVec 8)))
           (memory (Array (_ BitVec 64) (_ BitVec 8)))
           (s (_ BitVec 64))
           (c (_ BitVec 32))
           (count (_ BitVec 64))
           (result (_ BitVec 64)))
    (= (usmemset_post pmemory memory s c count result)
       (and (= result s)
          (forall ((p (_ BitVec 64)))
            (=> (and (bvule s p) (bvult p (bvadd s count)))
                (= (select pmemory p) ((_ extract 7 0) c)))))))))
```

```
;; The loop invariant: 0 <= count <= ocount
(declare-fun memset_inv_1 ((_ BitVec 64) (_ BitVec 64)) Bool)
(assert
  (forall ((count (_ BitVec 64)) (ocount (_ BitVec 64)))
    (= (memset_inv_1 count ocount)
        (and (bvule (_ bv0 64) count) (bvule count ocount)))))
```

Listing 1.6. A fragment of the SMT-LIB specification model of memset

It should be emphasized that the ACSL-to-SMT-LIB translation handles not only pre- and postconditions and loop invariants but also axiomatics, lemmas, and other verification hints, thus enabling their reuse at the binary code level.

3.4   Adapting Specification Model

The final step of the verification process is to reformulate the specification model in terms of the target ISA, link it to the implementation model, and generate the verification conditions. The function contract is bound to the machine code by connecting the function arguments and return value with the registers and the memory locations. Having knowledge of the application binary interface (ABI), this is easily automated. Such bindings for memset are shown in Listing 1.7 (XREG!n stands for the nth version of the XREG register array).

```
(declare-const _arg_s     (_ BitVec 64)) ;; void *s
(declare-const _arg_c     (_ BitVec 32)) ;; int c
(declare-const _arg_count (_ BitVec 64)) ;; size_t count
(declare-const _func_res  (_ BitVec 64)) ;; void *memset


;; Binding: void *s == XREG[10] (a0 in assembly syntax)
(assert (= _arg_s (select XREG!1 (_ bv10 5))))
;; Binding: int c == XREG[11] (a1 in assembly syntax)
(assert (= ((_ sign_extend 32) _arg_c)
            (select XREG!1 (_ bv11 5))))
;; Binding: size_t count == XREG[12] (a2 in assembly syntax)
(assert (= _arg_count (select XREG!1 (_ bv12 5))))
;; Binding: void *memset == XREG[10] (a0 in assembly syntax)
(assert (= _func_res (select XREG!48 (_ bv10 5))))
```

Listing 1.7. The ABI-based bindings for memset's arguments and return value

It is usually enough for loop-free programs. In practice, however, this is rare; the majority of programs contain loops, and we have to adapt the loop invariants (as well as variants) to the binary code level. This is the most tricky part of the job, implying that we know answers to the following three questions:

1. *Which points of the machine code the loop invariants should be applied to?*
   We recognize the loop hierarchy by finding the strongly connected components (SCCs) – and, recursively, the nested SCCs – in the CFG. For each SCC, the entry and backward edges are identified, to which we attach respectively the loop invariant's initialization and preservation conditions [34].

2. *How to bind the source code variables to the machine registers and locations?*
   Restoring the bindings goes together with finding correspondence between the
   loops and the invariants. We use heuristics for the both tasks. For example,
   to match an invariant with a loop, we correlate the number of the invariant
   arguments with the number of locations modified in the loop body [34].
3. *What if a compiler optimizes the loops and transforms the control flow?*
   Many loop optimizations, such as fission/fusion and reversal, make the source
   code invariants not working for the machine code. Our idea is to verify non-
   optimized code and then to prove its equivalence to the optimized one. We
   are experimenting with the equivalence checking techniques, such as [35,36].

As soon as the loop invariants are attached to the binary code and the bindings between the source code variables and the machine registers and locations
are restored, the verification conditions are generated as in Floyd's method [1].
Their negations represented in the SMT-LIB format are discharged with an SMT
solver, e.g. CVC4 [37]. The input function's machine code is considered to be
fully verified if for every verification condition the unsat verdict is returned.

4   Case Study

The approach described in this paper has been implemented in a tool prototype
called MicroVer [33]. It includes such components as the machine code extractor,
the CIL-to-WhyML translation plugin, and the verification condition generator
(see Fig. 1). Besides MicroVer, we used RISC-V GNU Compiler Toolchain [38],
MicroTESK [27], Frama-C [22], Why3 [11], and CVC4 [37]. The solution has
been applied to a number of small C functions (2–8 lines of code) supplied with
ACSL annotations and has allowed us to proof the total correctness of the non-
optimized binary code. Information on the functions is summarized in Table 3.

Table 3. The summary information on the verified functions

Function	C, LOC	Instructions	ACSL, LOC	Description
abs	2	22	3	Absolute value
swap	3	19	3	Swapping two pointers
x2	4	24	4	Multiplication by 2 in a loop
min	4	32	8	Index of minimum value
max	4	32	8	Index of maximum value
sum	5	26	9	Sum of integers from 0 to N
memset	5	27	7	*Naïve implementation*
memcpy	6	30	13	*Naïve implementation*
memchr	7	30	17	*Naïve implementation*
memscan	8	31	22	*Naïve implementation*

5 Conclusion

There are many methods and tools for source code verification. Unfortunately, most of compilers cannot be trusted; therefore, safety- and security-critical software needs to be verified at the binary code level. In this work, we have suggested an approach to deductive verification of (non-optimized) machine code that allows reusing source-code-level specifications. Being based on ISA specifications, the approach is relatively independent of the target platform. To date, several popular ISAs have been specified, including RISC-V, ARM, MIPS, and Power.

The work is in progress, and, obviously, many things are subject to improvement. Future work directions are as follows. First, we are planning to translate machine code (as well as the target ISA specification) into WhyML and/or Isabelle/HOL. This will allow us to reuse ACSL annotations in a more convenient way. Second, we are thinking on how to transform high-level loop invariants (and other verification hints) to fit binary code with modified control flow structure. It seems that it can be automated by providing bindings between the high- and low-level variables and by deriving additional invariants for the machine code entities (registers, stack locations, etc.). Finally, we are working on equivalence checking of optimized and non-optimized machine programs.

Acknowledgment. The authors would like to thank Russian Foundation for Basic Research (RFBR). The reported study was supported by RFBR, research project №17-07-00734.

References

1. Floyd, R.W.: Assigning meanings to programs. In: Proceedings of Symposia in Applied Mathematics, Mathematical Aspects of Computer Science, vol. 19, pp. 19–32 (1967). https://doi.org/10.1090/psapm/019/0235771
2. Hoare, C.A.R.: An axiomatic basis for computer programming. Commun. ACM **12**(10), 576–585 (1969). https://doi.org/10.1145/363235.363259
3. Klein, G., et al.: Comprehensive formal verification of an OS microkernel. ACM Trans. Comput. Syst. (TOCS) **32**(1), 21–270 (2014). https://doi.org/10.1145/2560537
4. Cohen, E., Paul, W., Schmaltz, S.: Theory of multi core hypervisor verification. In: van Emde Boas, P., Groen, F.C.A., Italiano, G.F., Nawrocki, J., Sack, H. (eds.) SOFSEM 2013. LNCS, vol. 7741, pp. 1–27. Springer, Heidelberg (2013). https://doi.org/10.1007/978-3-642-35843-2_1
5. Philippaerts, P., Mühlberg, J.T., Penninckx, W., Smans, J., Jacobs, B., Piessens, F.: Software verification with verifast: industrial case studies. Sci. Comput. Program. **82**, 77–97 (2014). https://doi.org/10.1016/j.scico.2013.01.006
6. Efremov, D., Mandrykin, M., Khoroshilov, A.: Deductive verification of unmodified Linux kernel library functions. In: Margaria, T., Steffen, B. (eds.) ISoLA 2018. LNCS, vol. 11245, pp. 216–234. Springer, Cham (2018). https://doi.org/10.1007/978-3-030-03421-4_15

7. Cok, D.R.: OpenJML: JML for Java 7 by extending OpenJDK. In: Bobaru, M., Havelund, K., Holzmann, G.J., Joshi, R. (eds.) NFM 2011. LNCS, vol. 6617, pp. 472–479. Springer, Heidelberg (2011). https://doi.org/10.1007/978-3-642-20398-5_35

8. CompCert Project. http://compcert.inria.fr

9. Sun, C., Le, V., Zhang, Q., Su, Z.: Toward understanding compiler bugs in GCC and LLVM. In: International Symposium on Software Testing and Analysis (ISSTA), pp. 294–305 (2016). https://doi.org/10.1145/2931037.2931074

10. Schoolderman, M.: Verifying branch-free assembly code in Why3. In: Paskevich, A., Wies, T. (eds.) VSTTE 2017. LNCS, vol. 10712, pp. 66–83. Springer, Cham (2017). https://doi.org/10.1007/978-3-319-72308-2_5

11. Filliâtre, J.-C., Paskevich, A.: Why3—where programs meet provers. In: Felleisen, M., Gardner, P. (eds.) ESOP 2013. LNCS, vol. 7792, pp. 125–128. Springer, Heidelberg (2013). https://doi.org/10.1007/978-3-642-37036-6_8

12. Myreen, M.O.: Formal Verification of Machine-Code Programs. Ph.D. Thesis. University of Cambridge (2009). 131 p

13. Slind, K., Norrish, M.: A brief overview of HOL4. In: Mohamed, O.A., Muñoz, C., Tahar, S. (eds.) TPHOLs 2008. LNCS, vol. 5170, pp. 28–32. Springer, Heidelberg (2008). https://doi.org/10.1007/978-3-540-71067-7_6

14. Fox, A.: Formal specification and verification of ARM6. In: Basin, D., Wolff, B. (eds.) TPHOLs 2003. LNCS, vol. 2758, pp. 25–40. Springer, Heidelberg (2003). https://doi.org/10.1007/10930755_2

15. Crary, K., Sarkar, S.: Foundational Certified Code in a Metalogical Framework. Technical report CMU-CS-03-108. Carnegie Mellon University (2003). 19 p

16. Leroy, X.: Formal certification of a compiler back-end or: programming a compiler with a proof assistant. In: Principles of Programming Languages (POPL), pp. 42–54 (2006). https://doi.org/10.1145/1111037.1111042

17. Bertot, Y.: A short presentation of coq. In: Mohamed, O.A., Muñoz, C., Tahar, S. (eds.) TPHOLs 2008. LNCS, vol. 5170, pp. 12–16. Springer, Heidelberg (2008). https://doi.org/10.1007/978-3-540-71067-7_3

18. Freericks, M.: The nML Machine Description Formalism. Technical report TR SM-IMP/DIST/08, TU Berlin CS Department (1993). 47 p

19. Baudin, P., et al.: ACSL: ANSI/ISO C Specification Language. Version 1.13 (2018). 114 p

20. Nguyen, T.M.T., Marché, C.: Hardware-dependent proofs of numerical programs. In: Jouannaud, J.-P., Shao, Z. (eds.) CPP 2011. LNCS, vol. 7086, pp. 314–329. Springer, Heidelberg (2011). https://doi.org/10.1007/978-3-642-25379-9_23

21. Barthe, G., Rezk, T., Saabas, A.: Proof obligations preserving compilation. In: Dimitrakos, T., Martinelli, F., Ryan, P.Y.A., Schneider, S. (eds.) FAST 2005. LNCS, vol. 3866, pp. 112–126. Springer, Heidelberg (2006). https://doi.org/10.1007/11679219_9

22. Frama-C Platform. http://frama-c.com

23. GCC, the GNU Compiler Collection. https://gcc.gnu.org

24. Tool Interface Standard (TIS) Executable and Linking Format (ELF), version 1.2 (1995)

25. Barrett, C., Fontaine, P., Tinelli, C.: The SMT-LIB Standard Version 2.6. Release 18 July 2017. 104 p

26. RISC-V Foundation. https://riscv.org

27. MicroTESK Framework. http://www.microtesk.org

28. Chupilko, M., Kamkin, A., Kotsynyak, A., Protsenko, A., Smolov, S., Tatarnikov, A.: Test Program Generator MicroTESK for RISC-V. In: International Workshop on Microprocessor and SOC Test and Verification (MTV) (2018). 6 p. https://doi.org/10.1109/MTV.2018.00011

29. GNU Binutils. https://www.gnu.org/software/binutils

30. Ottenstein, K., Ballance, R., MacCabe, A.: The program dependence web: a representation supporting control-, data-, and demand-driven interpretation of imperative languages. In: ACM SIGPLAN Conference on Programming Language Design and Implementation (PLDI), pp. 257–271 (1990). https://doi.org/10.1145/93542.93578

31. Havlak, P.: Construction of thinned gated single-assignment form. In: Banerjee, U., Gelernter, D., Nicolau, A., Padua, D. (eds.) LCPC 1993. LNCS, vol. 768, pp. 477–499. Springer, Heidelberg (1994). https://doi.org/10.1007/3-540-57659-2_28

32. Necula, G.C., McPeak, S., Rahul, S.P., Weimer, W.: CIL: intermediate language and tools for analysis and transformation of C programs. In: Horspool, R.N. (ed.) CC 2002. LNCS, vol. 2304, pp. 213–228. Springer, Heidelberg (2002). https://doi.org/10.1007/3-540-45937-5_16

33. MicroVer Project. https://forge.ispras.ru/projects/microver

34. Putro, P.A.: Applying high-level function loop invariants for machine code deductive verification. Proc. ISP RAS **31**(3), 123–134 (2019). https://doi.org/10.15514/ISPRAS-2019-31(3)-10

35. Churchill, B.R., Padon, O., Sharma, R., Aiken, A.: Semantic program alignment for equivalence checking. In: ACM SIGPLAN Conference on Programming Language Design and Implementation (PLDI), pp. 1027–1040 (2019). https://doi.org/10.1145/3314221.3314596

36. Dahiya, M., Bansal, S.: Black-box equivalence checking across compiler optimizations. In: Asian Symposium on Programing Languages and Systems (APLAS), pp. 127–147 (2017). https://doi.org/10.1007/978-3-319-71237-6_7

37. CVC4 Solver. https://github.com/CVC4/CVC4

38. RISC-V GNU Compiler Toolchain. https://github.com/riscv/riscv-gnu-toolchain

Spatio-Temporal Model-Checking of Cyber-Physical Systems Using Graph Queries

Hojat Khosrowjerdi[1](✉), Hamed Nemati[2], and Karl Meinke[1]

[1] KTH Royal Institute of Technology, Stockholm, Sweden
hojatk@kth.se
[2] Helmholtz Center for Information Security (CISPA), Saarbrücken, Germany

Abstract. We explore the application of *graph database technology* to *spatio-temporal model checking* of cooperating cyber-physical systems-of- systems such as vehicle platoons. We present a translation of *spatio-temporal automata* (STA) and the *spatio-temporal logic* STAL to semantically equivalent *property graphs* and *graph queries* respectively. We prove a sound reduction of the spatio-temporal verification problem to graph database query solving. The practicability and efficiency of this approach is evaluated by introducing *NeoMC*, a prototype implementation of our explicit model checking approach based on Neo4j. To evaluate NeoMC we consider case studies of verifying vehicle platooning models. Our evaluation demonstrates the effectiveness of our approach in terms of execution time and counterexample detection.

1 Introduction

In cooperating cyber-physical systems-of-systems (CO-CPS) such as vehicle platoons, with hard real-time and spatial requirements, even the slightest failure of a service may be catastrophic and endanger lives. Severe consequences of such failures reinforce the need for developing rigorous analysis techniques to increase the safety of CO-CPS. Recently, spatio-temporal verification [1–3] appears as a promising technique to verify advanced autonomous services that incorporate temporal and physical features to safely interact with the environment. The high complexity of such systems, however, makes scalable static analysis computationally challenging in practice. Therefore, to make safety certification practical, the analysis of CO-CPS also needs dynamic techniques for ensuring correct and safe functionality, such as model-based and learning-based testing.

There has been a large body of work related to specifying and verifying real-time systems. Examples include Timed Automata [4] and Duration Calculus [5]. None of these formalisms, however, are sufficient for problems with spatial requirements. We propose a new model checking approach based on *spatio-temporal automaton logic* (STAL) [1] to analyze systems having both temporal and spatial characteristics, e.g. CO-CPS. While several other works have also addressed this problem [2,3,6,7], a distinguishing feature of our approach is

W. Ahrendt and H. Wehrheim (Eds.): TAP 2020, LNCS 12165, pp. 59–79, 2020.
https://doi.org/10.1007/978-3-030-50995-8_4

the adoption of *graph databases* and *graph queries* [8] for model checking. This
enables us to gain advantages in terms of *counterexample detection, analysis time*
and *memory consumption*.

In [1], STAL was introduced as a requirements modeling language for systems of distributed dynamic objects, such as autonomous vehicles. (See Sect. 4).
STAL is based on a restricted subset of first-order linear temporal logic (FOLTL)
with dedicated real-valued spatial functions. To avoid undecidability problems
associated with infinite state spaces, STAL semantics is based on finite *spatio-
temporal automata* (STA) models. These properties of STAL make it a potentially practicable logic for modeling safety requirements on CO-CPS such as
collision avoidance and safety envelopes.

A finite state STA can be machine learned (ML) using techniques of finite
automaton learning [9]. By combining ML with the model checking methods for
STAL presented here, we can implement learning-based testing (LBT) [10,11]
as a dynamical safety assurance method for CO-CPS.

However, there are several problems with using off-the-shelf model checkers
to check STAL properties. Most existing model checkers do not support FOLTL
which is essential to verify spatial properties directly on the model and without
manually crafting new model features. Additionally, ML-generated STA models
are large, flat and unstructured. This prevents many model checkers from optimizing the search computation, or using compact internal representations of the
state space. We try to address these issues and show how the STAL model checking problem can be soundly implemented by graph database search (Sect. 6). We
show the practicability of this approach (Sect. 7) by developing an explicit state
model checker, called **NeoMC**, using the graph database *Neo4j* and its declarative query language *Cypher* [12,13] (Sect. 5). We apply our model checker to
large case studies and report the results in Sect. 7. Our benchmarking results
show the practicability and effectiveness of our approach in terms of counterexample detection and execution time. Most importantly, NeoMC has enabled us
to model check requirements and models that are otherwise not efficiently structured to be verified using other available model checkers.

2   Overview

Figure 1 depicts an application of STAL model checking in a dynamical safety
assurance toolchain based on learning-based testing (LBT) [11]. LBT uses
active automaton learning [14] to reverse engineer a state machine model of
an SUT that can be guaranteed to be both complete and correct. This model is
learned iteratively as a sequence of increasingly larger and more accurate models
$M_0, M_1, \ldots$, by alternating between active learning, model checking and equivalence checking queries. After each iteration, the current model M_i is checked
to find potential discrepancies with respect to functional requirements on the
SUT. If each M_i is an STA then these requirements can be spatio-temporal
requirements formalized in STAL [1].

In LBT, requirements testing is implemented by the model checker to evaluate whether an inferred model M_i complies with the given requirements.

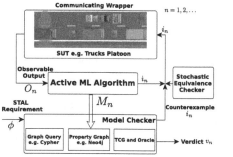

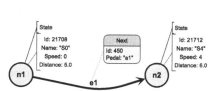

Fig. 1. LBT using graph queries.

Fig. 2. Example property graph showing part of a platoon state machine.

In this way, the model checker functions as the test oracle to generate pass or fail verdicts.

One of our main goals in implementing a dedicated model checker for STAL was to try to improve the performance of model checking for LBT. For this purpose we can represent an STA model M as a property graph data model $\mathcal{G}_M$ in Neo4j [12] and we can model a STAL requirement ϕ using the high level graph query language Cypher [13]. We can then use graph queries to search for potential counterexamples in $\mathcal{G}_M$ that falsify ϕ in M. Thus we can reduce model checking to a query matching problem.

Neo4j is a high-performance graph database that stores data in graphs (represented as a key-value database) rather than in tables. Using graph representation, Neo4j is able to capture the inherent graph structure of data appearing in applications such as geographic information systems (GIS), where data paths and navigational patterns are important [15]. The data processing engine in Neo4j utilizes *index-free adjacency* [16]. In this approach each node keeps micro-indexing of its adjacent nodes, thus reducing the query response time and making it independent of the total graph size. Neo4j is a fully transactional directed graph database and allows assigning attributes (key/value pairs) to nodes (vertices) and relationship (edges). It can efficiently handle connected data and supports various data-types (e.g. floating point, integer, strings). This makes Neo4j well suited for storing various types of automata models including STA, since nodes can represent states and edges naturally represent transitions.

Cypher [12,13] is a graph query language capable of specifying graph patterns between nodes that may span over arbitrary-length paths. Cypher is a declarative language allowing users to express queries without a deeper understanding of the underlying system. However, it is expressive enough to support complex query patterns related to graph analytics [17]. A Cypher query takes a property graph as the input and performs various computations on it, returning a table of values.

3 Preliminaries

A *Property Graph Model* (PGM) is a directed labeled graph in which nodes and edges have attributes, also called *properties*. A property is a pair of the form (*key, value*). Values can be basic data types, such as strings and integers, or composite, such as lists, maps and paths.

Let Σ be an alphabet, then Σ^* denotes the set of all strings over the alphabet. We let $K \subset \Sigma^*$ denote a finite set of property keys, and $\mathcal{A} \subseteq \Sigma^*$ denotes a possibly infinite set of variable names. We define node labels L and edge types T as countably infinite sets of strings from Σ^*. Also, V is the set of values and it contains:

- Node and edge identifiers.
- Base types: integers $\mathbb{Z}$, real numbers $\mathbb{R}$, and strings Σ^*.
- Booleans: $\mathbb{B} = \{\textbf{true}, \textbf{false}\}$.
- **null**: denoting an undefined value.
- Lists: an empty or non-empty list of values $list(v_1, v_2, ..., v_m)$.
- Maps: an empty or non-empty set of (*key, value*) pairs.
- Paths: a sequence of node and edge identifiers $(n_0, e_0, n_1, ..., n_{k-1}, e_{k-1}, n_k)$.

A *property graph* is an 8-tuple $\mathcal{G} = (N, E, L, T, \lambda, Lab, Typ, P_{node}, P_{edge})$ consisting of a set $N \subseteq \Sigma^*$ of *node identifiers*, and a set $E \subseteq \Sigma^*$ of *directed edge identifiers*. We associate a *label set* to each node by the function $Lab : N \to 2^L$. Similarly, we assign a *type* $t \in T$ (or possibly **null**) to each edge by the function $Typ : E \to T \cup \{\textbf{null}\}$. Furthermore, $\lambda : E \to N \times N$ is the function which yields the source and the target nodes for a given edge. Note that two edge identifiers may have the same source/target nodes.

By a *property* we mean a pair $p = (k, v) \in K \times V$ consisting of a key k and a value v. Then $P_{node} : N \times K \to V \cup \{\textbf{null}\}$ is the *property labelling* function for nodes which maps each node n and key k to the corresponding value (that could be **null**). Similarly, $P_{edge} : E \times K \to V \cup \{\textbf{null}\}$ is the *property labelling* function for edges which maps each edge e and key k to the corresponding value (possibly **null**).

Example 1. Figure 2 exemplifies a property graph. In this example, there are two nodes and one edge, namely n_1, n_2 and e_1. The node's label is "State" and the edge type is "Next". Node property keys are "Id", "Name", "Speed" and "Distance" and the edge property keys are "Id" and "Pedal". The value of the each property is given below.

$L = \{\texttt{State}\}$		
$N = \{n_1, n_2\}$	$Lab(n_1) = \{\texttt{State}\}$	$Lab(n_2) = \{\texttt{State}\}$
	$P_{node}(n_1, \texttt{Id}) = 21708$	$P_{node}(n_2, \texttt{Id}) = 21712$
	$P_{node}(n_1, \texttt{Name}) =$ "$S0$"	$P_{node}(n_2, \texttt{Name}) =$ "$S4$"
	$P_{node}(n_1, \texttt{Speed}) = 0$	$P_{node}(n_2, \texttt{Speed}) = 4$
	$P_{node}(n_1, \texttt{Distance}) = 5.0$	$P_{node}(n_2, \texttt{Distance}) = 6.0$
$T = \{\texttt{Next}\}$		
$E = \{e_1\}$	$\lambda(e_1) = (n_1, n_2)$	$Typ(e_1) = \{\texttt{Next}\}$
	$P_{edge}(e_1, \texttt{Id}) = 450$	$P_{edge}(e_1, \texttt{Pedal}) =$ "$a1$"

Having defined a property graph, we define a *path* in such a graph as follows. Let $n_i, n_k \in N$ and $e_j \in E$ be node and edge identifiers of a property graph $\mathcal{G}$. A *path* $\overline{w}$ from n_i to n_k denoted by $\overline{w} = (n_i \rightarrow^* n_k)$ is a finite sequence of nodes and edges $(n_i e_i n_{i+1}...n_{k-1} e_{k-1} n_k)$ such that $\forall i \le j < k : \lambda(e_j) = (n_j, n_{j+1})$.

We use $\prod_{type}^{size}(\mathcal{G})$ to denote the set of all paths in $\mathcal{G}$ of length *size* and a specific *type* in the input *model*. Then $\prod(\mathcal{G})$ denotes the set of all paths in $\mathcal{G}$ (of any finite length). If $\overline{w}_1 = (n_0 e_0 n_1...e_{k-1} n_k)$ and $\overline{w}_2 = (n_k e_k...e_{i-1} n_i)$, then we denote the order-preserving concatenation of $\overline{w}_1$ and $\overline{w}_2$ by $\overline{w}_1.\overline{w}_2 = (n_0 e_0 n_1...e_{k-1} n_k e_k...e_{i-1} n_i)$.

In a graph database, to create, read and update property graphs, graph queries are executed. A query $\mu \in \mathcal{Q}$ takes a graph $\mathcal{G}$ as an input and returns a table $\mathfrak{t} \in \mathbb{T}$. This table provides parameter bindings that match the query to a solution in the graph.

Let $u = \{a_1 : v_1, ..., a_n : v_n\}$ be an assignment(record) from variable names $\{a_1, ..., a_n\} \subset \mathcal{A}$ to values $\{v_1, ..., v_n\} \subset V$, and $dom(u)$ denotes the domain of u, i.e. $dom(u) = \{a_1, ..., a_n\}$. A table $\mathfrak{t} \in \mathbb{T}$ is a multiset (bag) of assignments that have a common domain $\mathcal{A}$. In other words, tables are partial mappings from names (columns) to values, without any specific ordering.

4   Spatio-Temporal Automaton Logic (STAL)

In [1] we presented a modal logic STAL suitable for describing the spatio-temporal behavior of a spatially distributed dynamical system of objects, such as autonomous vehicles or drones. Such systems have many dynamically changing properties such as object locations, distances and velocities. These properties may be expressed using relative or absolute coordinates. Following classical Newtonian physics, such properties are usually resolved into their vector components along 1, 2 or 3 spatial dimensions as appropriate.

Formally, STAL is a quantifier-free fragment[1] of first-order linear temporal logic (FOLTL). The semantics of STAL can therefore be defined in a similar

---

[1] To ensure decidability, STAL is syntactically restricted so that quantification over data types is not allowed.

way to FOLTL, in terms of a *spatio-temporal automaton* (STA) that interprets the spatial operators of the logic. A key requirement for learning-based testing (LBT) [11] is that spatio-temporal automata are amenable to machine learning in finite time in much the same way as finite automata [9]. Successful LBT also requires the existence of a decidable model checking problem and an efficient model checking algorithm such as the one presented in this work.

STAL can be used to describe a dynamically changing environment of spatially distributed objects by relativising spatio-temporal measurements to a distinguished object called the *ego object*. The ego object provides an origin and point of reference in each dimension for every *relative spatio-temporal property* (e.g. relative distance). Thus FOLTL provides an implicit temporal reference to *now*, while the ego object provides the corresponding spatial reference to *here*. Furthermore, by supporting the measurement of bounded relative properties, STA allow us to avoid infinite state automata models in many practical situations. This means that both machine learning and model checking of spatio-temporal automata can be achieved in finite time using regular inference and explicit state space search methods.

Taking the common case of 2 orthogonal spatial dimensions, the x and y axes, we can define a 2-dimensional[2] STA to be the following algebraic structure:

$$A = (\Sigma, Q, Obj, q_0, egoObj,$$
$$\delta : \Sigma \times Q \to Q, \; angle : Q \to [0, .., 360),$$
$$dist_x, \; dist_y, \; vel_x, \; vel_y : Obj \times Q \to \mathbb{R}).$$

Here $\Sigma = \{\sigma_1, \ldots, \sigma_m\}$ is a finite *input alphabet*, consisting of ordered key-value pairs[3] $p = (k, v) \in K \times V$, $Q = \{q_0, \ldots, q_n\}$ is a finite set of states, $Obj = \{o_1, \ldots, o_k\}$ is a finite set of objects, $q_0 \in Q$ is the distinguished initial state, $egoObj \in Obj$ is the distinguished ego object, $\delta : \Sigma \times Q \to Q$ is the state transition function, $angle : Q \to [0, .., 360)$ gives the *ego object orientation* relative to the x, y axes, $dist_x, dist_y : Obj \times Q \to \mathbb{R}$ are the *relative object distance* functions along the x, y axes measured from the ego object for each state, and $vel_x, vel_y : Obj \times Q \to \mathbb{R}$ are the *absolute object velocity* functions[4] measured along the x, y axes for each state.

Example 2. Figure 3 shows a simple STA consisting of three states q_0, q_1, q_2. It describes the movements of two vehicles in a platoon, namely *leader* and *follower*. The *leader* is controlled by a driver using gas and brake pedals. Then, the input alphabet Σ is a set consisting of $\sigma_0 = (Pedal, "gas")$ and $\sigma_1 = (Pedal, "brake")$. Both vehicles are driving along the x axis. The *follower* object, which is the ego object, tries to adapt its distance and speed to the *leader* object motion. This example STA is two dimensional and all distances are measured along x and y axes with respect to *follower* as the ego object. For all states of the automaton,

---

[2] This definition clearly generalises to the n-dimensional case.

[3] denoted as "(*key,value*)".

[4] Note: we can derive relative velocity from absolute velocity, and both measurements are always bounded in practise.

the angle of the ego vehicle, the inter-vehicle distance along the y axis of the ego object and the absolute vehicle velocities in the y dimension are zero. The transition function δ is defined as follows. Initially (in state q_0), the *leader* is 50 meters ahead of the *follower* along its x axis. This distance will be reduced to 20 and 10 meters if the *leader* accelerates (*Pedal, gas*) or brakes (*Pedal, brake*) respectively. If the driver pushes the gas pedal, the speed of the *leader* increases from zero to 50 km/h along the x axis. Should the brake pedal be pressed, the *leader* speed drops to 30 km/h. At the same time, the ego vehicle tries to follow this speed pattern at 48 km/h and 29 km/h.

The formal syntax of STAL is summarized in Fig. 4. In this Figure exp, exp_1 and exp_2 are arithmetic expressions, and ϕ, ϕ_1 and ϕ_2 are arbitrary STAL formulas. Let S denote the set of all STAL formulas.

$\sigma_0 = (Pedal, \text{``gas''}), \sigma_1 = (Pedal, \text{``brake''})$ $\Sigma = \{\sigma_0, \sigma_1\}$
$Q = \{q_0, q_1, q_2\}$ $Obj = \{leader, follower\}$
$egoObj = follower$

$\delta(\sigma_0, q_0) = q_1, \delta(\sigma_1, q_0) = q_0$ $\delta(\sigma_0, q_1) = q_1, \delta(\sigma_1, q_1) = q_2$
$\delta(\sigma_0, q_2) = q_1, \delta(\sigma_1, q_2) = q_2$

$angle(q_0) = 0, angle(q_1) = 0, angle(q_2) = 0$

$dist_x(leader, q_0) = 50, dist_x(leader, q_1) = 20,$ $dist_x(leader, q_2) = 10$
$dist_y(leader, q_0) = 0, dist_y(leader, q_1) = 0,$ $dist_y(leader, q_2) = 0$

$vel_x(leader, q_0) = 0, vel_x(leader, q_1) = 50,$ $vel_x(leader, q_2) = 30$
$vel_y(leader, q_0) = 0, vel_y(leader, q_1) = 0,$ $vel_y(leader, q_2) = 0$

$vel_x(follower, q_0) = 0, vel_x(follower, q_1) = 48,$ $vel_x(follower, q_2) = 29$
$vel_y(follower, q_0) = 0, vel_y(follower, q_1) = 0,$ $vel_y(follower, q_2) = 0$

Fig. 3. An example of an STA.

$exp ::= c \in \mathbb{R} \mid \texttt{next}(exp)$
    $\mid \texttt{Distance}_x(\texttt{o}) \mid \texttt{Distance}_y(\texttt{o}) \mid \texttt{Speed}_x(\texttt{o}) \mid \texttt{Speed}_y(\texttt{o}) \mid \texttt{Angle};$ where
$\texttt{o} \in Obj$
    $\mid exp_1 + exp_2 \mid exp_1 - exp_2 \mid exp_1 * exp_2 \mid exp_1/exp_2$
$\phi ::= \texttt{input} = \sigma, (\text{for } \sigma \in \Sigma)$
    $\mid (exp_1 < exp_2) \mid (exp_1 > exp_2) \mid (exp_1 \leq exp_2) \mid (exp_1 \geq exp_2) \mid (exp_1 \neq exp_2)$
    $\mid \neg(\phi) \mid (\phi_1 \wedge \phi_2) \mid (\phi_1 \vee \phi_2) \mid (\phi_1 \rightarrow \phi_2) \mid X(\phi) \mid F(\phi) \mid G(\phi)$

Fig. 4. Syntax of STAL.

For a given object $o \in Obj$, a STAL expression exp is either a floating point constant c, a distance expression $\texttt{Distance}_x(\texttt{o})$ or $\texttt{Distance}_y(\texttt{o})$, a speed expression $\texttt{Speed}_x(o)$ or $\texttt{Speed}_y(o)$, an angle expression $\texttt{Angle}$ or a binary arithmetic operation $(+, -, *, /)$ applied to two subexpressions exp_1, exp_2.

An *atomic STAL formula* is either an input expression ($\texttt{input} = \sigma$) for $\sigma \in \Sigma$ or a pair of arithmetic expressions connected by an arithmetic relation ($<, >, \leq,$

$\geq$). A *compound STAL formula* ϕ may be built up from subformulas by means of boolean operations (i.e. $\neg$, $\wedge$, $\vee$, or $\rightarrow$), and linear temporal operators (i.e. next X, eventually F, or always G).

The semantics of STAL is defined in Fig. 5. To define the satisfiability relation $\models$ we write $w = (\alpha_0, \alpha_1, ...) \in \prod^{\infty}(A)$ to denote an infinite path in A and we write its suffixes as $w^i = (\alpha_i, \alpha_{i+1}, ...)$ for $i \geq 0$. Note that a path in a spatio-temporal automaton is a sequence of input (σ) and state (q) pairs, i.e. $\alpha_i = (\sigma_i, q_i)$. We use $(\alpha_i \rightarrow^* \alpha_k)$ to indicate a path from q_i to q_k if $\forall i \leq j < k : q_{j+1} = \delta(\sigma_j, n_j)$ and the last input $\sigma_k = \epsilon$ is an empty string.

$$[\![c]\!]_\alpha = c$$
$$[\![Distance_x(o_i)]\!]_\alpha = dist_x(o_i, q)$$
$$[\![Distance_y(o_i)]\!]_\alpha = dist_y(o_i, q)$$
$$[\![Angle]\!]_\alpha = angle(q)$$
$$[\![Speed_x(o_i)]\!]_\alpha = vel_x(o_i, q)$$
$$[\![Speed_y(o_i)]\!]_\alpha = vel_y(o_i, q)$$
$$[\![next(exp)]\!]_{\alpha_i} = [\![exp]\!]_{\alpha_{i+1}}$$
$$[\![exp_1 \textbf{ bop } exp_2]\!]_\alpha = [\![exp_1]\!]_\alpha \textbf{ bop } [\![exp_2]\!]_\alpha$$
$$[\![\textbf{input} = \sigma]\!]_{\alpha_i} = \begin{cases} \textbf{true } if \sigma = \sigma_i \\ \textbf{false } if \sigma \neq \sigma_i \end{cases}$$

$$A, w \models (\textbf{input} = \sigma) \iff [\![\textbf{input} = \sigma]\!]_{\alpha_0}$$
$$A, w \models (exp_1 \textbf{ bop } exp_2) \iff [\![exp_1 \textbf{ bop } exp_2]\!]_{\alpha_0}$$
$$A, w \models \neg\phi \iff A, w \not\models \phi$$
$$A, w \models (\phi_1 \wedge \phi_2) \iff A, w \models \phi_1 \wedge A, w \models \phi_2$$
$$A, w \models (\phi_1 \vee \phi_2) \iff A, w \models \phi_1 \vee A, w \models \phi_2$$
$$A, w \models (\phi_1 \rightarrow \phi_2) \iff A, w \not\models \phi_1 \vee A, w \models \phi_2$$
$$A, w \models X(\phi) \iff A, w^1 \models \phi$$
$$A, w \models G(\phi) \iff \forall i \in \mathbb{N} : A, w^i \models \phi$$
$$A, w \models F(\phi) \iff \exists i \in \mathbb{N} : A, w^i \models \phi$$

Fig. 5. STAL semantics and its satisfiability relation over a path w of an STA A.

$exp ::= v \in V \mid a \in \mathcal{A} \mid f(exp), f \in F$	values/variables
$\quad \mid exp.k \mid \{\mathcal{P}\}$	
$mid[exp]$	maps/lists (for $k \in K$)
$\quad \mid exp_1 \textbf{ OR } exp_2 \mid exp_1 \textbf{ AND } exp_2 \mid \textbf{NOT } exp$	logic
$\quad \mid exp_1 \textbf{ bop } exp_2$	comparison

$pattern ::= \pi \mid a = \pi$ (for $a \in \mathcal{A}$)	$\mathcal{L} ::= :l \mid :l\mathcal{L}$ (for $l \in L$)
$\pi ::= \chi \mid \chi\rho\pi$	$\mathcal{P} ::= k{:}exp \mid k{:}exp, \mathcal{P} \mid \textbf{null}$
$\chi ::= (a \ \mathcal{L}? \ \{\mathcal{P}\}?)$	$\mathcal{T} ::= :t \mid \mathcal{T} \mid \textbf{null}$ (for $t \in T$)
$\rho ::= \text{-}[a \ \mathcal{T}? \ \mathcal{I}? \ \{\mathcal{P}\}?] \rightarrow$	$len ::= d \mid d_1.. \mid ..d_2 \mid d_1..d_2$
$\quad \mid \leftarrow [a \ \mathcal{T}? \ \mathcal{I}? \ \{\mathcal{P}\}?]\text{-}$	$\quad \mid \textbf{null}$ (for $d, d_1, d_2 \in \mathbb{N}$)
	$\mathcal{I} ::= *len?$

$ret ::= exp$
$query ::= \textbf{MATCH } pattern \textbf{ WHERE } exp \textbf{ RETURN } ret$

Fig. 6. Core syntax of Cypher for model checking

5   Cypher Syntax and Semantics

In this section we present a subset of the Cypher language which is sufficient for interpreting STAL formulas. Cypher includes *expressions*, *patterns*, *clauses*, and *queries*, which allow it to represent a data model represented as *values*, *graphs* and *tables*. The syntax of Cypher is depicted in Fig. 6. We present keywords in blue. The main concepts in Cypher are the notions of "pattern" and "pattern matching". The underlying data set for a query in Cypher is a property graph and the response is a table providing bindings for all query parameters representing solutions found in the property graph.

The MATCH clause denotes a matching function from tables to tables and may introduce new rows (synonymous with records) with bindings of the matched instances of the pattern in the queried graph. Similar to other query languages, the WHERE clause in Cypher filters the results of this matching based on the valid filter predicates. These predicates can be defined based on the properties of query elements. For example, Match (n) WHERE n.k = value is a query to match all nodes in a graph that satisfy the attribute restriction $k = value$ for a property $p : (k, value)$ of a node n. The binary operations, **bop**, are the standard ones and we use them to express the relation between two properties or properties and literals. The keyword RETURN expresses the projection of the result.

For model checking purposes, Cypher expressions are used in the WHERE clause to apply predicate conditions and filter search results. They also appear in the RETURN statement, e.g., to define how a counterexample should be structured and returned properly. Expressions can also be used in patterns to parameterize node and edge properties during a pattern matching search.

$$\llbracket v \rrbracket_{\mathcal{G},u} = v, \ v \in V \qquad\qquad \llbracket a \rrbracket_{\mathcal{G},u} = u(a), a \in dom(u)$$
$$\llbracket f(exp_1, ..., exp_m) \rrbracket_{\mathcal{G},u} = f(\llbracket exp_1 \rrbracket_{\mathcal{G},u}, ..., \llbracket exp_m \rrbracket_{\mathcal{G},u})$$

$\forall k, k_i \in K.$
$\llbracket exp.k \rrbracket_{\alpha_i} =$
$$\begin{cases} P_{node}(\llbracket exp \rrbracket_{\mathcal{G},u}, k) & \text{if } \llbracket exp \rrbracket_{\mathcal{G},u} \in N \\ P_{edge}(\llbracket exp \rrbracket_{\mathcal{G},u}, k) & \text{if } \llbracket exp \rrbracket_{\mathcal{G},u} \in E \\ v_i & \text{if } \llbracket exp \rrbracket_{\mathcal{G},u} = map((k_1, v_1), \ldots, (k_i, v_i), \ldots) \\ & \text{and } k = k_i \\ \textbf{null} & \text{if } \llbracket exp \rrbracket_{\mathcal{G},u} = map((k_1, v_1), \ldots, (k_i, v_i), \ldots) \\ & \text{and } k \notin \{k_1, \ldots, k_i\} \\ & \text{or } \llbracket exp \rrbracket_{\mathcal{G},u} = \{\} \\ & \text{or } \llbracket exp \rrbracket_{\mathcal{G},u} = \textbf{null} \end{cases}$$
$$\llbracket \{k_1 : exp_1, \ldots, k_i : exp_i\} \rrbracket_{\mathcal{G},u} = map((k_1, \llbracket exp_1 \rrbracket_{\mathcal{G},u}), \ldots, (k_i, \llbracket exp_i \rrbracket_{\mathcal{G},u}))$$

$$\llbracket NOT \, exp \rrbracket_{\mathcal{G},u} = \begin{cases} true & \text{if } \llbracket exp \rrbracket_{\mathcal{G},u} = false \\ false & \text{if } \llbracket exp \rrbracket_{\mathcal{G},u} = true \\ \textbf{null} & \text{if } \llbracket exp \rrbracket_{\mathcal{G},u} = \textbf{null} \end{cases}$$
$$\llbracket exp_1 \text{ AND } exp_2 \rrbracket_{\mathcal{G},u} = \begin{cases} true & \text{if } \llbracket exp_1 \rrbracket_{\mathcal{G},u} = \llbracket exp_2 \rrbracket_{\mathcal{G},u} = true \\ false & \text{if } \llbracket exp_1 \rrbracket_{\mathcal{G},u} = false \text{ or } \llbracket exp_2 \rrbracket_{\mathcal{G},u} = false \\ \textbf{null} & otherwise \end{cases}$$
$$\llbracket exp_1 \text{ OR } exp_2 \rrbracket_{\mathcal{G},u} = \begin{cases} true & \text{if } \llbracket exp_1 \rrbracket_{\mathcal{G},u} = true \text{ or } \llbracket exp_2 \rrbracket_{\mathcal{G},u} = true \\ false & \text{if } \llbracket exp_1 \rrbracket_{\mathcal{G},u} = \llbracket exp_2 \rrbracket_{\mathcal{G},u} = false \\ \textbf{null} & otherwise \end{cases}$$

Fig. 7. Cypher expression semantics.

5.1   Cypher Patterns

Syntax. Cypher supports three types of patterns: *node* (χ), *edge* (ρ) and *path* (π) patterns. In a path-based temporal logic such as FOLTL, path patterns can be used to describe a counterexample as a path to a node or group of nodes where some desired properties are violated. Patterns can be recursively defined using the derivation rules in Fig. 6. In this figure f is any m-ary function in F from values to values, e.g., `All` and `Any`, and *exp.k* returns a pair from a map with a matching key k, i.e. $v_i = map((k_1, v_1), \ldots, (k_i, v_i), \ldots).k_i$. We use "?" to denote optional (or "nullable") types, for which **null** represents missing (or None) values. Also "*" denotes a range $[d_1, d_2]$ with $d_1, d_2 \in \mathbb{N}$ specified by the optional *len* for the edge pattern ρ. The range is equal to $[1, \infty]$ if *len* is **null** or $[d, d]$, $[d_1, \infty]$, $[1, d_2]$, $[d_1, d_2]$ if other derivation rules are applied, respectively.

Definition 1 (Node Pattern). *A node pattern χ has the form $\chi = (a\ \mathcal{L}?\ \{\mathcal{P}\}?)$ where $a \in N$ is a node name, $\mathcal{L}$ is an optional finite set of node labels, and $\{\mathcal{P}\}$ is an optional partial mapping from property keys k to expressions exp. For example (x), $(x\!:\!State)$ and $(x\{Name\!:\ "S0"\})$ are node patterns.*

Definition 2 (Edge Pattern). *An edge pattern ρ has the form $\rho = (a\ \mathcal{T}?\ \mathcal{I}?\ \{\mathcal{P}\}?\ dir)$ where $a \in E$ is an edge name, $\mathcal{T}$ is an optional edge type, $\mathcal{I}$ indicates an optional range for the length of the edge between source/target nodes, $\mathcal{P}$ is an optional partial mapping from property keys to expressions and $dir \in \{\rightarrow, \leftarrow\}$ indicates the direction.*

Definition 3 (Path Pattern), *A path pattern π is a concatenation of node and edge patterns of the form $\chi_1 \rho_1 \chi_2 \rho_2 \cdots \chi_n$.*

Henceforth we write $\pi = (n_1)\text{-}[e]\!\!\rightarrow\!(n_2)$ where $n_1, n_2 \in N$ and $e \in E$, instead of $\pi = \chi_1 \rho \chi_2$ to denote the syntactic category pattern defined in Fig. 6. Using this notation, patterns can encode paths as nodes and edges with arrows between them to indicate the direction of a transition.

Semantics. The semantics of a pattern is the set of nodes, edges or paths which satisfy its conditions. For example, the semantics of a path pattern π is the path value $[\![\pi]\!]_{\mathcal{G},u} \in V$. Figure 7 shows the semantics of cypher expressions where the semantics of an expression *exp* is a value $[\![exp]\!]_{\mathcal{G},u} \in V$ determined by $\mathcal{G}$ and u. For example, for a constant $v \in V$, a variable name $a \in \mathcal{A}$ and an m-array function $f \in F$, the semantic values are $[\![v]\!]_{\mathcal{G},u} = v$, $[\![a]\!]_{\mathcal{G},u} = u(a)$ and $[\![f(exp_1, \ldots, exp_m)]\!]_{\mathcal{G},u} = f([\![exp_1]\!]_{\mathcal{G},u}, \ldots, [\![exp_m]\!]_{\mathcal{G},u})$ respectively. The complete semantics is given in [18].

Definition 4 (Path Value). *A path value for a pattern π in $\mathcal{G}$ given the assignment u which provides name bindings for π and $\mathcal{G}$, is a set of paths $\overline{w}$ in $\mathcal{G}$ such that, $[\![\pi]\!]_{\mathcal{G},u} = \{\overline{w} \in \prod(\mathcal{G}) \mid (\overline{w}, \mathcal{G}, u) \models \pi\}$.*

For example, the pattern $\pi = (n)\text{-}[e]\!\!\rightarrow\!(m)$ indicates a set of paths $\{(n_0 e_0 n_1) | n_0, n_1 \in N, e_0 \in E\}$ of length one in the graph $\mathcal{G}$ using the assignment

$u = (n : n_0, e : e_0, m : n_1)$, and n_0, e_0, n_1 are any node and edge identifiers in $\mathcal{G}$ with the relation $\lambda(e_0) = (n_0, n_1)$. Note that n_0, n_1 and e_0 can be any nodes and edges within the graph that satisfy this edge pattern.

Property 1. Let ρ be an edge pattern $(a\ \mathcal{T}?\ \mathcal{I}?\ \{\mathcal{P}\}?\ dir)$, χ be a node pattern $(a\ \mathcal{L}?\ \{\mathcal{P}\}?)$, $d_1 \le i \le d_2$ and $j \in \{1, ..., i\}$, then a path $\overline{w}$ in a graph $\mathcal{G}$ satisfies a pattern π (i.e., $(\overline{w}, \mathcal{G}, u) \models \pi$) if:

$$(n, \mathcal{G}, u) \models \chi \Leftrightarrow$$

$$\begin{cases} u(a) = n \\ \mathcal{L} \subseteq Lab(n) \\ \forall k \in K. \\ \quad [\![P_{node}(n, k) = \{\mathcal{P}\}.k]\!]_{\mathcal{G}, u} = true \end{cases}$$

and

$$(n_1...e_i n_{i+1}.\overline{w}, \mathcal{G}, u) \models \chi \rho \pi \Leftrightarrow$$

$$\begin{cases} (n_1, \mathcal{G}, u) \models \chi \\ (\overline{w}, \mathcal{G}, u) \models \pi \\ u(a) = list(e_1, ..., e_i) \\ Typ(e_j) \in \mathcal{T} \\ \forall k \in K. \\ \quad [\![P_{edge}(e_j, k) = \{\mathcal{P}\}.k]\!]_{\mathcal{G}, u} = true \\ \lambda(e_j) \in \begin{cases} \{(n_j, n_{j+1})\}; \text{ if } dir \text{ is } \rightarrow \\ \{(n_{j+1}, n_j)\}; \text{ if } dir \text{ is } \leftarrow \end{cases} \end{cases}$$

Example 3. Take the property graph $\mathcal{G}$ from Fig. 2 and assume a Cypher pattern $(x\{Name : \text{``}S0\text{''}\})-[y\{Pedal: \text{``}a1\text{''}\}]\mapsto(z)$, which is equivalent to:

$$\pi = \overbrace{(x\ \textbf{null}\ \{Name: \text{``}S0\text{''}\})}^{\chi_1}\ \overbrace{(y\ \textbf{null}\ \textbf{null}\ \{Pedal: \text{``}a1\text{''}\} \rightarrow)}^{\rho}\ \overbrace{(z\ \textbf{null}\ \textbf{null})}^{\chi_2}$$

where χ_1, χ_2 and ρ are the node and edge patterns. Say $u = (x: n_1, y: e_1, z: n_2)$, then one can show that $(n_1, \mathcal{G}, u) \models \chi_1$, $(e_1, \mathcal{G}, u) \models \rho$ and $(n_2, \mathcal{G}, u) \models \chi_2$. Also, for the path $\overline{w} = (n_1 e_1 n_2)$ it holds that $(\overline{w}, \mathcal{G}, u) \models \pi$ where $\pi = \chi_1 \rho \chi_2$.

Pattern Matching. Central to query satisfiability for a graph database is pattern matching, which is the problem of finding all subgraphs that match a given pattern. A match for a pattern is a function that maps variables to constants such that when applied to the pattern, the result is in the original graph database.

For a node pattern $\chi = (a, \mathcal{L}?, \{\mathcal{P}\}?)$, let $free(\chi) = \{a\}$ be the set of free variables of χ. Similarly, we define free variables of an edge pattern $\rho = (a, \mathcal{T}?, \mathcal{I}?, \mathcal{P}?, dir)$ by $free(\rho) = \{a\}$. Then, the free variables of a path pattern $\pi = \chi_1 \rho_1 \chi_2 \rho_2 ... \chi_n$ is defined to be the union of all free variables of individual node and edge patterns occurring in it, i.e., $free(\pi) = free(\chi_1) \cup free(\rho_1) \cup ... \cup free(\chi_n)$. We define pattern matching as the function which searches a graph $\mathcal{G}$ to find all paths p that satisfy a pattern π given a variable assignment u from values to variables for the *free variables* of π, i.e. $match(\pi, \mathcal{G}, u) = [\![\pi]\!]_{\mathcal{G}, u}$.

For brevity, we drop u and write $match(\pi, \mathcal{G})$ in the sequel. A Cypher matching query $\mu \in \mathcal{Q}$ can be defined as $\mu:: = $ MATCH *pattern* WHERE *exp* RETURN *ret*. The semantics of this query is to call $match(\pi, \mathcal{G})$, apply the predicate conditions of WHERE to filter the search results and project the results:

$$[\![\mu]\!]_{\mathcal{G}} = [\![\text{MATCH } \pi \text{ WHERE } exp]\!]_{\mathcal{G}} = \{\overline{w} \in match(\pi, \mathcal{G}) \mid [\![exp]\!]_{\mathcal{G}} = true\}$$

Definition 5. *We say a graph $\mathcal{G}$ satisfies a query μ if and only if there exists a path $\overline{w}$ in $\mathcal{G}$ that is in the semantics of the query. That is:*

$$\mathcal{G} \models \mu \iff \exists \overline{w} \in \prod(\mathcal{G}) \ such \ that \ \overline{w} \in [\![\mu]\!]_{\mathcal{G}}.$$

Graph pattern matching is a canonical NP-complete problem. Cypher allows pattern definitions with infinitely many matches (e.g., loops). This makes Cypher impractical in a homomorphism-based semantics [19]. For example, if $\mathcal{G}$ is a graph consisting of a single node n, a single edge e from n to n ($n \to n$), then patterns like $\pi = (n)\text{-}[*]\!\!\to\!(n)$ match $\mathcal{G}$ infinitely many times by iteratively traversing over e if there is no restriction on the number of iterations. Thus, for $i \geq 0$ there exists a match that iterates i times over e in $\mathcal{G}$. Cypher avoids this by using an isomorphism-based semantics [8] to disallow repeating edges while traversing edges in pattern matching. Hence, in the above example, the *match* function only returns two matches, one for $i = 0$ and one for $i = 1$.

6   Spatio-Temporal Model Checking

Spatio-temporal model checking is a variant of classical model checking that combines spatial reasoning with temporal reasoning. Given an STA model A, a STAL formula $\phi \in \mathcal{S}$, and a path $w \in \prod(A)$, model checking analyses whether $A, w \models \neg \phi$ holds. If it does, the path w is returned as a counterexample to ϕ in A. If no counterexample w can be found then model checking returns *true*, i.e., ϕ holds for all possible paths of A.

In traditional explicit state space model checking we usually construct a product automaton from the automaton model and the requirement formula and check this for voidness. By contrast, NeoMC uses *pattern matching* to find counterexamples. For this we translate the requirement into a graph query (*pattern*) and perform pattern matching on a graph model of the automaton to find matches (i.e. counterexamples).

Since STAL is an extension of FOLTL, its model checking problem is similar to that of FOLTL. Recalling the validity relation for an automaton and an LTL formula we define validity for STAL formulas as follows.

Definition 6. $A \models \phi \iff \nexists w \in \prod(A) \ such \ that \ A, w \models \neg \phi$

So STAL formulas are interpreted over infinite linear sequences of states (paths) and have linear counterexamples [20]. It follows that a counterexample of a specification $\phi \in \mathcal{S}$ is an infinite path $w \in \prod^{\infty}(A)$ such that $A, w \not\models \phi$ or $A, w \models \neg \phi$. One can show that w, as a counterexample to ϕ, can, w.l.o.g, be restricted to paths of the form $x.y^{\omega}$ [21]. Such a path is called a *"lasso"* and denoted by ℓ in this paper. A lasso consists of a finite prefix path x followed by an infinite loop over a finite suffix path y [20].

Lasso counterexamples are mainly counterexamples to *liveness properties* [22] which have a close relationship with infinite words over finite automata [23].

(i) *Node property keys are "Id", "Name", "Angle", "Speed_x"_o_i, "Speed_y"_o_i,*
   "Distance_x"_o_i and "Distance_y"_o_i for all $o_i \in Obj$.
(ii) *For all property keys k_i of $\sigma_i \in \Sigma$ pairs, edge property keys are "Id" and "input"_k_i.*
(iii) *For all $q_i \in Q$ there exists $n_i \in N$ such that $P_{node}(n_i, \text{"Name"}) = \text{"}q_i\text{"}$.*
(iv) *For all key-value pair (k_i, v_i) of $\sigma_i \in \Sigma$, q_i and $q_{i+1} = \delta(\sigma_i, q_i)$ there exists $e_i \in E$ such*
   that $\lambda(e_i) = (n_i, n_{i+1})$ and $P_{edge}(e_i, \text{"input"}\_k_i) = v_i$.
(v) *For all q_i and $o_i \in Obj$ then:*
   -$P_{node}(n_i, \text{"Speed\_x"}\_o_i) = vel_x(o_i, q_i),$
   -$P_{node}(n_i, \text{"Speed\_y"}\_o_i) = vel_y(o_i, q_i),$
   -$P_{node}(n_i, \text{"Distance\_x"}\_o_i) = dist_x(o_i, q_i)$
   -$P_{node}(n_i, \text{"Distance\_y"}\_o_i) = dist_y(o_i, q_i)$
   - and $P_{node}(n_i, \text{"Angle"}) = angle(q_i)$.

Fig. 8. Translation rules to convert an STA model A to its corresponding property graph $\mathcal{G}_A$.

For example, the formula $GF(\phi)$ specifies that the state property ϕ must hold infinitely often along an infinite path w. Clearly, a counterexample to this formula is an infinite path on which from some point on, ϕ does not hold. Intuitively, for a lasso counterexample $w = x.y^\omega$, this means ϕ never holds in the loop suffix, i.e., $A, y^\omega \nvDash \phi$.

As with FOLTL, not all STAL counterexamples are infinite. Certain formulas have finite length counterexamples, i.e. satisfiability depends only on a finite prefix of a path. Examples are *safety properties* [22] which specify unsafe behavior that should never happen. An *invariant* is the simplest example of a safety property, i.e. a formula of the form $G(\phi)$, where ϕ has no modal operators. For invariants, a counterexample is a finite path where the last state violates ϕ. We can model check an STA A against a STAL formula $\phi \in \mathcal{S}$ as follows:

1) Translate A to a property graph $\mathcal{G}$.
2) Negate the requirement formula ϕ and translate this into a path pattern compatible with the target representation, e.g., a lasso pattern.
3) Execute a query to find matches for the pattern inside the property graph, i.e., a MATCH query in Cypher.
4) Return the results of pattern matching, if these exist, as paths, otherwise return *true*.

6.1 Soundness of Model Checking

The expressiveness of Cypher as a declarative query language is equivalent to a subset of first-order logic with transitive closure [18,24]. This enables Cypher to capture complex structural conditions and dependencies of STAL, and makes Neo4j a powerful platform for model checking. Thus we can translate a given STAL formula into a lasso graph query such that when evaluated over a graph representation of an STA model A, the query matches identify counterexamples.

Let $\mathcal{G}_A = (N, E, L, T, \lambda, Lab, Typ, P_{node}, P_{edge})$ be a graph representation of an STA $A = (\Sigma, Q, Obj, q_0, egoObj, \delta, angle, dist_x, dist_y, vel_x, vel_y)$ obtained by applying the rules in Fig. 8[5]. For any path $w \in \prod(A)$ in A we let $\overline{w} \in \prod(\mathcal{G}_A)$ denote the isomorphic copy[6] of w in the property graph $\mathcal{G}_A$.

Then Theorem 1 establishes the soundness of our model checking approach.

Theorem 1. *For any STAL formula ϕ there exists a Cypher query $\mu_\phi = Trans(\phi)$ such that for every lasso path $w = x.y^\omega \in \prod(A)$ $A, w \models \phi \Leftrightarrow \overline{w} \in [\![\mu_\phi]\!]_\mathcal{G}$.*

To prove Theorem 1, we first define the translation function $Trans : \mathcal{S} \to \mathcal{Q}$ that converts a STAL formula $\phi \in \mathcal{S}$ to a Cypher query μ_ϕ. Since our approach to STAL model checking is to search for lasso counterexamples, $Trans$ coverts a given STAL formula into a *lasso query* which is composed of a lasso pattern

$$\pi_\ell = (\text{n\{Name: "}q_0\text{"\}})\text{-[}e_1\text{*0..]}\to\text{(m)-[}e_2\text{*1..]}\to\text{(m)}$$

and a WHERE condition, i.e.

$$\mu_\phi = Trans(\phi) = \text{MATCH } \pi_\ell \text{ WHERE condition}(\overline{w}, \phi).$$

In the condition $\text{condition}(\overline{w}, \phi)$ the path $\overline{w}$ is a generic solution to the structural lasso pattern π_ℓ that must be further filtered by the WHERE condition to satisfy the formula ϕ. Thus from Sect. 5.1, it follows that $[\![\mu_\phi]\!]_\mathcal{G} \subseteq [\![\pi_\ell]\!]_\mathcal{G}$. Since the Cypher structure of the lasso pattern is fixed, we need only define the Cypher expression $\text{condition}(\overline{w}, \phi)$ inductively based on the structure of the STAL formula ϕ. The base case is where ϕ is atomic and does not include any modal operators.

Let $w = (\alpha_0, \alpha_1...)$ and $w^i = (\alpha_i, \alpha_{i+1}...)$ where $\alpha_i = (\sigma_i, q_i)$ and $\sigma_i = (k_i, v_i)$ for $i \geq 0$. Notice that if w is a lasso then so is each w^i. Suppose $A, w \models \phi$ then we define $Trans$ as follows:

Base Case. Since no modality is involved, the condition of ϕ must hold for the initial state $\alpha_0 \in w$, i.e., $A, (\text{null}, q_0) \models \phi$. Similarly in $\overline{w} \in [\![Trans(\phi)]\!]_\mathcal{G}$, the condition of ϕ must hold for the initial state n_0 of $\overline{w}$. We define $\text{condition}(\overline{w}, \phi)$ for an atomic ϕ below.

$A, w \models (exp_1 \mathbf{bop} exp_2) \iff [\![exp_1]\!]_{\alpha_0} \mathbf{bop} [\![exp_2]\!]_{\alpha_0} \equiv$
$\overline{w} \in [\![\mu_\phi = \text{MATCH } \pi_\ell \text{ WHERE condition}(\overline{w}, (exp_1 \mathbf{bop} exp_2))]\!]_\mathcal{G}$
where $\text{condition}(\overline{w}, (exp_1 \mathbf{bop} exp_2)) = (n_0.exp_1 \mathbf{bop} n_0.exp_2)$

$A, w \models (\text{input} = \sigma) \iff [\![\text{input} = \sigma]\!]_{\alpha_0} \equiv$
$\overline{w} \in [\![\mu_\phi = \text{MATCH } \pi_\ell \text{ WHERE condition}(\overline{w}, (\text{input} = \sigma))]\!]_\mathcal{G}$
where $\text{condition}(\overline{w}, (\text{input} = \sigma)) = (e_0.\text{input}\_k = v)$

Inductive Case. For arbitrary formulas $\phi, \psi \in \mathcal{S}$ such that $w \models \phi$, $\overline{w} \in [\![Trans(\phi)]\!]_\mathcal{G}$, we define below $Trans$ for $\neg\phi$, $\phi \wedge \psi$, $\phi \vee \psi$, $X(\phi)$, $F(\phi)$, $G(\phi)$ cases.

---

[5] In this figure, $n_i \in N$, $e_i \in E$, $L = \{$ *"State"* $\}$, $T = \{$*"Next"*$\}$, $Lab(n_i) = $ *"State"* and $Typ(e_i) = $ *"Next"*.

[6] By the construction rules of Fig. 8, $\mathcal{G}_A$ is essentially structurally isomorphic to A.

- **cases** $(\neg\phi)$, $(\phi \wedge \psi)$ and $(\phi \vee \psi)$:

  $\text{Trans}(\neg\phi)\quad \equiv \text{MATCH } \pi_\ell \text{ WHERE NOT condition}(\overline{w}, \phi)$
  $\text{Trans}(\phi \wedge \psi) \equiv \text{MATCH } \pi_\ell \text{ WHERE condition}(\overline{w}, \phi) \text{ AND condition}(\overline{w}, \psi)$
  $\text{Trans}(\phi \vee \psi) \equiv \text{MATCH } \pi_\ell \text{ WHERE condition}(\overline{w}, \phi) \text{ OR condition}(\overline{w}, \psi)$

- **case** $X(\phi)$: According to the semantics of STAL,

  $A, w \models X(\phi) \iff A, w^1 \models \phi \equiv$
  $\overline{w} \in [\![\mu_\phi = \text{MATCH } \pi_\ell \text{ WHERE condition}(\overline{w}^1, \phi)]\!]_{\mathcal{G}}$

- **case** $F(\phi)$: The semantic of the *eventually* operator F concerns a finite path from a state q_i to a reachable state q_j where ϕ holds. Therefore,

  $A, w \models F(\phi) \iff \exists j \in \mathbb{N} : A, w^j \models \phi \equiv$
  $\overline{w} \in [\![\mu_\phi = \text{MATCH } \pi_\ell \text{ WHERE Any}(n_i, e_i \text{ in } [\![\pi_\ell]\!]_{\mathcal{G}} \text{ WHERE condition}(\overline{w}^i, \phi))]\!]_{\mathcal{G}}$

The `Any` function is a list predicate with boolean output which ensures that at least one element of a given list satisfies the conditions of its `WHERE` clause. Note that the index i of $\text{Any}(n_i, e_i \dots)$ is a position index and the `Any` function is actually a loop that breaks when the `condition` is satisfied.

- **case** $A, w \models G(\phi)$: Evaluating an *always* operator G requires to verify ϕ on an infinite path and for a *lasso* path $w = x.y^\omega$, ϕ must be valid for all states and transitions of the lasso. Therefore all nodes of a lasso path $\overline{w}$ should satisfy the `WHERE` conditions of ϕ. In Cypher, the `All` function is a list predicate with boolean output which ensures that all elements of a given list satisfy the conditions of its `WHERE` clause. Note that the index i of $\text{All}(n_i, e_i \dots)$ is a position index and the `All` function is actually a loop without any break condition.

  $A, w \models G(\phi) \iff \forall i \in \mathbb{N} : A, w^i \models \phi \equiv$
  $\overline{w} \in [\![\mu_\phi = \text{MATCH } \pi_\ell \text{ WHERE All}(n_i, e_i \text{ in } [\![\pi_\ell]\!]_{\mathcal{G}} \text{ WHERE condition}(\overline{w}^i, \phi))]\!]_{\mathcal{G}}$

Example 4. To clarify the translation procedure, below we provide two examples.

(i) $A, w \models GF(\phi) \rightarrow GF(\psi)$: This is a conjunction of GF and FG operators. If this formula is satisfiable by a lasso path $w = x.y^\omega$, then either all states of y must not satisfy ϕ, or at least one state of y must satisfy ψ.

  $A, w \models GF(\phi) \rightarrow GF(\psi) \equiv FG(\neg\phi) \vee GF(\psi)$
  $\iff (i, j \in \mathbb{N}, \exists i. \ \forall j, i \le j. \ w^j \not\models \phi) \vee (i, j \in \mathbb{N}, \forall i. \ \exists j, i \le j. \ w^j \models \psi) \equiv$
  $\overline{w} \in [\![\mu_\phi = \text{MATCH } \pi_\ell \text{ WHERE}$
  $\text{Any}(n_i, e_i \text{ in } [\![\pi_\ell]\!]_{\mathcal{G}} \text{ WHERE All}(n_j, e_j \text{ in } [\![\pi_\ell]\!]_{\mathcal{G}} \text{ WHERE NOT condition}(\overline{w}^{i+j}, \phi)))$
  $\text{OR All}(n_i, e_i \text{ in } [\![\pi_\ell]\!]_{\mathcal{G}} \text{ WHERE Any}(n_j, e_j \text{ in } [\![\pi_\ell]\!]_{\mathcal{G}} \text{ WHERE condition}(\overline{w}^{i+j}, \phi)))]\!]_{\mathcal{G}}$

(ii) $A, w \models GFX(\phi)$: One of the complex structures is the combination of the *liveness* GF and the *next* X operators. However, the translation to a lasso query is straightforward.

  $A, w \models GFX(\phi) \iff i, j \in \mathbb{N}, \forall i. \ \exists j, i \le j. \ w^{j+1} \models \phi \equiv$
  $\overline{w} \in [\![\mu_\phi = \text{MATCH } \pi_\ell \text{ WHERE All}(n_i, e_i \text{ in } [\![\pi_\ell]\!]_{\mathcal{G}} \text{ WHERE Any}(n_j, e_j \text{ in } [\![\pi_\ell]\!]_{\mathcal{G}} \text{ WHERE}$
  $\text{condition}(\overline{w}^{i+j+1}, \phi)))]\!]_{\mathcal{G}}$

Having defined the translation Trans, the proof of Theorem 1 is straightforward and relies on the definition of $\overline{w}$, $\overline{w} \in [\![\mu_\phi]\!]_{\mathcal{G}}$.

7   NeoMC Implementation and Evaluation

Figure 9 shows the architecture of our Neo4j-based model checker NeoMC that checks STAL formulas against STA models. As we have seen in Sect. 6, to check a STAL formula, NeoMC first converts an STA model to a Neo4j property graph. Then, it negates the formula and converts it into a Cypher pattern and uses this to perform a pattern matching query. If the query matches any paths in the graph, counterexamples are returned. Otherwise the verdict *true* is returned.

The Neo4j database (DB) is a stand-alone Java application that can be instantiated through the Neo4j API. It is responsible for performing all database queries and populating the results. The communication between NeoMC and the database is carried out over a TCP connection known as a *"Bolt url"*.

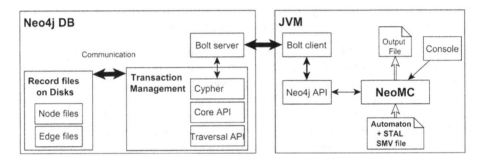

Fig. 9. Architecture of NeoMC integrated with Neo4j DB

To evaluate NeoMC we constructed a number of large STAs by machine learning using the platooning simulator of [25] to simulate a distributed multi-object dynamical system. These STAs ranged in size from 1 K to 71 K states. The largest STA had about 1.5 million transitions.

Our specific case study is a two vehicle platoon consisting of a leader (the ego object) and a follower. The leader is under manual control, and the follower is autonomously controlled using a cooperative adaptive cruise control (CACC) algorithm [25] for longitudinal control. The simulator accepts two input signals to control the brake and throttle of the lead vehicle. These continuous inputs were discretized to 10 different levels. In total, there were 21 discretized input values, called Pedal values. The outputs of the simulator used to construct the STA models were the speed of the leader and the relative distance between leader and the follower in the x dimension only, i.e., $\mathrm{Speed}_x(leader)$ and $\mathrm{Distance}_x(follower)$, denoted by Speed_x and $\mathrm{Distance}_x$.

To benchmark NeoMC on the STAs derived from the platooning simulation, we defined a set of spatio-temporal requirements on the platooning vehicles themselves using STAL. Some of these requirements are presented in Table 1. A positive **Pedal** value in the table means pressing the lead vehicle gas pedal and a negative value means braking pedal level. Case (1) is to capture a near collision and means: "The distance between the follower and the lead vehicles should never be less than five meters. Case (2) means: "Gassing up the lead vehicle should eventually result in a speed greater than 30 km/h", and Case (3) means that, "Eventually the leader speed should stay at a high speed value greater than 70 km/h if the gas pedal is nearly fully pressed infinitely often".

Benchmarking tests of NeoMC were performed on an Ubuntu 16.4 LTS machine with Intel Core i5-6260U ×4 running at 1.80 GHz and 16Gb available RAM.

Table 2 summarizes our benchmark results for NeoMC model checking based on 10 different sized STA models and 7 different STAL requirements. Table 2 shows both the number of counterexamples found (lhs) and the execution time

Table 1. Platoon requirements in STAL.

Req	STAL formula ϕ	Cypher query $\mu = \mathbf{Trans}(\neg\phi)$
(1)	$G\neg(Distance_x < 5)$	`WHERE m.Distance_x < 5`
(2)	$FG(Pedal > 0) \rightarrow FG(Speed_x > 30)$	`WHERE Any(`n_i, e_i` in `$[\![\pi_\ell]\!]_G$` WHERE`
		`All(`n_j, e_j` in `$[\![\pi_\ell]\!]_G$` WHERE `e_{i+j}`.input_Pedal>0))`
		`AND All(`n_i, e_i` in `$[\![\pi_\ell]\!]_G$` WHERE Any(`n_j, e_j` in `$[\![\pi_\ell]\!]_G$`
		`WHERE NOT `n_{i+j}`.Speed_x>30) )`
(3)	$GF(Pedal > 7) \rightarrow GF(Speed_x > 70)$	`WHERE All(`n_i, e_i` in `$[\![\pi_\ell]\!]_G$` WHERE`
		`Any(`n_j, e_j` in `$[\![\pi_\ell]\!]_G$` WHERE `e_{i+j}`.input_Pedal>7))`
		`AND Any(`n_i, e_i` in `$[\![\pi_\ell]\!]_G$` WHERE All(`n_j, e_j` in `$[\![\pi_\ell]\!]_G$`
		`WHERE NOT `n_{i+j}`.Speed_x>70) )`
(4)	$G(Pedal > 0 \rightarrow X(acc^* > 0))$	`WHERE Any(`n_i, e_i` in `$[\![\pi_\ell]\!]_G$` WHERE `e_i`.input_Pedal>0`
		`AND NOT `n_{i+1}`.Speed_x - `n_i`.Speed_x>0)`
(5)	$G(Pedal < 0 \rightarrow X(acc < 0))$	`WHERE Any(`n_i, e_i` in `$[\![\pi_\ell]\!]_G$` WHERE `e_i`.input_Pedal<0`
		`AND NOT `n_{i+1}`.Speed_x - `n_i`.Speed_x<0)`
(6)	$G\neg(Pedal = -10 \rightarrow$	`WHERE Any(`n_i, e_i` in `$[\![\pi_\ell]\!]_G$` WHERE NOT `e_i`.input_Pedal=-10`
	$(Next(Speed_x) - Speed_x) > 0)$	`OR `n_{i+1}`.Speed_x - `n_i`.Speed_x < 20) )`
(7)	$G\neg(Speed_x > 120)$	`WHERE m.Speed > 120`

* The Leader acceleration.

Table 2. Number of identified counterexamples and the execution time for model checking of requirements in Table 1 for different model sizes (1.1 K–71 K states). Here ϵ means the execution time is less than 0.5 s.

Req	#Counterexamples on K-state models										Execution Time* (in seconds)									
	1.1	1.7	2.1	2.5	3.4	4	7.8	12.6	25	71	1.1	1.7	2.1	2.5	3.4	4	7.8	12.6	25	71
(1)	8	4	2	5	7	7	28	28	100	35	ϵ	ϵ	ϵ	ϵ	ϵ	ϵ	1	1	3	1
(2)	0	0	0	0	0	0	0	0	0	0	3	4	5	6	8	9	39	40	102	784
(3)	0	0	0	0	0	15	1	1	16	0	2	3	4	5	7	9	25	41	107	793
(4)	1	1	1	1	1	2	6	6	11	1	ϵ	ϵ	ϵ	ϵ	ϵ	ϵ	ϵ	ϵ	1	1
(5)	27	32	43	64	98	100	100	100	100	57	ϵ	ϵ	ϵ	ϵ	ϵ	ϵ	ϵ	ϵ	ϵ	1
(6)	0	0	0	0	0	0	0	2	0	8	ϵ	ϵ	ϵ	ϵ	ϵ	ϵ	ϵ	ϵ	1	1
(7)	0	0	0	0	0	0	0	0	0	0	ϵ	ϵ	ϵ	ϵ	ϵ	ϵ	ϵ	ϵ	1	ϵ

in each case (rhs). We limited the maximum number of counterexamples to 100 to make the table concise and readable. In general, as the learned model grows in size, more violations of a requirement can be observed, because the model captures more execution paths with bad sequences of states. Table 2 shows that the execution time increases linearly with respect to model size.

We were unable to easily compare NeoMC performance with existing model checkers. One reason is that we could not find an efficient and scalable representation of large STA models for tools such as NuXMV [26], Spin [27] and LTSmin [28]. These tools parse the input models into their internal data representation and as the models grow in size, they either fail to read the files or construct the state space efficiently. Even for a medium size STA of 4k states, the model parsing times of Spin and the model checking time of NuXMV are beyond any acceptable figures. The memory usage of NuXMV is huge, of the order of tens of Gigabytes. Spin also consumes a lot of memory to generate its internal verifier. Only the built-in symbolic format (i.e. ETF) of LTSmin matches the STA models and quickly performs the model checking. However, the ETF format only works for symbolic datatypes and does not support FO STAL expressions and formulas.

8   Related Work

There is a large body of work on spatio-temporal logic. A rather complete list of related work in this area is provided in [1]. Verification of spatial and temporal modalities is studied in different domains such as in biochemistry [29], biology [30,31] and air traffic management [32]. Research on spatio-temporal model checking is often tailored to specific applications. SpaTeL [6] uses statistical model checking to estimate the probability of events in networked systems that relate different regions of space at different times. Statistical model checking has also been applied to collective adaptive systems where spatio-temporal properties expressed in STLCS [33] are verified against discrete, geographical models of a smart public transportation system [34]. In [7] a shape calculus based spatio-temporal model checking is introduced for the verification of a real-time railroad crossing system. A second order model checker is used to perform reachability checks on BDDs representing transition relations.

Verification of vehicle platooning is also studied by Kamali et al. [2] where timed and untimed automata models of a spatial controller are model checked using AJPF and UPPAAL. Schwammberger [3] introduced MLSL logic to verify safety of traffic maneuvers. Similarly to STAL, MLSL is using the snapshot concept which captures the state of objects at a given moment in time. However, our work differs from [2,3]. While they tried to verify safety of controller algorithms using timed-automata models in UPPAAL, our model checking technique is developed to verify a learned behavior of CO-CPSs using graph queries. Also, AJPF does not support temporal analysis and is resource-heavy, whereas graph databases scale with ease. The most closely related work to ours is [24] which used declarative graph queries for the verification of CPSs. They developed a runtime monitoring for railway systems against spatial requirements expressed in a 3-valued logic, but, this work lacks exhaustive verification and model checking.

9   Conclusions

We have proposed an approach to spatio-temporal model checking based on using the graph database Neo4j and its declarative query language Cypher. We have established the theoretical soundness of this approach, and implemented and evaluated it on a large case study. NeoMC shows that query solving for Cypher is an efficient way to implement model-checking. To the best of our knowledge, our work is the first attempt to apply graph database technology to model checking. Furthermore, Neo4j enabled us to quickly prototype a model checker for STAL that was scalable to large models. The efficiency of NeoMC is partly due to efficient search algorithms employed in modern graph databases, and also the fact that we could avoid constructing large product automata.

Acknowledgments. This research has been supported by KTH ICT-TNG project STaRT (Spatio-Temporal Planning at Runtime), as well as the German Federal Ministry of Education and Research (BMBF) through funding for the CISPA-Stanford Center for Cybersecurity (FKZ: 13N1S0762).

References

1. Khosrowjerdi, H., Meinke, K.: Learning-based testing for autonomous systems using spatial and temporal requirements. In: Proceedings of the 1st International Workshop on Machine Learning and Software Engineering in Symbiosis, MASES@ASE 2018, Montpellier, France, 3 September 2018, pp. 6–15 (2018). https://doi.org/10.1145/3243127.3243129
2. Kamali, M., Linker, S., Fisher, M.: Modular verification of vehicle platooning with respect to decisions, space and time. In: Artho, C., Ölveczky, P.C. (eds.) FTSCS 2018. CCIS, vol. 1008, pp. 18–36. Springer, Cham (2019). https://doi.org/10.1007/978-3-030-12988-0_2
3. Schwammberger, M.: An abstract model for proving safety of autonomous urban traffic. Theor. Comput. Sci. **744**, 143–169 (2018). https://doi.org/10.1016/j.tcs.2018.05.028
4. Alur, R., Dill, D.L.: A theory of timed automata. Theor. Comput. Sci. **126**(2), 183–235 (1994). https://doi.org/10.1016/0304-3975(94)90010-8
5. Chaochen, Z., Hoare, C., Ravn, A.P.: A calculus of durations. Inf. Process. Lett. **40**(5), 269–276 (1991). http://www.sciencedirect.com/science/article/pii/002001909190122X
6. Haghighi, I., Jones, A., Kong, Z., Bartocci, E., Grosu, R., Belta, C.: Spatel: a novel spatial-temporal logic and its applications to networked systems. In: Proceedings of the 18th International Conference on Hybrid Systems: Computation and Control, HSCC 2015, Seattle, WA, USA, 14–16 April 2015, pp. 189–198 (2015). https://doi.org/10.1145/2728606.2728633

7. Quesel, J.-D., Schäfer, A.: Spatio-temporal model checking for mobile real-time systems. In: Barkaoui, K., Cavalcanti, A., Cerone, A. (eds.) ICTAC 2006. LNCS, vol. 4281, pp. 347–361. Springer, Heidelberg (2006). https://doi.org/10.1007/11921240_24

8. Angles, R., Arenas, M., Barceló, P., Hogan, A., Reutter, J.L., Vrgoc, D.: Foundations of modern query languages for graph databases. ACM Comput. Surv. **50**(5), 68:1–68:40 (2017). http://doi.acm.org/10.1145/3104031

9. Bennaceur, A., Hähnle, R., Meinke, K. (eds.): Machine Learning for Dynamic Software Analysis: Potentials and Limits. LNCS, vol. 11026. Springer, Cham (2018). https://doi.org/10.1007/978-3-319-96562-8

10. Meinke, K., Niu, F.: A learning-based approach to unit testing of numerical software. In: Petrenko, A., Simão, A., Maldonado, J.C. (eds.) ICTSS 2010. LNCS, vol. 6435, pp. 221–235. Springer, Heidelberg (2010). https://doi.org/10.1007/978-3-642-16573-3_16

11. Meinke, K., Sindhu, M.A.: Incremental learning-based testing for reactive systems. In: Gogolla, M., Wolff, B. (eds.) TAP 2011. LNCS, vol. 6706, pp. 134–151. Springer, Heidelberg (2011). https://doi.org/10.1007/978-3-642-21768-5_11

12. Webber, J.: A programmatic introduction to neo4j. In: Conference on Systems, Programming, and Applications: Software for Humanity, SPLASH 2012, Tucson, AZ, USA, 21–25 October 2012, pp. 217–218 (2012). https://doi.org/10.1145/2384716.2384777

13. Francis, N., et al.: Cypher: an evolving query language for property graphs. In: Proceedings of the 2018 International Conference on Management of Data, SIGMOD Conference 2018, Houston, TX, USA, 10–15 June 2018, pp. 1433–1445 (2018). http://doi.acm.org/10.1145/3183713.3190657

14. de la Higuera, C.: Grammatical Inference: Learning Automata and Grammars. Cambridge University Press, (2010). iv + 417 pages, Machine Translation, vol. 24, no. 3–4, pp. 291–293, 2010. https://doi.org/10.1007/s10590-011-9086-9

15. Angles, R., Gutiérrez, C.: Survey of graph database models. ACM Comput. Surv. **40**(1), 11–139 (2008). https://doi.org/10.1145/1322432.1322433

16. Robinson, I., Webber, J., Eifrem, E.: Graph Databases: New Opportunities for Connected Data, 2nd edn. O'Reilly Media Inc., Sebastopol (2015)

17. Hölsch, J., Schmidt, T., Grossniklaus, M.: On the performance of analytical and pattern matching graph queries in neo4j and a relational database. In: Proceedings of the Workshops of the EDBT/ICDT 2017 Joint Conference (EDBT/ICDT 2017), Venice, Italy, 21–24 March 2017 (2017). http://ceur-ws.org/Vol-1810/GraphQ_paper_01.pdf

18. Francis, N., et al.: Formal semantics of the language cypher. CoRR, vol. abs/1802.09984 (2018). http://arxiv.org/abs/1802.09984

19. Junghanns, M., Kießling, M., Averbuch, A., Petermann, A., Rahm, E.: Cypher-based graph pattern matching in gradoop. In: Proceedings of the Fifth International Workshop on Graph Data-management Experiences & Systems, GRADES@SIGMOD/PODS 2017, Chicago, IL, USA, 14–19 May 2017, pp. 3:1–3:8 (2017). http://doi.acm.org/10.1145/3078447.3078450

20. Clarke, E.M., Henzinger, T.A., Veith, H., Bloem, R. (eds.): Handbook of Model Checking. Springer, Cham (2018). https://doi.org/10.1007/978-3-319-10575-8

21. Wolper, P., Vardi, M.Y., Sistla, A.P.: Reasoning about infinite computation paths (extended abstract). In: 24th Annual Symposium on Foundations of Computer Science, Tucson, Arizona, USA, 7–9 November 1983, pp. 185–194 (1983). https://doi.org/10.1109/SFCS.1983.51

22. Alpern, B., Schneider, F.B.: Defining liveness. Inf. Process. Lett. **21**(4), 181–185 (1985). https://doi.org/10.1016/0020-0190(85)90056-0
23. Vardi, M.Y., Wolper, P.: An automata-theoretic approach to automatic program verification (preliminary report). In: Proceedings of the Symposium on Logic in Computer Science (LICS 1986), Cambridge, Massachusetts, USA, June 16–18, 1986, pp. 332–344 (1986)
24. Búr, M., Szilágyi, G., Vörös, A., Varró, D.: Distributed graph queries for runtime monitoring of cyber-physical systems. In: Russo, A., Schürr, A. (eds.) FASE 2018. LNCS, vol. 10802, pp. 111–128. Springer, Cham (2018). https://doi.org/10.1007/978-3-319-89363-1_7
25. Meinke, K.: Learning-based testing of cyber-physical systems-of-systems: a platooning study. In: Reinecke, P., Di Marco, A. (eds.) EPEW 2017. LNCS, vol. 10497, pp. 135–151. Springer, Cham (2017). https://doi.org/10.1007/978-3-319-66583-2_9
26. Cavada, R., Cimatti, A., Dorigatti, M., Griggio, A., Mariotti, A., Micheli, A., Mover, S., Roveri, M., Tonetta, S.: The NUXMV symbolic model checker. In: Biere, A., Bloem, R. (eds.) CAV 2014. LNCS, vol. 8559, pp. 334–342. Springer, Cham (2014). https://doi.org/10.1007/978-3-319-08867-9_22
27. Holzmann, G.J.: The SPIN Model Checker - Primer and Referencemanual. Addison-Wesley, Boston (2004)
28. Kant, G., Laarman, A., Meijer, J., van de Pol, J., Blom, S., van Dijk, T.: LTSmin: high-performance language-independent model checking. In: Baier, C., Tinelli, C. (eds.) TACAS 2015. LNCS, vol. 9035, pp. 692–707. Springer, Heidelberg (2015). https://doi.org/10.1007/978-3-662-46681-0_61
29. Chiarugi, D., Falaschi, M., Hermith, D., Olarte, C.: Verification of spatial and temporal modalities in biochemical systems. Electr. Notes Theor. Comput. Sci. **316**, 29–44 (2015). https://doi.org/10.1016/j.entcs.2015.06.009
30. Parvu, O., Gilbert, D.R.: Automatic validation of computational models using pseudo-3D Spatio-temporal model checking. BMC Syst. Biol. **8**, 124 (2014). https://doi.org/10.1186/s12918-014-0124-0
31. Grosu, R., Smolka, S.A., Corradini, F., Wasilewska, A., Entcheva, E., Bartocci, E.: Learning and detecting emergent behavior in networks of cardiac myocytes. Commun. ACM **52**(3), 97–105 (2009). https://doi.org/10.1145/1467247.1467271
32. de Oliveira, Í.R., Cugnasca, P.S.: Checking safe trajectories of aircraft using hybrid automata. In: Anderson, S., Felici, M., Bologna, S. (eds.) SAFECOMP 2002. LNCS, vol. 2434, pp. 224–235. Springer, Heidelberg (2002). https://doi.org/10.1007/3-540-45732-1_22
33. Ciancia, V., Grilletti, G., Latella, D., Loreti, M., Massink, M.: An experimental spatio-temporal model checker. In: Bianculli, D., Calinescu, R., Rumpe, B. (eds.) SEFM 2015. LNCS, vol. 9509, pp. 297–311. Springer, Heidelberg (2015). https://doi.org/10.1007/978-3-662-49224-6_24
34. Ciancia, V., Gilmore, S., Grilletti, G., Latella, D., Loreti, M., Massink, M.: Spatio-temporal model checking of vehicular movement in public transport systems. STTT **20**(3), 289–311 (2018). https://doi.org/10.1007/s10009-018-0483-8

SAT Modulo Differential Equation Simulations

Tomáš Kolárik[1] and Stefan Ratschan[2]([⊠]) [ID]

[1] Faculty of Information Technology, Czech Technical University in Prague,
Prague, Czech Republic
[2] Institute of Computer Science of the Czech Academy of Sciences,
Prague, Czech Republic
stefan.ratschan@cs.cas.cz

Abstract. Differential equations are of immense importance for modeling physical phenomena, often in combination with discrete modeling formalisms. In current industrial practice, properties of the resulting models are checked by testing, using simulation tools. Research on SAT solvers that are able to handle differential equations has aimed at replacing tests by correctness proofs. However, there are fundamental limitations to such approaches in the form of undecidability, and moreover, the resulting solvers do not scale to problems of the size commonly handled by simulation tools. Also, in many applications, classical mathematical semantics of differential equations often does not correspond well to the actual intended semantics, and hence a correctness proof wrt. mathematical semantics does not ensure correctness of the intended system.

In this paper, we head at overcoming those limitations by an alternative approach to handling differential equations within SAT solvers. This approach is usually based on the semantics used by tests in simulation tools, but still may result in mathematically precise correctness proofs wrt. that semantics. Experiments with a prototype implementation confirm the promise of such an approach.

1 Introduction

The design of cyber-physical systems is more and more being based on models that can be simulated before the actual system even exists. Here, the most natural way of modeling the physical part is based on differential equations. The resulting models can then be simulated using numerical solvers for ordinary differential equations (ODEs), or tools such as Xcos or Simulink. However, the computational support for automatically analyzing (e.g., testing, verifying) such models is still far from satisfactory.

This has been addressed by SAT solvers [10,11] that do not only offer efficient discrete (i.e., Boolean) reasoning, but that, in addition, are also able to handle differential equations by integrating interval ODE solvers [17,19]. Handling ODEs in such a way is extremely difficult, and most related verification problems are undecidable [5]. The resulting SAT modulo ODE solvers can handle

© Springer Nature Switzerland AG 2020
W. Ahrendt and H. Wehrheim (Eds.): TAP 2020, LNCS 12165, pp. 80–99, 2020.
https://doi.org/10.1007/978-3-030-50995-8_5

benchmark examples that are impressive, but still quite far away from the size of the problems that may occur in industrial practice.

A further reason why such tools are a poor fit to the needs coming from industrial applications is the fact that classical mathematical solutions usually do *not* correctly represent the intended behavior of industrial models [16], since the design process is based on the results of numerical simulations, and *not* on a mathematical analysis of the underlying differential equations. The numerical simulations differ from mathematical solutions due to discretization and floating-point computation. Hence, the output of the used simulation tool is the authoritative description of the behavior of the model, *not* traditional mathematical semantics. This holds even in cases when the model was designed based on ODEs corresponding to physical laws ("from first principles"), because even in such cases, the parameters of the model are estimated based on simulations. This is becoming all the more important due to the increasing popularity of data driven modeling approaches, for example, based on machine learning.

Therefore, the existing SAT modulo ODE approaches prove correctness wrt. semantics that differs from the notion of correctness used during simulation and testing. We overcome this mismatch by formalizing the semantics of SAT modulo ODE based on numerical simulations. We prove decidability of the resulting problem, and design a simple solver. We provide a syntactical characterization of the kind of inputs for which one can expect an efficient solution from such a solver, and support this by experiments using a prototype implementation.

We also address another restriction of existing SAT modulo ODE approaches. Their support for differential equations has the form of monolithic building blocks that contain a full system of ordinary differential equations within which no Boolean reasoning is allowed. In contrast to that, in this paper we provide a direct integration of ODEs into a standard SAT modulo theory (SMT) framework [3], which results in a tight integration of the syntax of the theory into Boolean formulas, as usual for theories in SMT-LIB [1].

The problem of verifying differential equations wrt. simulation semantics has been addressed before [4,16], but not in a SAT modulo theory context. Also floating point arithmetic has been realized to be an important domain for verification tools [6,14], resulting in a floating point theory in SMT-LIB. However, this concentrates on the intricacies of floating point arithmetic, which we largely ignore here, and concentrate instead on the handling of ODEs.

In the next section, we will introduce an illustrative toy example. Then we will present our integration of ODEs into SMT, first using classical mathematical semantics (Sect. 3), then using simulation semantics (Sect. 4). In the next three sections, we prove decidability of the resulting theory, design a simple solver, and study its theoretical properties. In Sect. 8, we present some computational experiments with a prototype implementation, and in Sect. 9, we conclude the paper.

2   Example

For explaining the intuition behind the syntax of our language and the structure of formulas that we expect to handle, we describe an illustrative toy example.

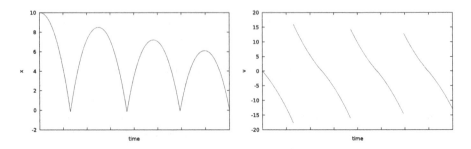

Fig. 1. Example Trajectories

The example corresponds to a bounded model checking problem for a bouncing ball with linear drag—Fig. 1 shows the height of the ball on the left-hand side and its speed on the right-hand side.

$g = 9.81 \wedge K = 0.9 \wedge \neg up_1 \wedge init(x_1) = 10 \wedge init(v_1) = 0 \wedge$
$\dot{x}_1 = v_1 \wedge \left(up_1 \Rightarrow \dot{v}_1 = -g - \frac{v_1}{100} \right) \wedge \left(\neg up_1 \Rightarrow \dot{v}_1 = -g + \frac{v_1}{100} \right) \wedge$
$x_1 \geq 0 \wedge (up_1 \Rightarrow v_1 \geq 0) \wedge (\neg up_1 \Rightarrow v_1 \leq 0) \wedge$
$up_1 \Rightarrow (final(v_1) \leq 0 \wedge \neg up_2 \wedge init(x_2) = final(x_1) \wedge init(v_2) = 0) \wedge$
$\neg up_1 \Rightarrow (final(x_1) \leq 0 \wedge up_2 \wedge init(x_2) = 0 \wedge init(v_2) = -Kfinal(v_1)) \wedge$
$\dot{x}_2 = v_2 \wedge \left(up_2 \Rightarrow \dot{v}_2 = -g - \frac{v_2}{100} \right) \wedge \left(\neg up_2 \Rightarrow \dot{v}_2 = -g + \frac{v_2}{100} \right) \wedge$
$x_2 \geq 0 \wedge (up_2 \Rightarrow v_2 \geq 0) \wedge (\neg up_2 \Rightarrow v_2 \leq 0) \wedge$
$up_2 \Rightarrow (final(v_2) \leq 0 \wedge \neg up_3 \wedge init(x_3) = final(x_2) \wedge init(v_3) = 0) \wedge$
$\neg up_2 \Rightarrow (final(x_2) \leq 0 \wedge up_3 \wedge init(x_3) = 0 \wedge init(v_3) = -Kfinal(v_2)) \wedge$
$\cdots$
$final(x_{23}) \geq 8$

In the example, the variables $up_1, \ldots$ range over the Booleans, the variables K and g range over real numbers, and the variables $x_i, v_i, i \in \{1, \ldots, 23\}$ range over functions from corresponding intervals $[0, \tau_i]$ to the real numbers, where the lengths τ_i are *not* fixed a priori. The example does not provide this information explicitly—we will introduce notation to do so, later. Also, all constraints on those variables (i.e., all invariants) are intended to hold *for all* elements of those intervals. Again we will introduce formal details later.

The dot operator denotes differentiation, *init* denotes the value of the argument function at 0 and *final* the value at τ_i. Note that the example uses the Boolean variables $up_1, \ldots$ to activate different differential equations and bounds on the variables $x_1, v_1, x_2, v_2, \ldots$.

The ball starts at height 10 with speed zero, and for each $x_i, v_i, i \in \{1, \ldots, 23\}$ the pair x_i, v_i models one falling or rising phase of the ball (the figure shows 7 of those). The update $init(v_{i+1}) = -Kfinal(v_i)$ results in a non-continuous change between the last point of v_i and the initial point of v_{i+1}. The example checks whether a state with height greater or equal 8 is reached after falling and rising a certain number of times. For illustrative purposes, the modeled behavior is completely deterministic, although our method can also handle non-determinism.

We want to check whether there are values for the variables that satisfy such formulas when interpreting the differential equations using simulation tools. Before going into details we will analyze the structure of the above formula.

First of all, the variables have indices 1, 2, and 3 corresponding to stages of a bounded model checking problem. The indices are just part of the names of the corresponding variables, but still, they clarify the fact that the variables in the formulas also occur in stages. Especially, the variables with the same index belong to the same stage, and within stage i, each functional variable, that is, x_i and v_i, is determined by a differential equation.

Further, understanding that x_i models the height of a bouncing ball, we see that if the ball is moving down, the constraints $x_i \geq 0$ eventually must be violated, bounding the length of the functional variables. If the ball is moving up, this is ensured by the constraints $v_i \geq 0$.

And finally, the stages also define a specific order on how one can assign values to variables: The first line of the formula assigns values to the variables g and K, and initial values of x_1 and v_1. Then it states differential equations describing the evolution of x_1 and v_1. Moreover, it states invariants that should hold on those solutions. Next, it describes how the initial value of x_2 and v_2 depends on the final value of x_1 and v_1. Then it analogously repeats the above statements for x_2 and v_2, and so on. In other words, solving the real part of the above formula may proceed in stages, avoiding any circular reasoning.

3   Formalization: SAT Modulo ODE

In this section, we will tightly integrate ODEs into SAT, roughly following the SMT framework of Barrett and Tinelli [3]. Note that SMT uses *first-order* predicate logic as its basis, while here we want to reason about functions (the solutions of ODEs). We overcome this seeming mismatch by simply handling those functions as first-order objects[1].

The signature of our theory contains the sort symbols $\mathcal{R}$ and $(\mathcal{F}_k)_{k \in \kappa}$ for a finite index set κ. Intuitively, the sort $\mathcal{R}$ corresponds to real numbers, and each sort symbol $\mathcal{F}_k$, $k \in \kappa$ to real functions, with the argument modeling time over a certain time interval. In the illustrative example, the variables x_1, v_1 belong to the same sort (e.g., $\mathcal{F}_1$), the variables x_2, v_2 to another one (e.g., $\mathcal{F}_2$), and so on.

The allowed predicate symbols are $\{=, \geq\}$ and the function symbols include $\{0, 1, +, -, \cdot, \exp, \log, \sin, \cos, \tan\}$, all of the usual arity. All of those predicate and function symbols are defined on all sorts (i.e., not only on $\mathcal{R}$, but also on $(\mathcal{F}_k)_{k \in \kappa}$). Still, we always require all arguments and results to be from the same sort.

We will have additional function symbols that we will also call *functional operators*: The function symbols $init_k : \mathcal{F}_k \to \mathcal{R}$ and $final_k : \mathcal{F}_k \to \mathcal{R}$, $k \in \kappa$

---

[1] While this is new in the context of SAT modulo ODE, this is quite common in mathematics. For example, Zermelo-Fraenkel set theory uses such an approach to define sets, relations, etc. within *first-order* predicate logic.

model the initial and final value of the argument function. The function symbol $diff_k : \mathcal{F}_k \to \mathcal{F}_k$, $k \in \kappa$, models differentiation, and hence we will usually write $diff(z)$ as $\dot{z}$. We also assume the function symbols $embed_k : \mathcal{R} \to \mathcal{F}_k$, $k \in \kappa$, that convert real numbers to functions. However, we will not write the function symbols $embed_k$, $k \in \kappa$ explicitly, but implicitly assume them whenever an argument from $\mathcal{F}_k$ is expected and an argument from $\mathcal{R}$ present. In the example, this is the case in the differential equation $\dot{v}_2 = -g$ which would actually read $\dot{v}_2 = -embed_2(g)$, or $\dot{v}_2 = embed_2(-g)$. For all functional operators we will not write the index, if clear from the context.

Since we do not allow quantifiers, we will not work with a separate set of variables, but simply call 0-ary predicate symbols *Boolean variables*, 0-ary function symbols from $\mathcal{R}$ *numerical variables*, and 0-ary function symbols from $\mathcal{F}_k$, $k \in \kappa$, *k-function variables* and often just *function variables*. We denote the set of Boolean variables by $\mathcal{V}_\mathcal{B}$, and for every sort $\mathcal{S}$, we denote the corresponding set of variables by $\mathcal{V}_\mathcal{S}$. We also define the set of all such variables $\mathcal{V} := \mathcal{V}_\mathcal{B} \cup \mathcal{V}_\mathcal{R} \cup \bigcup_{k \in \kappa} \mathcal{V}_{\mathcal{F}_k}$.

Definition 1. *An* atomic formula *is either a Boolean variable or an atomic theory formula. An* atomic theory formula *is of one of the three following kinds:*

- *An atomic* real-valued formula *is a formula of the form $p(\eta_1, \ldots, \eta_n)$ where p is an n-ary predicate symbol from $\mathcal{R}$ and $\eta_1, \ldots, \eta_n$ are terms built in the usual way using function symbols from $\mathcal{R}$ and the functional operators init and final, whose argument is allowed to be a function variable.*
- *An atomic* k-differential formula *is a differential equation of the form $\dot{z} = \eta$ where z is a function variable from $\mathcal{F}_k$, and η is a term of type $\mathcal{F}_k$ not containing any functional operator except for $embed_k$.*
- *An atomic* k-function formula *is a formula of the form $p(\eta_1, \ldots, \eta_n)$, where p is an n-ary predicate symbol from $\mathcal{F}_k$ and $\eta_1, \ldots, \eta_n$ are terms built in the usual way using function symbols from $\mathcal{F}_k$, and not containing any functional operators except for $embed_k$.*

A literal *is either an atomic formula or the negation of an atomic formula. A* formula *is an arbitrary Boolean combination of literals. A* theory formula *is a formula without Boolean variables.*

For example, $g = 9.81$ and $init(v_2) = -K final(v_1)$ are examples of atomic real-valued formulas, $\dot{x}_1 = v_1$ is an example of an atomic differential formula, and $x_1 \geq 0$ is an example of an atomic function formula.

The resulting formulas have the usual mathematical semantics where we interpret the sort $\mathcal{R}$ over the real numbers $\mathbb{R}$ and $\mathcal{F}_k$, $k \in \kappa$ over smooth functions in $[0, \tau_k] \to \mathbb{R}$, where $\tau_k \in \mathbb{R}^{\geq 0}$. Hence the length τ_k will be the same for all elements belonging to the same sort $\mathcal{F}_k$. These functions will usually arise as solutions of differential equations, hence the domain $[0, \tau_k]$ usually models time.

We interpret all symbols in $\mathcal{R}$ according to their usual meaning over the real numbers. To extend this to arithmetical predicate and function symbols with function arguments, that is, with arguments from $\mathcal{F}_k$, we simply lift their meaning over the reals to the whole domain $[0, \tau_k]$ of our functions in $[0, \tau_k] \to \mathbb{R}$. For example, the constant 1 in $\mathcal{F}_k$ is the function that assigns to each element of $[0, \tau_k]$ the constant 1. The atomic function formula $z \geq 1$ expresses the fact that the k-function variable z is greater or equal than the constant function 1 at every element of $[0, \tau_k]$. In general, for a function symbol f of type $\mathcal{F}_k \times \cdots \times \mathcal{F}_k \to \mathcal{F}_k$, its interpretation $f_{\mathcal{F}_k}$ is such that for $z_1, \ldots, z_n : [0, \tau_k]$, for all $t \in [0, \tau_k]$, $f_{\mathcal{F}_k}(z_1, \ldots, z_n)(t) = f_{\mathcal{R}}(z_1(t), \ldots, z_n(t))$, where $f_{\mathcal{R}}$ is the interpretation of the corresponding function symbol f of type $\mathcal{R} \times \cdots \times \mathcal{R} \to \mathcal{R}$. For a predicate symbol p of type $\mathcal{F}_k \times \cdots \times \mathcal{F}_k$, its interpretation $p_{\mathcal{F}_k}$ is such that $p_{\mathcal{F}_k}(z_1, \ldots, z_n)$ iff for all $t \in [0, \tau_k]$, $p_{\mathcal{R}}(z_1(t), \ldots, z_n(t))$, where again $p_{\mathcal{R}}$ is the interpretation of the corresponding predicate symbol p of type $\mathcal{R} \times \cdots \times \mathcal{R}$.

Note that, as a result, $\neg z \geq 1$ is *not* equivalent to $z < 1$: The former means that not all the time z is greater or equal one, whereas the latter means that all the time z is less than one. Due to this, we will also call such atomic function formulas *invariants*.

Finally, we interpret the function operators as follows: The interpretation of $init_k$ takes a function $z : [0, \tau_k] \to \mathbb{R}$ and returns $z(0)$, whereas the interpretation of $final_k$ returns $z(\tau_k)$. The interpretation of $embed_k$ takes a real number x, and returns the constant function that takes the value x on its whole domain $[0, \tau_k]$. Finally, we interpret $diff_k$ as the usual differential operator from mathematical analysis.

We call a function that assigns values of corresponding type to all elements of $\mathcal{V}$, and the above meaning to all other function and predicate symbols, an $ODE_{\mathbb{R}}$-*interpretation*. Based on this, we get the usual semantical notions from predicate logic. The main problem is to check, for a given formula, whether it is satisfiable by an $ODE_{\mathbb{R}}$-interpretation.

4   Formalization: SAT Modulo ODE Simulations

In this section, we will introduce alternative semantics to formulas based on floating point arithmetic. Since there are various variants of floating point arithmetic (e.g., 32 and 64 bit IEEE 754 arithmetic), including different formalizations [6,14], and moreover, a plethora of methods for solving differential equations [12], the resulting semantics will be parametric in the used variant of floating point arithmetic and ODE solver.

Now we interpret the $\mathcal{R}$-variables over the floating point numbers $\mathbb{F}$, and the $\mathcal{F}_k$-variables over functions from $\{t\Delta \mid t \in \{0, \ldots, \frac{\tau_k}{\Delta}\}\} \to \mathbb{F}$ (*trajectories*), for a given $k \in \kappa$. Here, we require τ_k to be a multiple of the step size Δ. We interpret all function and predicate symbols—including the functional operators—in the obvious floating point analogue to the formalization from the previous section, with the usual rounding to the nearest floating point number. Especially, we interpret function symbols on $\mathcal{F}_k$, $k \in \kappa$ point-wise on the elements of $\{t\Delta \mid t \in \{0, \ldots, \frac{\tau_k}{\Delta}\}\}$. However, when lifting predicates to type $\mathcal{F}_k$, we only require the lifted predicate to hold for $t \in \{0, \ldots, \frac{\tau_k}{\Delta} - 1\}$, that is, without the final point. For explaining why we refer to the illustrative example. If $\neg up$, it uses an invariant $x \geq 0$. At the same time it allows switching to up if and only if $x \leq 0$. When interpreting x as a continuous function, this makes perfect sense: the switch occurs exactly when both $x \geq 0$ and $x \leq 0$, that is, when $x = 0$. This does not work in our approximate interpretation because it is highly unlikely that, after discretization, a point is reached for which precisely $x = 0$. To circumvent this problem, we allow the invariant to be violated at the very final point of x which at the same time is the first point that allows switching.

To concentrate on our main point, we will ignore special floating point values modeling overflow and similar intricacies of floating point arithmetic. Still, our approach is compatible with such values, since we do not require that every floating point number have a corresponding real number.

Before turning to differential equations, we first describe how they are usually solved in practice [12]. The input to such a solver is a *system* of differential equations which, in our terminology, is a conjunction of n atomic k-differential formulas in n variables. Solvers then compute a solution for the *whole system*, using discrete steps in time. For example, writing the system of differential equations as $\dot{z} = F(z)$, where boldface indicates vectors, Euler's method—the most widely known explicit solution method for ODEs—uses the rule $z(t + \Delta) = z(t) + F(z(t))\Delta$. As a result, the solution satisfies this equality at each point in time.

Since in our case, differential equations do not directly occur in systems, but in individual atomic formulas, we separate this rule into conditions for the individual formulas, instead of conditions for the individual time steps. In the case of Euler's method, denoting the individual $\mathcal{F}_k$-variables by $z_1, \ldots, z_n$, for a differential formula $\dot{z}_i = f(z_1, \ldots, z_n)$, the resulting condition is

$$\forall t \in \{0, \ldots, \frac{T_k}{\Delta} - 1\} \,.\, z_i((t+1)\Delta) = z_i(t\Delta) + f(z_1(t\Delta), \ldots, z_n(t\Delta))\Delta.$$

In general, the rules used by explicit solvers are based on an equality with left-hand side $z(t + \Delta)$ which allows an analogical natural separation into conditions on the individual components of the solution.

We call a function that assigns Boolean values to the elements of $\mathcal{V}_\mathcal{B}$, floating point numbers to the elements of $\mathcal{V}_\mathcal{R}$, trajectories to the elements of $\mathcal{V}_{\mathcal{F}_k}, k \in \kappa$ and the above meaning to all other function and predicate symbols, an $ODE_\mathbb{F}$-*interpretation*. This again defines all the usual semantical notions from predicate logic using the same notation as in the previous section. For any interpretation $\mathcal{I}$ we denote by $\mathcal{I}(\eta)$ the value of the term η in $\mathcal{I}$, by $\mathcal{I} \models \phi$ the satisfiability of ϕ in $\mathcal{I}$, and so on. For the rest of the paper we assume a floating point interpretation $\mathcal{I}_\mathbb{F}$ for $\mathcal{V} = \emptyset$ that we will extend with values for a non-empty set $\mathcal{V}$.

In the rest of the paper, we design and analyze tools for checking whether a given formula is satisfiable by an $ODE_\mathbb{F}$-interpretation, in which case we will also simply say that it is satisfiable.

5   Theory Solver

The common SMT approaches use separate solvers for handling the Boolean part and the specific logical theory, respectively. In this section we concentrate on the latter. So, for a given theory formula ϕ (i.e., formula without Boolean variables), we want to check whether ϕ is satisfiable by an $ODE_\mathbb{F}$-interpretation.

As an example consider the formula $g = 9.81 \wedge init(v) = 10 \wedge v \geq 0 \wedge final(v) \leq 0 \wedge \dot{v} = -g - \frac{v}{100}$ which is satisfiable by an interpretation that assigns to g the value 9.81 and to v a trajectory that starts with the value 10, then decreases according to the given differential equation, and stays non-negative, except for the very last step which is non-positive.

We first prove that unlike $ODE_\mathbb{R}$, in our case there is no fundamental theoretical hurdle caused by undecidability.

Theorem 1. $ODE_\mathbb{F}$-*satisfiability is algorithmically decidable.*

Proof. Assume a theory formula ϕ. W.l.o.g. we assume ϕ to be a conjunction. Let $|\mathbb{F}|$ be the cardinality of the set of floating point numbers. The key observation is that $|\mathbb{F}|$ is finite. The problem is that $ODE_\mathbb{F}$-interpretations satisfying ϕ may assign trajectories of arbitrary length to function variables. However, if there is an interpretation that satisfies ϕ then there is also an interpretation satisfying ϕ that has length smaller than $|\mathbb{F}|^{\max\{\frac{T_k}{\Delta} | k \in \kappa\}}$: Assume an interpretation $\mathcal{I}$ satisfying ϕ that for some $k \in \kappa$ assigns trajectories longer than this bound to the variables in $\mathcal{F}_k$. Due to the finite cardinality of $|\mathbb{F}|$, there must be t, t' s.t. $t \neq t'$ and for every $z \in V_k$, $\mathcal{I}(z)(t) = \mathcal{I}(z)(t')$. This means that the interpretation that coincides with $\mathcal{I}$, but for every $z \in V_k$, the section between $t + 1$ and t' is removed, also satisfies ϕ. We can repeat this process until the interpretation satisfying ϕ is short enough.

Due to this we can check the satisfiability of ϕ using brute force search, checking whether the finite set of interpretations assigning trajectories of length smaller than $|\mathbb{F}|^{\max\{\frac{T_k}{\Delta} | k \in \kappa\}}$ contains an element that satisfies ϕ. $\square$

This proof is based on the fact that the set of floating point numbers has finitely many elements. However, due to the sheer number of those elements, the algorithm used in the proof is far from practically useful.

In the rest of the section we will design a solver that is able to solve theory formulas that arise from the specific structure identified in Sect. 2 much more efficiently. This structure will allow each step of the solver to assign a value to a variable. Since we will also want to compute initial values of function variables, we introduce a set $V_{init} := \{init(z) \mid z \in V_{\mathcal{F}_k}, k \in \kappa\}$ each ranging over the floating point numbers $\mathbb{F}$. We can represent the computed values as follows:

Definition 2. *A* state σ *is a function that assigns to each element of* $V_\mathcal{R} \cup V_\mathcal{F} \cup V_{init}$ *either an object of the corresponding type or the special value* undef.

For a state σ, we denote the extension of $\mathcal{I}_\mathbb{F}$ with the values defined by σ on $V_\mathcal{R} \cup V_\mathcal{F}$ (ignoring the values for V_{init}) by $\mathcal{I}_\sigma$. Our theory solver will use inference rules to fill the state σ with values until those values allow us to evaluate the given formula. For this we define for a term η, $ev_\sigma(\eta)$ to be *undef*, if the term η contains a variable v for which $\sigma(v) = undef$, and the result of term evaluation $\mathcal{I}_\sigma(\eta)$, otherwise. For example, for a state $\sigma = \{K \mapsto 0.5, v_1 \mapsto undef\}$, $ev_\sigma(-Kfinal(v_1)) = undef$, but for $\sigma = \{K \mapsto 0.5, v_1 \mapsto \rho\}$, where ρ is a trajectory whose final value is 2.0, $ev_\sigma(-Kfinal(v_1)) = -1.0$.

In a similar way, for an atomic formula A we define $ev_\sigma(A) = undef$, if σ assigns *undef* to a variable in A, and otherwise $ev_\sigma(A) = \top$, if $\mathcal{I}_\sigma \models A$, and $ev_\sigma(A) = \bot$, if $\mathcal{I}_\sigma \not\models A$. For example, for the state σ just mentioned, $ev_\sigma(-Kfinal(v_1) \geq 0) = \bot$.

Based on the usual extension of the Boolean operators $\neg, \wedge, \vee$ to three values, in our case $\{\bot, undef, \top\}$, this straightforwardly extends to formulas, in general. For example, $ev_{\{x \mapsto 0, y \mapsto undef\}}(x = 1 \wedge y = 1) = ev_{\{x \mapsto 0, y \mapsto undef\}}(x = 1) \wedge ev_{\{x \mapsto 0, y \mapsto undef\}}(y = 1) = \bot \wedge undef = \bot$. This implies that whatever value y has, the formula will not be satisfiable.

Theorem 2. *ϕ is ODE$_\mathbb{F}$-satisfiable iff there is a state σ with $ev_\sigma(\phi) = \top$.*

Proof. If $ev_\sigma(\phi) = \top$ then $\mathcal{I}_\sigma \models \phi$ and hence ϕ is satisfiable. In the other direction, if ϕ is satisfiable by an ODE$_\mathbb{F}$-interpretation $\mathcal{I}$, then for the state σ with $\sigma(x) = \mathcal{I}(x)$, for $x \in \mathcal{V}_\mathcal{R} \cup \mathcal{V}_\mathcal{F}$, and $\sigma(init(z)) = \mathcal{I}(z)(0)$, for every $z \in \mathcal{V}_{\mathcal{F}_k}, k \in \kappa$, $ev_\sigma(\phi) = \top$. $\square$

The question is, how to find such a state efficiently, if ϕ is satisfiable, and how to decide that it does not exist in the case where it is unsatisfiable. We will assume the input formula to be a conjunction of literals, since disjunctions will be handled by the Boolean solver (see Sect. 7). By misuse of notation we will also view ϕ as the set of its literals.

As already discussed, we will use inference rules on states. The first rule uses the fact that both sides of an equality have to evaluate to the same value in σ:

Definition 3. *For two states σ and σ', $\sigma \rightarrow_\mathcal{R} \sigma'$ iff*

- *there is a literal of the form $x = \eta$ or $\eta = x$ in ϕ with $x \in \mathcal{V}_\mathcal{R} \cup \mathcal{V}_{init}$,*
- *$\sigma(x) = undef$,*
- *$ev_\sigma(\eta) \neq undef$, and*
- *σ' is s.t. for all $v \in \mathcal{V}_\mathcal{R} \cup \mathcal{V}_\mathcal{F} \cup \mathcal{V}_{init}$, $\sigma'(v) = \begin{cases} ev_\sigma(\eta), & \text{if } v = x, \text{ and} \\ \sigma(v), & \text{otherwise.} \end{cases}$*

For example, if $\sigma = \{K \mapsto 0.5, v_1 \mapsto \rho, init(v_2) \mapsto undef\}$, with ρ again a trajectory with final value 2.0, and the input formula contains the literal $init(v_2) = -Kfinal(v_1)$, then $\sigma \rightarrow_\mathcal{R} \sigma'$, where $\sigma' = \{K \mapsto 0.5, v_1 \mapsto \rho, init(v_2) \mapsto -1.0\}$.

The second inference solves differential equations. For a state σ and $k \in \kappa$ we define $IVP_\phi(\sigma, k)$ (for "initial value problem") as the formula

$$\bigwedge_{\dot{z} = \eta \in \phi, z \in \mathcal{V}_{\mathcal{F}_k}} \dot{z} = \eta \wedge \bigwedge_{z \in \mathcal{V}_{\mathcal{F}_k}} init(z) = \sigma(init(z)) \wedge \bigwedge_{x \in \mathcal{V}_\mathcal{R}, \sigma(x) \neq undef} x = \sigma(x).$$

Here we assume for all $z \in \mathcal{F}_k$, $\sigma(init(z)) \neq undef$, and for all $x \in \mathcal{V}_\mathcal{R}$ occurring in a k-differential equation in ϕ, $\sigma(x) \neq undef$. Then one can find an assignment to the variables in $\mathcal{V}_{\mathcal{F}_k}$ satisfying the formula $IVP_\phi(\sigma, k)$ using a numerical ODE solver whose method corresponds to the one used for defining formula semantics. This assignment is unique up to the length of the assigned trajectories. In practice, the solver might fail, e.g. due to floating point overflows, but we ignore this complication for simplicity of exposition.

Definition 4. *For two states σ and σ', $k \in \kappa$ and $t \in \mathbb{N}_{\geq 0}$, $\sigma \rightarrow_{\mathcal{F}_k, t} \sigma'$ iff*

- *for every variable $z \in \mathcal{V}_{\mathcal{F}_k}$, $\sigma(z) = undef$,*
- *for every variable $z \in \mathcal{V}_{\mathcal{F}_k}$, $\sigma(init(z)) \neq undef$,*
- *for every variable $x \in \mathcal{V}_\mathcal{R}$ occurring in a k-differential equation in ϕ, $\sigma(x) \neq undef$*
- *for every variable $z \in \mathcal{V}_{\mathcal{F}_k}$, ϕ contains exactly one literal of the form $\dot{z} = \eta$*
- *σ' is identical to σ except that it assigns to the variables $z \in \mathcal{V}_{\mathcal{F}_k}$ the corresponding trajectories of length t satisfying $IVP_\phi(\sigma, k)$.*

It would not be difficult to also handle the case when ϕ contains more than one differential literal with the same left-hand side. But usually this is not practically useful, and hence the rules does not consider this case.

Now we can apply several inference steps in a row, starting from the everywhere undefined state σ_{undef}. This always terminates, since every inference step creates a state with less undefined elements and $\mathcal{V}_\mathcal{R} \cup \mathcal{V}_\mathcal{F} \cup \mathcal{V}_{init}$ is finite.

Remember that our goal is to use the inference rules to arrive at a state σ, for which $ev_\sigma(\phi) = \top$ or to decide that no such state exists. Since the inferences do not introduce new undefined values, it does not make sense to do further inferences on a state σ, for which $ev_\sigma(\phi) \neq undef$.

If we arrive at a state σ for which $ev_\sigma(\phi) = \bot$, can we conclude that ϕ is unsatisfiable? Certainly not: A different sequence of inferences might have found a state that evaluates to $\top$, showing satisfiability. For example, for the formula $init(z) = 0 \wedge \dot{z} = 1 \wedge final(z) \geq 10$, one inference step from σ_{undef} wrt. $\rightarrow_\mathcal{R}$ results in the state $\{init(z) \mapsto 0, z \mapsto undef\}$, but from this state, an inference wrt. $\rightarrow_{\mathcal{F}, t}$ only results in a state that evaluates to $\top$, if t is big enough for the final state of the assigned trajectory to be larger of equal 10.

Still, for given fixed lengths t of inferences $\rightarrow_{\mathcal{F}, t}$, the order of inferences does not matter.

Theorem 3. *Let $\lambda : \kappa \rightarrow \mathbb{N}_{\geq 0}$. Let σ_1 and σ_2 be the final states of two sequences of inferences using $\rightarrow_\mathcal{R}$ and $\rightarrow_{\mathcal{F}_k, \lambda(k)}, k \in \kappa$ s.t. neither from σ_1 nor from σ_2, further inferences are possible. Then $ev_{\sigma_1}(\phi) = ev_{\sigma_2}(\phi)$.*

So it may be necessary to try different trajectory lengths for arriving at a state that evaluates to $\top$, showing satisfiability. We represent this search using a tree:

Definition 5. *An* inference tree *is a tree whose vertices are formed by states, where the root is σ_{undef}, and every vertex state σ that is no leaf either has*

– *precisely one successor vertex σ' with $\sigma \to_{\mathcal{R}} \sigma'$ or*
– *successor vertices $\sigma'_0, \sigma'_1, \ldots, \sigma'_n$ s.t. for an arbitrary, but fixed $k \in \kappa$*
  • *for every $i \in \{0, \ldots, n\}$, $\sigma \to_{\mathcal{F}_k,i} \sigma'_i$, , and*
  • *there is an $m < n$ s.t. for all $z \in V_{\mathcal{F}_k}$, $\sigma'_n(z)(m) = \sigma'_n(z)(n)$.*

For example, for the formula $init(v) = 10 \land v \geq 0 \land final(v) \leq 0 \land \dot{v} = -9.81 - \frac{v}{100}$, and the tree root σ_{undef}, the inference rule $\to_{\mathcal{R}}$, results in the successor state $\sigma = \{init(v) \mapsto 10, v \mapsto undef\}$. Now we use the second inference rule which branches the tree. For the successor state wrt. $\to_{\mathcal{F}_k,0}$, the final state of the trajectory computed for v is equal to its initial state 10, which violates the condition $final(v) \leq 0$, and hence this successor state evaluates to $\bot$. The successor states wrt. $\to_{\mathcal{F}_k,1}$, $\to_{\mathcal{F}_k,2}$, ... will have longer trajectories with the respective final states getting smaller and smaller, until—at the point when the trajectory has become long enough—the final state will finally satisfy $final(v) \leq 0$. The resulting successor state then evaluates to $\top$ which shows satisfiability of the formula.

Even if we would not find a state that evaluates to $\top$, we would not have to search infinitely many successors, since an inference tree includes only a finite subset of the infinite set of possible inferences wrt. $\to_{\mathcal{F}_k,t}$, $t \in \mathbb{N}_0$. The termination condition $\sigma'_n(z)(m) = \sigma'_n(z)(n)$ must be satisfied for some m, again due to the finite cardinality of the set of floating point numbers. Still, inference trees cover the search space completely, allowing us to conclude the input to be unsatisfiable in some cases:

Theorem 4. *Assume an inference tree such that for all leaves σ, $ev_\sigma(\phi) = \bot$. Then ϕ is unsatisfiable.*

The theorem follows from two facts: First, for states σ and $\sigma'_1, \sigma'_1, \ldots$ s.t. $\sigma \to_{\mathcal{F}_k,1} \sigma'_1, \sigma \to_{\mathcal{F}_k,2} \sigma'_2, \ldots$, and ϕ is satisfiable by an $ODE_\mathbb{F}$-interpretation that coincides with a state σ on its defined elements, there is an $i \in \mathbb{N}_0$ s.t. ϕ is satisfiable by σ'_i. Second, due to the same reasoning as used in the proof of Theorem 1, if this is the case for an arbitrary $i \in \mathbb{N}_0$ then this is also the case for an $i < n$, since $\sigma'_n(z)(m) = \sigma'(z)(n)$.

Now an algorithm can simply check all leaves of such an inference tree to check satisfiability. There is various possibilities to do so, for example using simple recursive depth-first search:

$ODESAT(\sigma)$
let Σ be the set of successor vertices of σ in an inference tree.
if $\Sigma = \emptyset$ **then return** $ev_\sigma(\phi)$
else if there is a $\sigma' \in \Sigma$ s.t. $ODESAT(\sigma') = \top$ **then return** $\top$
else if for all $\sigma' \in \Sigma$ s.t. $ODESAT(\sigma') = \bot$ **then return** $\bot$
else return *undef*

The initial call should be $ODESAT(\sigma_{undef})$, and the result $\top$ can be interpreted as SAT, the result *undef* as UNKNOWN, and the result $\bot$ as UNSAT.

We call any such algorithm that returns its result based on application of Theorems 4 and 2 to the leaves of an inference tree an *evaluation based $ODE_\mathbb{F}$-solver*. Here we may encounter two problems:

- The tree might have some leaves σ with $ev_\sigma(\phi) = undef$, resulting in the answer UNKNOWN.
- The tree may be huge, resulting in a long run-time of the algorithm.

The first problem may happen, for example, if a numerical variable is constrained by an equation such as $x^2 = 1$ that cannot be solved by our rules (of course, such an equation can be easily solved, for example by methods for solving polynomial equations, but here we are interested in getting as far as possible without such techniques). In such a case, one can fall back to brute-force search of Theorem 1. Of course, this is inefficient, and we want to avoid it, which leads us back to the second problem, the problem of a large search tree.

One possibility is to simply give up on completeness by not exploring the full search space. For example, as usual for SAT modulo ODE solvers [10,11], we might only search for trajectories up to a certain length, that is, use the strategy of bounded model checking. In this case, the solver will not decide satisfiability, but satisfiability by trajectories up to a certain length.

Also, in some cases, we might have good heuristics available. Especially, for a given inference tree, finding a vertex σ with $ev_\sigma(\phi) = \top$ is a tree search problem which enables the usage of well-known tree search algorithms [9], allowing us to efficiently find a leaf that shows satisfiability of the input.

In any case, we will see in the next section, that for formulas having a structure similar to the toy example, these problems can be avoided.

6   Formula Structure

In the previous section we identified a search tree that allows us to replace brute-force search by inferences. In this section we show how to use syntactical restrictions on the input formula to

- ensure that the inference tree does not end in undefined leaves, and to
- restrict the size of the inference tree.

First we will show how to avoid undefined leaves by ensuring that the value of every non-Boolean variable be deducible from the value of another variable without the need for circular reasoning.

Definition 6. *A formula ϕ is* orientable *iff there is a total order $r_1, \ldots, r_{|\mathcal{V}_\mathcal{R} \cup \mathcal{V}_\mathcal{F}|}$ on the variables in $\mathcal{V}_\mathcal{R} \cup \mathcal{V}_\mathcal{F}$ s.t. for every $i \in \{1, \ldots, |\mathcal{V}_\mathcal{R} \cup \mathcal{V}_\mathcal{F}|\}$,*

- *if $r_i \in \mathcal{V}_\mathcal{R}$, then there is a literal in ϕ that is of the form $r_i = \eta$ or $\eta = r_i$, where η does not contain any variable from $r_i, \ldots, r_{|\mathcal{V}_\mathcal{R} \cup \mathcal{V}_\mathcal{F}|}$, and*
- *if $r_i \in \mathcal{V}_\mathcal{F}$, then*
  - *there is a literal in ϕ that is of the form $init(r_i) = \eta$ or $\eta = init(r_i)$, where η does not contain any variable from $r_i, \ldots, r_{|\mathcal{V}_\mathcal{R} \cup \mathcal{V}_\mathcal{F}|}$ and*
  - *there is exactly one literal in ϕ that has the form $\dot{r}_i = \eta$, and the term η does not contain any variable that is both in $\mathcal{V}_\mathcal{R}$ and in $r_i, \ldots, r_{|\mathcal{V}_\mathcal{R} \cup \mathcal{V}_\mathcal{F}|}$.*

Note that the non-circularity condition for atomic differential formulas only includes variables in $\mathcal{V}_\mathcal{R}$ but not variables in $\mathcal{V}_\mathcal{F}$, allowing the formulation of systems of ordinary differential equations. For illustration of Definition 6, consider the formula $x = \sin y \wedge y = 2x \wedge \dot{z}_1 = z_1 + z_2 \wedge \dot{z}_2 = z_1 - z_2 \wedge init(z_1) = 10 \wedge init(z_2) = 10$ that is not orientable, but $\Psi \wedge x = 0$, where Ψ is the previous formula, is orientable using the order x, y, z_1, z_2.

Theorem 5. *Assume a formula ϕ that is orientable, and a corresponding inference tree Ω whose leaves do not allow further inferences. Then for every state σ at a leaf of Ω, for every variable $v \in \mathcal{V}_\mathcal{R} \cup \mathcal{V}_\mathcal{F}$, $\sigma(v) \neq undef$.*

Hence, in such a case, we can decide satisfiability of the input formula using inferences alone, never returning UNKNOWN.

Theorem 6. *Every evaluation based $ODE_\mathbb{F}$-solver that is based on an inference tree whose leaves do not allow further inferences, is a decision procedure for all orientable $ODE_\mathbb{F}$-formulas.*

Still, the inference tree may be huge, since we might have to search for extremely long trajectories. To avoid this, we analyze the example from Sect. 2 once more. Here, the invariant $x_1 \geq 0$ ensures, that the ball will eventually stop falling. In a similar way, the invariant $v_1 \geq 0$ detects that the ball stops rising. As soon as those two invariants stop to hold, we do not have to search for longer trajectories. The following theorem generalizes this.

Theorem 7. *If ϕ contains an atomic k-functional formula A with $ev_\sigma(A) = \bot$ then for every state σ' s.t. for every function variable z, $\sigma'(z)$ is at least as long as $\sigma(z)$, and σ' is equal to σ for all elements defined in σ, including function variables up to their length, $ev_{\sigma'}(A) = \bot$.*

Hence, as soon as the application of the inference rule $\sigma \to_{\mathcal{F}_k, t} \sigma'$ results in a state σ' such that $ev_{\sigma'}(A) = \bot$, we do not have to expand further successors of σ using the same rule with bigger t.

7   Solver Integration

Now we also allow disjunctions and Boolean variables in the input formula ϕ. We follow the common architecture [18] of SMT solvers where a SAT solver handles the Boolean structure, a theory solver (in our case the one from Sect. 5) handles conjunctions of non-Boolean literals, and the integrating SMT solver handles communication between the two.

We include the case where either the Boolean solver or the theory solver is incomplete, in which the combination may return UNKNOWN. Even though many SMT schemes expect the underlying theory solver to be complete, one can usually use an incomplete solver, as well, by letting the theory solver return UNSAT in the place of UNKNOWN. If this happens during execution of the SMT solver, it should return UNKNOWN when it would otherwise have returned UNSAT. In any case, if the input is identified to be satisfiable, the solver still can reliably return SAT as the final result.

The usual SMT solvers proceed by replacing all atomic formulas from the theory by elements of a set of fresh Boolean variables V_A, and finding a Boolean assignment $\alpha : V_B \cup V_A \rightarrow \{\bot, \top\}$ satisfying the resulting purely Boolean formula. Denoting by $\gamma(A)$ the atomic formula in ϕ corresponding to the variable $A \in V_A$ one can then use the theory solver to check whether the formula

$$\Sigma(\alpha) := \bigwedge_{A \in V_A, \alpha(A) = \top} \gamma(A) \ \wedge \bigwedge_{A \in V_A, \alpha(A) = \bot} \neg\gamma(A)$$

is satisfiable. If this is the case, the original input formula ϕ is satisfiable, as well.

If we want to ensure that $\Sigma(\alpha)$ fulfills the syntactical restrictions of Sect. 6, we have to ensure that for every such Boolean assignment the formula $\Sigma(\alpha)$ fulfills those restrictions. Returning to the illustrative example from Sect. 2, the order $g, K, x_1, v_1, x_2, v_2, x_3, v_3$ ensures that $\Sigma(\alpha)$ is always orientable. Here, the variables up_1, up_2 always activate the necessary atomic formulas.

In the case of our theory, in practically reasonable formulas, in a similar way as in our illustrative example, atomic differential and function formulas occur positively, without a negation. If a Boolean assignment satisfies the abstraction of such a formula, then also any Boolean assignment that assigns $\top$ instead of $\bot$ to a Boolean variable in V_A that corresponds to a differential or function literals. Hence, whenever the SMT solver asks the theory solver to check satisfiability of a formula where such a literal occurs negatively, then the theory solver may ignore those, and check the rest of the formula for satisfiability.

When integrating the theory solver into SMT [18], several levels of integration are possible. Following the classification of Nieuwenhuis et. al. [18], the lowest level is the naive lazy approach. Here a SAT solver finds a satisfiable Boolean assignment α of the Boolean abstraction of the input formula, and the theory solver checks the formula $\Sigma(\alpha)$. If the answer is SAT, the input formula is satisfiable. If the answer is UNSAT, the solver should identify a sub-formula of $\Sigma(\alpha)$ that is still unsatisfiable. The negation of the abstraction of this formula is formed (a so-called *conflict clause*) and added to the original input formula. Then the whole process is repeated with restarting the SAT solver from scratch. All of this can be easily supported by our theory solver described in Sect. 5 by recording inference in the usual way into a so-called implication graph.

A further level of integration is to use an incremental theory solver. This means that in the case where the theory solver answers either SAT or UNKNOWN for some input formula ϕ, the SMT solver may later ask us to check satisfiability of an extended formula $\phi \wedge \psi$. Later, the SMT solver might ask the theory solver to backtrack to an earlier state. Again, it is no problem for our theory solver to support all of this. The new part ψ of the extended formula may allow additional inferences and the algorithm can simply continue from the state where it finished the analysis of the original formula ϕ.

Note that here the SMT solver might associate a certain strength with the query [18, Section 4.1], asking for a definitive answer only in the situation when the formula will not further be extended. Here it makes sense to wait with using the $\rightarrow_{\mathcal{F}_k}$-inferences until all k-function literals appear in the formula to check since those literals may play an essential role in keeping the inference tree small by applying Theorem 7. Ideally, the SMT solver supports this by adding such literals always together with the corresponding differential equations.

So-called online SMT solvers do not restart the SAT solver from scratch in further iterations, but only backtrack to an earlier point that did not yet result into an unsatisfiable theory formula.

A further feature of advanced SMT solvers is theory propagation. In this case, the SMT solver not only asks the theory solver to check satisfiability of some formula ϕ but, in addition, to also identify elements from a set of literals that are entailed by ϕ. This is easy to do in the case of inferences that have only one successor state, especially, inferences wrt. $\rightarrow_{\mathcal{R}}$, but will probably not pay off for inferences that require search.

8   Computational Experiments

In this section we will study the behavior of a prototype implementation of the techniques introduced in this paper. Especially, we are interested in how far our theoretical finding that the SAT modulo ODE problem is easier for simulation semantics than for classical mathematical semantics (Theorem 1) also holds in practice. Our solver (UN/SOT) is based on the naive lazy approach to SMT, the simplest possible one described in Sect. 7, using the SAT solver Minisat[2] and our theory solver implementation which currently uses the ODE solver ODEINT[3]. It avoids the full evaluation of its input formula after each inference step: Instead it cycles through all literals in the input formula, handling all k-differential literals and k-function literals for each $k \in \kappa$ as one block. Whenever the current literal or k-block allows an inference, the corresponding inference rule is applied, and whenever the current literal can be evaluated based on the current state, it is evaluated. As soon as a literal evaluates to $\perp$ or all literals evaluate to $\top$, the corresponding result is returned to the SMT solver. If no more inferences are possible, and no result has been found up to this point, the solver returns UNKNOWN. This happens only in cases not following the structure identified in Sect. 6. In the case where the answer is UNSAT, the theory solver forms conflict clauses from the sub-formula involved in the inferences necessary to arrive at the answer. We only do simple backtracking, no backjumping.

As a solver with classical mathematical semantics we used dReal[4], that is based on the ODE solver CAPD[5] that builds on decades of research on validated ODE integration [15,17,19]. But again, the goal of this section is *not* to measure the efficiency of the used algorithms, but rather, the inherent practical difficulty of the respective problems.

---

[2] http://minisat.se
[3] http://www.odeint.com
[4] http://dreal.github.io
[5] http://capd.ii.uj.edu.pl

We present experiments based on a hybrid system model of inpatient glycemic control of a patient with type 1 diabetes [7]. The patient is represented by 18 specific parameters and by initial values of the insulin system (5 function variables) and the glucose system (2 function variables). The whole process is divided into two phases. In the first phase, the patient is being monitored to ensure his or her stability for the surgery. If this fails, the surgery is canceled and the process ends. Otherwise, the second phase (and the surgery) follows, where the controller starts operating—it drives insulin and glucose inputs—wrt. observed condition of the patient. The patient's condition is sampled approximately every 30 min (using 1 min timing jitter). We have two verification tasks, safety—surgery starts, and the glucose level stays in a certain set of safe states, and unsafety—surgery starts, and the set of safe states is left.

For translating the hybrid system to an SMT problem, we unrolled it wrt. its discrete transitions. We did two types of experiments for both solvers, first with fixing a certain initial state, and second with intervals of initial states. For experiments of the second type we equidistantly cover the initial states with a number of sample points and specify the initial state using a disjunction over these sample points. For dReal, we use the original interval. The same applies also for modeling the timing jitter (for both types of experiments), where, in the case of our solver, the equidistance is an input parameter.

The results of the first case, with a fixed initial state, can be seen in the following tables. We examined two different scenarios, where satisfiability amounts to the terminal state being safe and unsafe, respectively. The tables on the top show a variant with an initial state for which the system stays within the safe states, the tables at the bottom a variant where it reaches an unsafe state after the fifth unrollment, and stays there. The column N lists the number of unrollments, s the equidistance of the timing jitter, and the column headed by the tool names the run-time in seconds. The time-ratio should not serve for any efficiency comparison between the two tools but across different test cases.

"Safe" init. state

		Verifying safety						Verifying unsafety			
N	s	Result	UN/SOT	dReal	Ratio	N	s	Result	UN/SOT	dReal	Ratio
3	1	sat	0.15	26	172	3	1	unsat	0.14	6	44.1
3	$\frac{1}{4}$	sat	0.13	26	197	3	$\frac{1}{4}$	unsat	0.33	6	18
6	1	sat	0.88	50000	56804	6	1	unsat	4.04	52119	12911
6	$\frac{1}{4}$	sat	1.51	50000	33101	6	$\frac{1}{4}$	unsat	363	52119	143
12	1	sat	4.71	×	×	8	1	unsat	28	×	×
12	$\frac{1}{4}$	sat	7.12	×	×	8	$\frac{1}{4}$	unsat	36761	×	×

"Unsafe" init. state

N	s	Result	UN/SOT	dReal	Ratio	N	s	Result	UN/SOT	dReal	Ratio
3	1	sat	0.18	26.2	145	3	1	unsat	0.14	5.8	40.8
3	$\frac{1}{4}$	sat	0.11	26.2	230	3	$\frac{1}{4}$	unsat	0.31	5.8	18.6
6	1	unsat	0.78	107980	138809	6	1	sat	0.65	5428	8296
6	$\frac{1}{4}$	unsat	8.95	107980	12064	6	$\frac{1}{4}$	sat	1.19	5428	4545
12	1	unsat	0.87	×	×	8	1	sat	1.00	×	×
12	$\frac{1}{4}$	unsat	10.2	×	×	8	$\frac{1}{4}$	sat	1.07	×	×

Here, not unexpectedly, our approach scales quite well against the parameter N. This contrasts the behavior of methods based on interval computation, that have to fight with the so-called dependency problem that tends to blow up intervals over long time horizons.

The results of the second case, with intervals of initial points, are shown in the following tables. This time, the tables on the top show a variant with smaller ranges of possible initial states, and the tables at the bottom a variant with larger ones.

<table>
<tr><th colspan="6">Verifying safety</th><th colspan="6">Verifying unsafety</th></tr>
<tr><th>N</th><th>s</th><th>Result</th><th>UN/SOT</th><th>dReal</th><th>Ratio</th><th>N</th><th>s</th><th>Result</th><th>UN/SOT</th><th>dReal</th><th>Ratio</th></tr>
<tr><td>3</td><td>1</td><td>sat</td><td>0.2</td><td>24045</td><td>122261</td><td>3</td><td>1</td><td>unsat</td><td>4455</td><td>6.3</td><td>0.001</td></tr>
<tr><td>3</td><td>$\frac{1}{2}$</td><td>sat</td><td>5.04</td><td>24045</td><td>4770</td><td>3</td><td>$\frac{1}{2}$</td><td>unsat</td><td>7776</td><td>6.3</td><td>0.001</td></tr>
<tr><td>6</td><td>1</td><td>sat</td><td>2.38</td><td>×</td><td>×</td><td>4</td><td>1</td><td>unsat</td><td>25042</td><td>124</td><td>0.005</td></tr>
<tr><td>6</td><td>$\frac{1}{2}$</td><td>sat</td><td>2.17</td><td>×</td><td>×</td><td>4</td><td>$\frac{1}{2}$</td><td>unsat</td><td>> 36000</td><td>124</td><td>×</td></tr>
<tr><td>12</td><td>1</td><td>sat</td><td>5.83</td><td>×</td><td>×</td><td>5</td><td>1</td><td>unsat</td><td>> 36000</td><td>2478</td><td>×</td></tr>
<tr><td>12</td><td>$\frac{1}{2}$</td><td>sat</td><td>8.28</td><td>×</td><td>×</td><td>5</td><td>$\frac{1}{2}$</td><td>unsat</td><td>×</td><td>2478</td><td>×</td></tr>
</table>

(Left block: *Smaller intervals*)

<table>
<tr><th>N</th><th>s</th><th>Result</th><th>UN/SOT</th><th>dReal</th><th>Ratio</th><th>N</th><th>s</th><th>Result</th><th>UN/SOT</th><th>dReal</th><th>Ratio</th></tr>
<tr><td>3</td><td>1</td><td>sat</td><td>29.9</td><td>> 82800</td><td>×</td><td>3</td><td>1</td><td>unsat</td><td>overflow</td><td>9.3</td><td>×</td></tr>
<tr><td>3</td><td>$\frac{1}{2}$</td><td>sat</td><td>28.2</td><td>> 82800</td><td>×</td><td>3</td><td>$\frac{1}{2}$</td><td>unsat</td><td>×</td><td>9.3</td><td>×</td></tr>
<tr><td>6</td><td>1</td><td>sat</td><td>1.04</td><td>×</td><td>×</td><td>4</td><td>1</td><td>?</td><td>> 36000</td><td>> 54000</td><td>×</td></tr>
<tr><td>6</td><td>$\frac{1}{2}$</td><td>sat</td><td>70.6</td><td>×</td><td>×</td><td>4</td><td>$\frac{1}{2}$</td><td>?</td><td>×</td><td>> 54000</td><td>×</td></tr>
<tr><td>12</td><td>1</td><td>sat</td><td>58.9</td><td>×</td><td>×</td><td>5</td><td>1</td><td>sat</td><td>887</td><td>> 86400</td><td>×</td></tr>
<tr><td>12</td><td>$\frac{1}{2}$</td><td>sat</td><td>6.96</td><td>×</td><td>×</td><td>5</td><td>$\frac{1}{2}$</td><td>sat</td><td>8598</td><td>> 86400</td><td>×</td></tr>
</table>

(Left block: *Larger intervals*)

Here, in the case with intervals, the unsafe state can be reached only with the larger ranges. Also, of course, with the intervals and with the unsatisfiable result, the performance of our tool degrades heavily, when choosing more sample points in the interval. In the worst case, it has to check the finite set of all floating point numbers in the interval, while dReal uses more sophisticated techniques. The result "overflow" means that the program crashed due to restrictions of our implementation.

All experiments were performed on a personal laptop machine with CPU Intel® i7-4702MQ, 8GB memory, running on OS Arch Linux with 4.19.60 Linux kernel.

Note that the original model [7] contains a few mistakes, which we had to correct. The main problem is that the dynamics can block switching between adjacent modes, leading to unintended UNSAT results.

We showed that the (corrected) model is *not* safe. This contradicts the original results [7] that proved the model to be safe, apparently only due the mentioned modeling mistakes. To support our statement, we attach a trajectory of a concrete counterexample in Fig. 2. Here, a dangerous glucose level is reached (variable G_p, the dotted curve) for the initial values $I_p(0) = 29, X(0) = 290, I_1(0) = 120, I_d(0) = 144, I_l(0) = 10, G_p(0) = 238, G_t(0) = 50$.

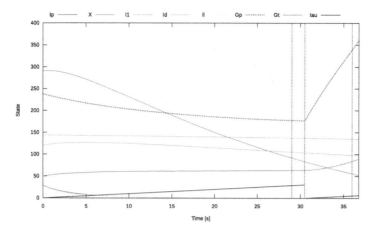

Fig. 2. Unsafety witness for the glucose model

We refer curious readers to our experimental report [13] for more details. The input data of these and many further experiments, along with the source code of the tool, are available on the website of the tool[6].

Finally, we would like to mention that we found the dReal immensely useful for developing, tuning, and debugging our own tool.

9   Conclusion

In this paper we introduced an alternative approach to handling differential equations in a SAT context. Motivated by industrial practice, the approach uses the semantics of simulation tools instead of classical mathematical semantics as its basis. Also, the approach allows inputs that integrate ODEs more tightly into SAT problems than was the case for existing methods. Computational experiments with a simple prototype implementation indicate that this problem formulation allows the efficient solution of problems that are highly difficult for start-of-the-art tools based on classical mathematical semantics, especially in satisfiable cases.

In the future, we intend to work on a tighter algorithmic integration between the Boolean and the theory solver [2,8,18], on search techniques for efficient handling of satisfiable inputs, and on deduction techniques to prune the inference tree for unsatisfiable inputs. Finally, it will be important to support advanced ODE solving techniques such as root finding (for locating events happening between two simulation steps) and adaptive step sizes.

Acknowledgements. This work was funded by institutional support of the Institute of Computer Science (RVO:67985807) and by CTU project SGS20/211/OHK3/3T/18.

---

6 https://gitlab.com/Tomaqa/unsot, subdirectory doc/experiments/v0.7

References

1. Barrett, C., Fontaine, P., Tinelli, C.: The Satisfiability Modulo Theories Library (SMT-LIB). www.SMT-LIB.org (2016)
2. Barrett, C., Nieuwenhuis, R., Oliveras, A., Tinelli, C.: Splitting on demand in SAT modulo theories. In: Hermann, M., Voronkov, A. (eds.) LPAR 2006. LNCS (LNAI), vol. 4246, pp. 512–526. Springer, Heidelberg (2006). https://doi.org/10.1007/11916277_35
3. Barrett, C., Tinelli, C.: Satisfiability modulo theories. Handbook of Model Checking, pp. 305–343. Springer, Cham (2018). https://doi.org/10.1007/978-3-319-10575-8_11
4. Bouissou, O., Mimram, S., Chapoutot, A.: Hyson: set-based simulation of hybrid systems. In: 23rd IEEE International Symposium on Rapid System Prototyping (RSP), pp. 79–85. IEEE (2012)
5. Bournez, O., Campagnolo, M.L.: A survey on continuous time computations. In: Cooper, S., Löwe, B., Sorbi, A. (eds.) New Computational Paradigms, pp. 383–423. Springer, New York (2008)
6. Brain, M., Tinelli, C., Rümmer, P., Wahl, T.: An automatable formal semantics for IEEE-754 floating-point arithmetic. In: 22nd IEEE Symposium on Computer Arithmetic, pp. 160–167. IEEE (2015)
7. Chen, S., O'Kelly, M., Weimer, J., Sokolsky, O., Lee, I.: An intraoperative glucose control benchmark for formal verification. In: Analysis and Design of Hybrid Systems ADHS, vol. 48 of IFAC-PapersOnLine, pp. 211–217. Elsevier (2015)
8. de Moura, L., Jovanović, D.: A model-constructing satisfiability calculus. In: 14th International Conference on Verification, Model Checking, and Abstract Interpretation, VMCAI, Rome, Italy (2013)
9. Edelkamp, S., Schroedl, S.: Heuristic Search: Theory and Applications. Morgan Kaufmann, Burlington (2012)
10. Eggers, A., Fränzle, M., Herde, C.: SAT modulo ODE: a direct SAT approach to hybrid systems. In: Automated Technology for Verification and Analysis, vol. 5311, LNCS (2008)
11. Gao, S., Kong, S., Clarke, E.M.: Satisfiability modulo ODEs. In: 2013 Formal Methods in Computer-Aided Design, pp. 105–112. IEEE (2013)
12. Hairer, E., Nørsett, S.P., Wanner, G.: Solving Ordinary Differential Equations I. Springer, Heidelberg (1987). https://doi.org/10.1007/978-3-540-78862-1
13. Kolárik, T.: UN/SOT v0.7 experiments report. https://gitlab.com/Tomaqa/unsot/blob/master/doc/experiments/v0.7/report.pdf (2020)
14. Melquiond, G.: Floating-point arithmetic in the Coq system. Inf. Comput. **216**, 14–23 (2012)
15. Moore, R.E., Kearfott, R.B., Cloud, M.J.: Introduction to interval analysis. In: SIAM (2009)
16. Mosterman, P.J., Zander, J., Hamon, G., Denckla, B.: A computational model of time for stiff hybrid systems applied to control synthesis. Control Eng. Pract. **20**(1), 2–13 (2012)
17. Nedialkov, N.S.: Implementing a rigorous ODE solver through literate programming. In: Rauh, A., Auer, E. (eds.) Modeling Design and Simulation of Systems with Uncertainties, pp. 3–19. Springer, Heidelberg (2011). https://doi.org/10.1007/978-3-642-15956-5_1

18. Nieuwenhuis, R., Oliveras, A., Tinelli, C.: Solving SAT and SAT modulo theories: from an abstract Davis-Putnam-Logemann-Loveland procedure to DPLL(T). J. ACM (JACM) **53**(6), 937–977 (2006)
19. Wilczak, D., Zgliczyński, P.: $\mathcal{C}^r$-Lohner algorithm. Schedae Informaticae **20**, 9–46 (2011)

Verified Runtime Assertion Checking
for Memory Properties

Dara Ly[1,4(✉)], Nikolai Kosmatov[1,2], Frédéric Loulergue[3,4],
and Julien Signoles[1]

[1] CEA, LIST, Software Security and Reliability Laboratory, Palaiseau, France
{dara.ly,nikolai.kosmatov,julien.signoles}@cea.fr,
nikolaikosmatov@gmail.com
[2] Thales Research & Technology, Palaiseau, France
[3] School of Informatics Computing and Cyber Systems, Northern Arizona University,
Flagstaff, USA
frederic.loulergue@nau.edu
[4] INSA Centre Val de Loire, Université d'Orléans, LIFO EA 4022, Orléans, France

Abstract. Runtime Assertion Checking (RAC) for expressive specification languages is a non-trivial verification task, that becomes even more complex for memory-related properties of imperative languages with dynamic memory allocation. It is important to ensure the soundness of RAC verdicts, in particular when RAC reports the absence of failures for execution traces. This paper presents a formalization of a program transformation technique for RAC of memory properties for a representative language with memory operations. It includes an observation memory model that is essential to record and monitor memory-related properties. We prove the soundness of RAC verdicts with regard to the semantics of this language.

1 Introduction

Runtime assertion checking (RAC) [7] is a well-established verification technique whose goal is to evaluate specified program properties (assertions, or more generally, annotations) during a particular program run and to report any detected failures. It is particularly challenging for languages like C, where memory-related properties (such as pointer validity or variable initialization) cannot be directly expressed in terms of the language, while their evaluation is crucial to ensure the soundness of the program and to avoid the numerous cases of *undefined behavior* [12]. Indeed, memory-related errors, such as invalid pointers, out-of-bounds memory accesses, uninitialized variables and memory leaks, are very common. C is still widely used, e.g. in embedded software, and a study from IBM [29] reports that about 50% of detected software errors were related to pointers and array accesses.

Recent tools addressing memory safety of C programs, such as Valgrind and MemCheck [23,26], DrMemory [5] or AddressSanitizer [25], have become very popular and successful in detecting bugs. However, their soundness is usually not

© Springer Nature Switzerland AG 2020
W. Ahrendt and H. Wehrheim (Eds.): TAP 2020, LNCS 12165, pp. 100–121, 2020.
https://doi.org/10.1007/978-3-030-50995-8_6

formally established, and often does not hold, since most of them rely on very efficient but possibly unsound heuristics [31]. While for a reported bug, it can be possible—at least, in theory—to carefully analyze the execution and check whether an error is correctly reported, the soundness of the "no-bug" verdict cannot be checked.

For runtime assertion checking, soundness becomes a major concern: because this technique is used to verify the absence of failures, often in complement to sound deductive verification on parts of annotated code which were not (yet) proved, ensuring the soundness of tools implementing it is crucial. E-ACSL[1] is one of these tools [28], as part of the Frama-C verification platform [16] for static and dynamic analyses of C programs. A *formal proof of soundness* for E-ACSL is highly desirable with regard to the complexity of verification of memory-related properties, that requires numerous instrumentation steps to record memory related operations—often in a complex, highly optimized *observation memory model* [13,17,32]—and to evaluate them thanks to this record. In this context, the proof of soundness is highly non-trivial: it requires to formalize not only the semantics of the considered programming and specification languages, but also the program transformation and the observation memory.

The purpose of the present work is to formalize and prove the soundness of a runtime assertion checker for memory-related properties. We consider a simple but representative imperative programming language with dynamic memory allocation and a specification language with a complete set of memory-related predicates, including pointer validity, variable initialization, as well as pointer offset, base address and size of memory blocks. We define their semantics and formalize a runtime assertion checker for these languages, including the underlying program transformation and observation memory model. Finally, we state and prove the soundness result ensuring that the resulting verdicts are correct with respect to the semantics.

The contributions of the paper include:

- a formalization of all major steps of a runtime assertion checker for a simple but representative language;
- a definition of a dedicated memory model for RAC with an observation memory, suitable for a modular definition and verification of program transformations injecting non-interfering code, and an associated proof technique;
- a proof of soundness of a runtime verifier for memory properties.

Outline. Section 2 gives an overview of the work and a motivating example. Section 3 defines the considered languages. The runtime assertion checker is formalized in Sect. 4, while Sect. 5 states and proves the soundness result. Finally, Sects. 6 and 7 give some related work and conclusion.

2 Overview and Motivating Example

At a first glance, runtime assertion checking might be considered as an easy task: just directly translate each logic term and predicate from the source specification

---

[1] Available as open-source software at https://frama-c.com/eacsl.html.

```
1   int search(int *t, int len, int x) {   // search x in array t of size len
2       int lo = 0, hi = len - 1;           // initial search interval bounds
3       while (lo <= hi) {                   // while search interval non empty
4           int mid = lo + (hi - lo) / 2;    // take the middle value
5           /*@ assert(\valid(t + mid)); */
6           if (t[mid] == x) return mid;     // element found
7           else if (t[mid] < x) lo = mid + 1;
8           else hi = mid - 1;               // reduce the search interval
9       }
10      return -1;                           // element not found
11  }
12
13  int main(void) {
14      int t[5] = { -3, 2, 4, 7, 10 };
15      return search(t, 5, 7);
16  }
```

Fig. 1. Binary search annotated with a memory-related property.

language to the corresponding expression of the target programming language and that's it. In that spirit, Barnett et al. [2] explain how they enforce Spec# contracts, but only a short paragraph is dedicated to their runtime checker (all the others being dedicated to static verifications). Here it is *in extenso*:

> The run-time checker is straightforward: each contract indicates some particular program points at which it must hold. A run-time assertion is generated for each, and any failure causes an exception to be thrown.

However, this statement is not true for complex properties such as *memory properties*. Consider for instance the C function implementing binary search in Fig. 1. It contains an assertion at line 5, written in the E-ACSL specification language [9,27], stating that t+mid of type **int*** refers to a "valid memory location", ensuring that it is safe to dereference it at lines 6 and 7. For this program, the assertion is satisfied and runtime assertion checking of this program with the E-ACSL tool will not detect any failure.

To illustrate a failure, let us assume that **search** is called at line 15 with an erroneous length argument, say, 10 instead of 5. Then during the first iteration of the loop, **mid** would take the value 5 (at line 4) and the assertion at line 5 would fail because $t + 5$ is out of **t**'s bounds (as defined on line 14). In this case, runtime assertion checking of this program with the E-ACSL tool would halt the program execution and report the failure.

Checking such a property at runtime is not trivial: in particular, it requires to know at the annotation's program point (line 5) whether the **sizeof(int)** bytes starting from the address t+mid have been properly allocated by the program earlier in the execution, in the same memory block, without being freed in the meantime. For that purpose, runtime memory checkers (also called memory debuggers) need to store at runtime pieces of information about program memory in a disjoint memory space, named *observation memory* in this paper. For instance, the instrumented version of Fig. 1 created by the E-ACSL runtime assertion checker [28] is 111-lines long (when deactivating its static optimization described in [21]) for tracking the program's memory manipulation. In particu-

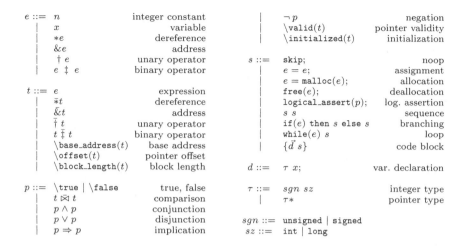

Fig. 2. Syntax of the source language, with expressions e, logical terms t, predicates p, statements s, declarations d, types τ, signedness sgn and size sz.

lar, for the block t created and initialized at line 14, E-ACSL adds the following lines of code (assuming that **sizeof**(**int**) = 4, so t is 20-byte long):

```
__e_acsl_store_block((void *)(t),(size_t)20); //record new block
__e_acsl_full_init((void *)(& t)); //mark it as initialized
```

Optimized implementations of such functions are also pretty complex, as explained by Vorobyov et al. [32]. In this work, assuming their correct implementation, we *formalize* the whole instrumentation performed by a RAC tool, and *prove its soundness*. For that purpose, we provide a model for such functions.

Moreover, RAC often has to manipulate additional variables, e.g. to evaluate annotations. We also prove that the instrumentation has no effect on the functional behavior of the input program as long as no annotation is violated. For that purpose, we add a new memory space, named *instrumentation* (or *monitor*) *memory*, that helps to prove non-interference in a modular way.

3 The Considered Languages

We model the instrumentation operated by RAC as a program transformation from a source language with logical assertions to a destination one with program assertions and observation memory primitives. We describe both languages in this section, before defining the program transformation in the next section.

3.1 Source Language

Our source language is a small C-like imperative language extended with formal annotations. It focuses on memory-related constructs and properties.

Syntax. Figure 2 presents the syntax of this source language. Expressions are (integer) constants, variables and operators (e.g. arithmetic operators), as well as the distinguished reference (&) and dereference (∗) operators. Variables are implicitly type-annotated, and all programs are supposed well-typed with respect to a type system that we do not detail here.

Statements include assignment of a value to a memory location (variable or dereferenced pointer) and basic control flow (sequence, conditional branching, loop). Beside these, notable constructs are primitives for dynamic memory allocation and deallocation, the `logical_assert(p);` statement (which does nothing if predicate p evaluates to true and halts the execution otherwise), and code blocks with (possibly multiple) local variable declarations (denoted $\vec{d}$).

Predicates form a propositional calculus (with the usual conjunction, disjunction, negation, and implication connectives), whose atoms are pointer validity, pointed value initialization, and logical term comparison. Terms are a superset of C expressions, extended with block-level memory attributes such as the length of the block containing the pointer, the base address of the pointer (i.e. the address of the first byte of its block), or the offset of the pointer with regards to the base address. To express this extension, terms have to include syntactical constructs mapping those of expressions, denoted with an overline: for instance $\bar{*}$ denotes pointer dereferencing *for terms*.

Semantics Overview. We give our language a big-step operational semantics adapted from that of CompCert's Clight [4]. The choice of this style (rather than, say, small-step operational semantics) is motivated by its ease of use when reasoning about program transformations. Moreover, the semantics is *blocking* [8]: in case of an error, the evaluation cannot evolve.

The evaluation context is composed of a variable environment $\widehat{E}$ (mapping variables' names to memory block identifiers) and a memory state $\widehat{M}$ (mapping memory locations to values, as explained below). Five inductive relations define our semantics:

- $\widehat{E}, \widehat{M} \models_e e \Rightarrow v$, evaluation of an expression e in the context of a variable environment $\widehat{E}$ and a memory state $\widehat{M}$, yielding a value v;
- $\widehat{E}, \widehat{M} \models_{lv} e \Rightarrow b, \delta$, evaluation of an expression e as a left-value, yielding a memory location (b, δ) in a memory block b with an offset δ;
- $\widehat{E}, \widehat{M} \models_t t \Rightarrow v$, evaluation of a logical term t, similarly yielding a value v;
- $\widehat{E}, \widehat{M} \models_p p \Rightarrow \mathbf{b}$, evaluation of predicate p to a Boolean truth value $\mathbf{b}$;
- $\widehat{E}, \widehat{M_1} \models_s s \Rightarrow \widehat{M_2}$, evaluation of statement s in the context of a variable environment $\widehat{E}$ and an initial memory state $\widehat{M_1}$; the evaluation results in a final memory state $\widehat{M_2}$, while the environment $\widehat{E}$ remains the same.

As later theorems and proofs in this paper involve both source and destination language constructs, and in order to visually differentiate them, we take the convention to write objects related to a source program—such as environments, memory states or values—with a hat; as of destination language constructs, they are written normally, without a hat. For instance, a variable environment $\widehat{E}$ could appear in a *source* program evaluation, while a memory state M would be used in a *destination* program evaluation. Readers should keep in mind that this is a pure convention, and this notation bears no formal meaning: in particular, $\widehat{E}$ and E (for example) have the same type. The inference symbol ($\widehat{\vDash}$ or $\vDash$) is also written with a hat for the source language and without it for the destination one (where its usage will be slightly different).

Memory Model. In accordance with our choice of using CompCert as an inspiration for our semantics, we reuse the (first) memory model of CompCert [20], based on the notion of memory blocks. In this model, a memory location is a couple (b, δ) where b is an abstract block identifier (or *block* for short), and $\delta \in \mathbb{N}$ an offset within the associated block. Blocks have a *size* defined at allocation time, which determines the maximum possible offset (starting from 0) where a value may actually be stored.

Following [20], the type of such a memory state is left abstract. However, it may be thought of as a map from blocks to their content, which is itself a map from offsets to values, resulting in the following type:

$$\text{mem} : \text{block} \to \mathbb{N} \to \text{value}.$$

This type supports four axiomatized operations, which we describe informally below using the following notations: M (or $\widehat{M}$) denotes a memory state, b a block, δ an offset, v a value, and τ a type. As some memory operations may fail, their return value has an option type, meaning that such a value is either ε (no return value) or $\lfloor v \rfloor$ (some value v).

Thus, $\text{alloc}(M, n) = (b, M')$ means that the allocation of a new block in memory state M returns its identifier b, along with the new memory state M'; in M', b is allocated with a size of n bytes. Data in the new block is uninitialized, i.e. the values stored in the block are Undef. $\text{length}(M, b)$ returns the byte size recorded for b.

Conversely, $\text{free}(M, b)$ deallocates a block b from M. If b was allocated in M and not previously deallocated, a new memory state $\lfloor M' \rfloor$ is returned. Otherwise, the deallocation fails and returns ε.

$\text{store}(\tau, M, b, \delta, v)$ stores value v with type τ at location (b, δ) in M, returning a new memory state $\lfloor M' \rfloor$ if it succeeds. The store fails and returns ε if the block does not exist, or if the attempt is made to store data out of b's bounds.

Finally, $\text{load}(\tau, M, b, \delta)$ reads from M at (b, δ) a value of type τ, returning a value $\lfloor v \rfloor$ upon success and ε upon failure. A failure occurs when loading from a non-existing block or from an existing block, but out of its bounds. Notice that a value v may be Undef despite being successfully loaded: for instance $\text{load}(\tau, M, b, 0) = \lfloor \text{Undef} \rfloor$ when b is a newly allocated block, containing uninitialized data, or more generally, when a value of the same type[2] was not previously stored at the same offset (or was completely or partially overwritten since it was stored).

---

[2] For simplicity, we do not allow type conversion here and refer the reader to [20] for a more general definition with type conversion.

$\widehat{E_3}$ and $\widehat{E_4}$: $\widehat{M_3}$ and $\widehat{M_4}$:

variable		block
t	$\mapsto$	b_2
len	$\mapsto$	b_3
x	$\mapsto$	b_4
lo	$\mapsto$	b_5
hi	$\mapsto$	b_6
mid	$\mapsto$	b_7

block		content	byte size
b_1	$\mapsto$	$\boxed{-3\,|\,2\,|\,4\,|\,7\,|\,10}$	20
b_2	$\mapsto$	$\boxed{\text{Ptr}(b_1,0)}$	4
b_3	$\mapsto$	$\boxed{5}$	4
b_4	$\mapsto$	$\boxed{7}$	4
b_5	$\mapsto$	$\boxed{0}$	4
b_6	$\mapsto$	$\boxed{4}$	4
b_7	$\mapsto$	$\boxed{2}$	4

Fig. 3. Environment $\widehat{E_3}$ and memory state $\widehat{M_3}$ (above the single line) show the context at line 3 at the start of the binary search (cf. Fig. 1). Environment $\widehat{E_4}$ and memory state $\widehat{M_4}$ show the context after line 4 and contain in addition the elements below the single line. The Int constructor is omitted around integer values in the content column.

We say that accesssing (b, δ) with type τ is valid, and we write $M \vDash \tau @ b, \delta$, if data of type τ may be safely accessed at (b, δ) in M, that is, load(τ, M, b, δ) would return some value $\lfloor v \rfloor$ (possibly with $v = $ Undef).

Memory Model Usage. Let us consider the example code from Fig. 1. We detail memory operations performed during the first iteration of the loop (lines 3 to 9), when **search** is called from **main** (line 15). At the beginning of the loop (line 3), the program has variable environment $\widehat{E_3}$ and memory state $\widehat{M_3}$, represented in Fig. 3. Let us illustrate that after line 4, the program has variable environment $\widehat{E_4}$ and memory state $\widehat{M_4}$, having both an additional line as shown in Fig. 3.

Line 4 contains a declaration of mid followed by an assignment: let us denote by $\widehat{E_3'}$ and $\widehat{M_3'}$ the variable environment and memory state between them. The loop body introduces a local variable mid, which requires an allocation: alloc$(\widehat{M_3}, \text{sizeof}(\text{int})) = (b_7, \widehat{M_3'})$, where $\widehat{M_3'}$ is equal to $\widehat{M_4}$ except that, as no data has yet been stored to b_7 in this state, $\widehat{M_3'}$ contains Undef at each offset $\delta \in [0; 4[$. Variable mid is also added into the variable environment $\widehat{E_3'}$ accordingly (as shown on the last line of $\widehat{E_3'} = \widehat{E_4}$, cf. Fig. 3).

Then, lo + (hi − lo)/2 is evaluated (line 4). This requires reading lo's value: load$(\text{int}, \widehat{M_3'}, b_5, 0) = \lfloor \text{Int}(0) \rfloor$. hi's value is read similarly.

After evaluation of the right-hand side expression, its result is written to mid: store$(\text{int}, \widehat{M_3'}, b_7, 0, \text{Int}(2)) = \lfloor \widehat{M_4} \rfloor$. The resulting memory state $\widehat{M_4}$ is shown in Fig. 3, where the Int constructor is omitted for short.

Thereafter, in this first loop iteration, the condition on line 6 (i.e., $t[2] = 5$) is false, and that on line 7 ($t[2] < 5$) is true, so the then branch on line 7 is executed. Similar load and store operations occur at lines 6 and 7, bringing the

E_INT:

$$\overline{\widehat{E}, \widehat{M} \vDash_e n \Rightarrow \text{Int}(n)}$$

E_VAR:
$$\frac{\widehat{E}(x) = b}{\widehat{E}, \widehat{M} \vDash_{lv} x \Rightarrow b, 0}$$

E_DEREF:
$$\frac{\widehat{E}, \widehat{M} \vDash_e e \Rightarrow \text{Ptr}(b, \delta)}{\widehat{E}, \widehat{M} \vDash_{lv} *e \Rightarrow b, \delta}$$

E_ADDR:
$$\frac{\widehat{E}, \widehat{M} \vDash_{lv} e \Rightarrow b, \delta}{\widehat{E}, \widehat{M} \vDash_e \&e \Rightarrow \text{Ptr}(b, \delta)}$$

E_LVAL:
$$\frac{\widehat{E}, \widehat{M} \vDash_{lv} e \Rightarrow b, \delta \quad \text{typeof}(e) = \tau}{\widehat{E}, \widehat{M} \vDash_e e \Rightarrow v}$$
$$\text{load}(\tau, \widehat{M}, b, \delta) = \lfloor v \rfloor \quad v \neq \text{Undef}$$

Fig. 4. Semantics of expressions.

memory into some state $\widehat{M_7}$, equal to $\widehat{M_4}$ except for the line for b_5 where 0 is replaced by 3, the new value of lo. Finally, as the control flow reaches the end of this loop iteration, mid is deallocated: $\text{free}(\widehat{M_7}, b_7) = \lfloor \widehat{M_9} \rfloor$, where $\widehat{M_9}$ is equal to $\widehat{M_3}$ except for the line for b_5 where 0 is replaced by 3. The variable environment at the end of the block is equal to that before the block, i.e. $\widehat{E_9} = \widehat{E_3}$: local variable mid is removed.

Semantics Inference Rules. The relations expressing the semantics of our source language are defined by a set of inference rules. Expressions (see Fig. 4) evaluate either to a value, or, as left-values, to a memory location. A value is either an integer, a pointer to a memory location (that is, in our memory model, a block and an offset), or an undefined value: $v ::= \text{Int}(n) \mid \text{Ptr}(b, \delta) \mid \text{Undef}$.

Figure 5 defines the semantics of statements. Rule E_ASSIGN is an example of use of the memory model: the right-hand side of the assignment is evaluated to a value v, while the left-hand side is evaluated to a memory location (b, δ). A store() operation is then performed to write v into $\widehat{M_1}$ at location (b, δ), and must lead to a final memory state $\widehat{M_2}$ (recall our semantics is blocking). Selected rules defining the semantics of predicates and terms are given in Fig. 6. The reader can see how these rules are applied following the steps in the Memory Model Usage example above, illustrated on Fig. 3.

3.2 Destination Language

The destination language is quite close to the source language: it has the same expressions, and mostly the same statements (see Fig. 7). The first difference is the absence of assertions over logical predicates, therefore removing the need for terms and predicates. These are substituted with a weaker, program assertion over expressions, similar to the C assert macro. The other difference is the addition of a set of primitives to interact with an additional *observation memory*. In order to give these primitives a semantics, we extend the evaluation relation with the state of the observation memory (denoted $\overline{M}$). Consequently, evaluation relations for the destination language take the following shapes:

E_MALLOC:
$$\frac{\widehat{E}, \widehat{M_1} \vDash_e e_2 \Rightarrow \mathrm{Int}(n) \qquad \mathrm{alloc}(\widehat{M_1}, n) = (b', \widehat{M_2}) \qquad \widehat{E}, \widehat{M_1} \vDash_{lv} e_1 \Rightarrow b, \delta \qquad \mathrm{typeof}(e_1) = \tau* \qquad \mathrm{store}(\tau*, \widehat{M_2}, b, \delta, \mathrm{Ptr}(b', 0)) = \lfloor \widehat{M_3} \rfloor}{\widehat{E}, \widehat{M_1} \vDash_s e_1 = \mathtt{malloc}(e_2); \Rightarrow \widehat{M_3}}$$

E_ASSIGN:
$$\frac{\widehat{E}, \widehat{M_1} \vDash_e e_2 \Rightarrow v \qquad \widehat{E}, \widehat{M_1} \vDash_{lv} e_1 \Rightarrow b, \delta \qquad \mathrm{typeof}(e_2) = \tau \qquad \mathrm{store}(\tau, \widehat{M_1}, b, \delta, v) = \lfloor \widehat{M_2} \rfloor}{\widehat{E}, \widehat{M_1} \vDash_s e_1 = e_2; \Rightarrow \widehat{M_2}}$$

E_FREE:
$$\frac{\widehat{E}, \widehat{M_1} \vDash_e e \Rightarrow \mathrm{Ptr}(b, 0) \qquad \mathrm{free}(\widehat{M_1}, b) = \lfloor \widehat{M_2} \rfloor}{\widehat{E}, \widehat{M_1} \vDash_s \mathtt{free}(e); \Rightarrow \widehat{M_2}}$$

E_LOGICAL_ASSERT:
$$\frac{\widehat{E}, \widehat{M} \vDash_p p \Rightarrow \mathrm{true}}{\widehat{E}, \widehat{M} \vDash_s \mathtt{logical\_assert}(p); \Rightarrow \widehat{M}}$$

E_SEQ:
$$\frac{\widehat{E}, \widehat{M_1} \vDash_s s_1 \Rightarrow \widehat{M_2} \qquad \widehat{E}, \widehat{M_2} \vDash_s s_2 \Rightarrow \widehat{M_3}}{\widehat{E}, \widehat{M_1} \vDash_s s_1 \, s_2 \Rightarrow \widehat{M_3}}$$

E_IF_FALSE:
$$\frac{\widehat{E}, \widehat{M_1} \vDash_e e \Rightarrow \mathrm{Int}(0) \qquad \widehat{E}, \widehat{M_1} \vDash_s s_2 \Rightarrow \widehat{M_2}}{\widehat{E}, \widehat{M_1} \vDash_s \mathtt{if}\ (e)\ \mathtt{then}\ s_1\ \mathtt{else}\ s_2 \Rightarrow \widehat{M_2}}$$

E_IF_TRUE:
$$\frac{\widehat{E}, \widehat{M_1} \vDash_e e \Rightarrow \mathrm{Int}(n) \qquad n \neq 0 \qquad \widehat{E}, \widehat{M_1} \vDash_s s_1 \Rightarrow \widehat{M_2}}{\widehat{E}, \widehat{M_1} \vDash_s \mathtt{if}\ (e)\ \mathtt{then}\ s_1\ \mathtt{else}\ s_2 \Rightarrow \widehat{M_2}}$$

E_WHILE_FALSE
$$\frac{\widehat{E}, \widehat{M} \vDash_e e \Rightarrow \mathrm{Int}(0)}{\widehat{E}, \widehat{M} \vDash_s \mathtt{while}\ (e)\ s \Rightarrow \widehat{M}}$$

E_WHILE_TRUE:
$$\frac{\widehat{E}, \widehat{M_1} \vDash_e e \Rightarrow \mathrm{Int}(n) \qquad n \neq 0 \qquad \widehat{E}, \widehat{M_1} \vDash_s s \Rightarrow \widehat{M_2} \qquad \widehat{E}, \widehat{M_2} \vDash_s \mathtt{while}\ (e)\ s \Rightarrow \widehat{M_3}}{\widehat{E}, \widehat{M_1} \vDash_s \mathtt{while}\ (e)\ s \Rightarrow \widehat{M_3}}$$

E_BLOCK:
$$\frac{\widehat{E_2}, \widehat{M_2} = \mathrm{alloc\_vars}(\vec{d}, \widehat{E_1}, \widehat{M_1}) \qquad \widehat{E_2}, \widehat{M_2} \vDash_s s \Rightarrow \widehat{M_3} \qquad \widehat{M_4} = \mathrm{dealloc\_vars}(\vec{d}, \widehat{E_2}, \widehat{M_3})}{\widehat{E_1}, \widehat{M_1} \vDash_s \{\vec{d}\ s\} \Rightarrow \widehat{M_4}}$$

Fig. 5. Semantics of the source language statements, where alloc_vars() allocates memory for the list of local variable declarations $\vec{d}$ using the alloc() operation, and adds the corresponding bindings into the environment. dealloc_vars() is the converse function.

- $E, M \vDash_e e \Rightarrow v$, evaluation of an expression (unchanged);
- $E, M \vDash_{lv} e \Rightarrow b, \delta$, evaluation of an expression as a left-value (unchanged);
- $E, M_1, \overline{M_1} \vDash_s s \Rightarrow M_2, \overline{M_2}$, evaluation of a statement; in addition to the final execution memory M_2, it also returns a final observation memory $\overline{M_2}$.

In the same way as the execution memory model is a prerequisite to the definition of the source language semantics, the observation memory must be defined prior to the semantics of the above primitives. The observation memory is basically a data structure for the runtime monitor to store metadata about the (execution) memory of the program under monitoring. As for the execution memory model, we define it with an abstract type, a set of functions over this type, and an axiomatization of these functions. Four of them are the observation counterparts of the execution memory operations. store_block($\overline{M}, b, n$) records block

b as being allocated with byte size n, returning an updated observation memory state. delete_block($\overline{M}, b$) marks b as deallocated and returns an updated observation memory. initialize($\tau, \overline{M}, b, \delta$) marks the data with type τ at location (b, δ) as initialized and returns an updated observation memory. Conversely, is_initialized($\tau, \overline{M}, b, \delta$) returns 1 if location (b, δ) with type τ is marked as initialized in $\overline{M}$, and 0 otherwise. Two other functions provide information about *metadata* stored in the memory state: is_valid($\tau, \overline{M}, b, \delta$) returns 1 if accessing data with type τ at location (b, δ) is legal, and 0 otherwise, while length($\overline{M}, b$) returns the size that was recorded for b with store_block(). Vorobyov et al. explain how all these operations can be implemented [32].

Figure 8 presents the semantics of the destination language's additional statements, and their relation with the observation memory operations. Evaluation rules for the statements already present in the source language are omitted, as they are similar and only adapted to include observation memory states, which remain unchanged in these evaluation rules.

E_OR1:
$$\frac{\widehat{E}, \widehat{M} \vDash_p p_1 \Rightarrow \text{true}}{\widehat{E}, \widehat{M} \vDash_p p_1 \vee p_2 \Rightarrow \text{true}}$$

E_OR2:
$$\frac{\widehat{E}, \widehat{M} \vDash_p p_1 \Rightarrow \text{false} \quad \widehat{E}, \widehat{M} \vDash_p p_2 \Rightarrow b}{\widehat{E}, \widehat{M} \vDash_p p_1 \vee p_2 \Rightarrow b}$$

E_INIT_TRUE:
$$\frac{\widehat{E}, \widehat{M} \vDash_t t \Rightarrow \text{Ptr}(b, \delta) \quad \text{typeof}(t) = \tau* \quad \text{load}(\tau, \widehat{M}, b, \delta) = \lfloor v \rfloor \quad v \neq \text{Undef}}{\widehat{E}, \widehat{M} \vDash_p \text{\textbackslash initialized}(t) \Rightarrow \text{true}}$$

E_INIT_FALSE:
$$\frac{\widehat{E}, \widehat{M} \vDash_t t \Rightarrow \text{Ptr}(b, \delta) \quad \text{typeof}(t) = \tau* \quad \text{load}(\tau, \widehat{M}, b, \delta) = \lfloor \text{Undef} \rfloor}{\widehat{E}, \widehat{M} \vDash_p \text{\textbackslash initialized}(t) \Rightarrow \text{false}}$$

E_VALID_TRUE:
$$\frac{\widehat{E}, \widehat{M} \vDash_t t \Rightarrow \text{Ptr}(b, \delta) \quad \text{typeof}(t) = \tau* \quad \widehat{M} \vDash \tau @ b, \delta}{\widehat{E}, \widehat{M} \vDash_p \text{\textbackslash valid}(t) \Rightarrow \text{true}}$$

E_VALID_FALSE:
$$\frac{\widehat{E}, \widehat{M} \vDash_t t \Rightarrow \text{Ptr}(b, \delta) \quad \text{typeof}(t) = \tau* \quad \widehat{M} \nvDash \tau @ b, \delta}{\widehat{E}, \widehat{M} \vDash_p \text{\textbackslash valid}(t) \Rightarrow \text{false}}$$

E_BASE_ADDR:
$$\frac{\widehat{E}, \widehat{M} \vDash_t t \Rightarrow \text{Ptr}(b, \delta)}{\widehat{E}, \widehat{M} \vDash_t \text{\textbackslash base\_address}(t) \Rightarrow \text{Ptr}(b, 0)}$$

E_OFS:
$$\frac{\widehat{E}, \widehat{M} \vDash_t t \Rightarrow \text{Ptr}(b, \delta)}{\widehat{E}, \widehat{M} \vDash_t \text{\textbackslash offset}(t) \Rightarrow \text{Int}(\delta)}$$

E_BLOCK_LENGTH:
$$\frac{\widehat{E}, \widehat{M} \vDash_t t \Rightarrow \text{Ptr}(b, \delta) \quad \text{length}(\widehat{M}, b) = \lfloor n \rfloor}{\widehat{E}, \widehat{M} \vDash_t \text{\textbackslash block\_length}(t) \Rightarrow \text{Int}(n)}$$

E_EXPR:
$$\frac{\widehat{E}, \widehat{M} \vDash_e e \Rightarrow v}{\widehat{E}, \widehat{M} \vDash_t e \Rightarrow v}$$

Fig. 6. Semantics of predicates and terms.

$s ::=$	...	source lang. stmts		$e = \text{is\_initialized}(e);$	is $(*e)$ initialized
	~~logical_assert(p);~~	no assert. over pred.		$\text{initialize}(e);$	mark $*e$ as initialized
	$\text{assert}(e);$	assert. over exp.		$e = \text{base\_address}(e);$	e's block base address
	$\text{store\_block}(e, e);$	record new block		$e = \text{offset}(e);$	get pointer offset
	$\text{delete\_block}(e);$	remove recorded bl.		$e = \text{block\_length}(e);$	e's block length
	$e = \text{is\_valid}(e);$	is e valid			

Fig. 7. Additional statements of the destination language.

4   Program Transformation

We now turn to the implementation of a runtime monitor by program transformation. This transformation has two purposes: first, translating logical predicates (and terms) into chunks of executable code evaluating them; and second, inserting statements into the original code, in order to track the state of the execution memory; that is, updating the observation memory whenever a memory related operation occurs.

The general idea underlying this transformation is the following: atomic predicates and terms are translated into dedicated primitives of the target language, while composite ones (logical connectors, comparison operators...) are encoded with non-logical constructs of the source language. The translation of each term and predicate introduces a specific variable res that stores its results for later use by subsequent computations.

Formally, we express the transformation as a set of three recursive functions over statements (denoted $[\![\cdot]\!]_s$), predicates ($[\![\cdot]\!]_p$) and terms ($[\![\cdot]\!]_t$). Notice that indices s, p, t are here part of notation (and not a reference to a specific statement s, predicate p or term t). These functions have the following types: $[\![\cdot]\!]_s$: statement $\rightarrow$ statement; $[\![\cdot]\!]_p$: predicate $\rightarrow$ $\{code : statement; res : variable\}$; $[\![\cdot]\!]_t$: term $\rightarrow$ $\{code : statement; res : variable\}$. While $[\![\cdot]\!]_s$ is a straightforward translation from statement to statement, the other two translation functions

E_STOREBLOCK:
$$\frac{E, M_1 \vDash_e p \Rightarrow \mathrm{Ptr}(b,0) \qquad E, M_1 \vDash_e e \Rightarrow n \qquad \mathrm{store\_block}(\overline{M_1}, b, n) = \lfloor \overline{M_2} \rfloor}{E, M_1, \overline{M_1} \vDash_s \texttt{store\_block}(p, e); \Rightarrow M_1, \overline{M_2}}$$

E_DELETEBLOCK:
$$\frac{E, M_1 \vDash_e p \Rightarrow \mathrm{Ptr}(b,0) \qquad \mathrm{delete\_block}(\overline{M_1}, b) = \lfloor \overline{M_2} \rfloor}{E, M_1, \overline{M_1} \vDash_s \texttt{delete\_block}(p); \Rightarrow M_1, \overline{M_2}}$$

E_ISVALID:
$$\frac{E, M_1 \vDash_{lv} e_1 \Rightarrow b_1, \delta_1 \quad E, M_1 \vDash_e e_2 \Rightarrow \mathrm{Ptr}(b_2, \delta_2) \quad \mathrm{typeof}(e_2) = \tau* \quad \mathrm{is\_valid}(\tau, \overline{M_1}, b_2, \delta_2) = n \quad \mathrm{store}(\mathrm{int}, M_1, b_1, \delta_1, n) = \lfloor M_2 \rfloor}{E, M_1, \overline{M_1} \vDash_s e_1 = \texttt{is\_valid}(e_2); \Rightarrow M_2, \overline{M_1}}$$

E_ISINITIALIZED:
$$\frac{E, M_1 \vDash_{lv} e_1 \Rightarrow b_1, \delta_1 \quad E, M_1 \vDash_e e_2 \Rightarrow \mathrm{Ptr}(b_2, \delta_2) \quad \mathrm{typeof}(e_2) = \tau* \quad \mathrm{is\_initialized}(\tau, \overline{M_1}, b_2, \delta_2) = n \quad \mathrm{store}(\mathrm{int}, M_1, b_1, \delta_1, n) = \lfloor M_2 \rfloor}{E, M_1, \overline{M_1} \vDash_s e_1 = \texttt{is\_initialized}(e_2); \Rightarrow M_2, \overline{M_1}}$$

E_INITIALIZE:
$$\frac{\mathrm{typeof}(e) = \tau* \quad E, M_1 \vDash_e e \Rightarrow \mathrm{Ptr}(b, \delta) \quad \mathrm{initialize}(\tau, \overline{M_1}, b, \delta) = \lfloor \overline{M_2} \rfloor}{E, M_1, \overline{M_1} \vDash_s \texttt{initialize}(e); \Rightarrow M_1, \overline{M_2}}$$

E_BASEADDR:
$$\frac{E, M_1 \vDash_{lv} e_1 \Rightarrow b_1, \delta_1 \quad E, M_1 \vDash_e e_2 \Rightarrow \mathrm{Ptr}(b_2, \delta_2) \quad \mathrm{typeof}(e_1) = \tau* \quad \mathrm{store}(\tau*, M_1, b_1, \delta_1, \mathrm{Ptr}(b_2, 0)) = \lfloor M_2 \rfloor}{E, M_1, \overline{M_1} \vDash_s e_1 = \texttt{base\_address}(e_2); \Rightarrow M_2, \overline{M_1}}$$

E_BLOCKLENGTH:
$$\frac{E, M_1 \vDash_{lv} e_1 \Rightarrow b_1, \delta_1 \quad E, M_1 \vDash_e e_2 \Rightarrow \mathrm{Ptr}(b_2, \delta_2) \quad \mathrm{length}(\overline{M_1}, b_2) = \lfloor n \rfloor \quad \mathrm{store}(\mathrm{int}, M_1, b_1, \delta_1, n) = \lfloor M_2 \rfloor}{E, M_1, \overline{M_1} \vDash_s e_1 = \texttt{block\_length}(e_2); \Rightarrow M_2, \overline{M_1}}$$

E_OFFSET:
$$\frac{E, M_1 \vDash_{lv} e_1 \Rightarrow b_1, \delta_1 \quad E, M_1 \vDash_e e_2 \Rightarrow \mathrm{Ptr}(b_2, \delta_2) \quad \mathrm{store}(\mathrm{int}, M_1, b_1, \delta_1, \delta_2) = \lfloor M_2 \rfloor}{E, M_1, \overline{M_1} \vDash_s e_1 = \texttt{offset}(e_2); \Rightarrow M_2, \overline{M_1}}$$

Fig. 8. Semantics of destination-specific statements.

$[\![\texttt{skip};]\!]_s =$ skip;
$[\![p = \texttt{malloc}(e);]\!]_s =$
    $p = \texttt{malloc}(e);$
    store_block$(p, e);$
    initialize$(\&p);$
$[\![\texttt{free}(p);]\!]_s =$ free(p);
    delete_block$(p);$
$[\![l = e;]\!]_s =$ $l = e;$
    initialize$(\&l);$
$[\![\texttt{logical\_assert}(p);]\!]_s = \{$
    mkdecl$([\![p]\!]_p.res)$
    $[\![p]\!]_p.code;$
    assert$([\![p]\!]_p.res);$ }

$[\![s_1 \ s_2]\!]_s =$ $[\![s_1]\!]_s \ [\![s_2]\!]_s$
$[\![\texttt{if} \ (e) \ \texttt{then} \ s_1 \ \texttt{else} \ s_2]\!]_s =$
    if (e) then $[\![s_1]\!]_s$ else $[\![s_2]\!]_s$
$[\![\texttt{while}(e) \ s]\!]_s =$ while$(e) \ [\![s]\!]_s$
$[\![\{\tau_1 \ x_1; \dots \tau_n \ x_n; \ s\}]\!]_s = \{$
    $\tau_1 \ x_1; \dots \tau_n \ x_n;$
    store_block$(\&x_1, \texttt{sizeof}(\tau_1));$
    $\dots$
    store_block$(\&x_n, \texttt{sizeof}(\tau_n));$
    $[\![s]\!]_s$
    delete_block$(\&x_1);$
    $\dots$
    delete_block$(\&x_n);$ }

Fig. 9. Translation of statements.

$[\![\backslash\texttt{false}]\!]_p.code =$ $[\![p]\!]_p.res = 0;$
$[\![t_1 \bowtie t_2]\!]_p.code =$ {
    mkdecl$([\![t_1]\!]_t.res)$
    mkdecl$([\![t_2]\!]_t.res)$
    $[\![t_1]\!]_t.code$
    $[\![t_2]\!]_t.code$
    $[\![p]\!]_p.res = [\![t_1]\!]_t.res \bowtie [\![t_2]\!]_t.res;$ }
$[\![p_1 \lor p_2]\!]_p.code =$ {
    mkdecl$([\![p_1]\!]_p.res)$
    $[\![p_1]\!]_p.code$
    if$([\![p_1]\!]_p.res)$ then
        $[\![p]\!]_p.res = 1;$
    else {
        mkdecl$([\![p_2]\!]_p.res)$

$[\![p_2]\!]_p.code$
$[\![p]\!]_p.res = [\![p_2]\!]_p.res;$ } }
$[\![\neg p_1]\!]_p.code =$
$[\![p_1]\!]_p.code$
$[\![p]\!]_p.res = 1 - [\![p_1]\!]_p.res;$
$[\![\backslash\texttt{valid}(t)]\!]_p.code =$ {
    mkdecl$([\![t]\!]_t.res)$
    $[\![t]\!]_t.code$
    $[\![p]\!]_p.res =$ is_valid$([\![t]\!]_t.res);$ }
$[\![\backslash\texttt{initialized}(t)]\!]_p.code =$ {
    mkdecl$([\![t]\!]_t.res)$
    $[\![t]\!]_t.code$
    $[\![p]\!]_p.res =$ is_initialized$([\![t]\!]_t.res);$ }

Fig. 10. Translation of predicates, where p denotes the currently translated predicate for short. Omitted cases are similar to those displayed.

return records; their fields are a statement (the *code* field of the record type) performing computation of the translated term or predicate, and distinguished variable *res* to store the result of the computation.

4.1 Statement Translation

The statement translation (see Fig. 9) is the top-level transformation function. It simply follows the structure of the source program, only adding observation memory manipulation primitives where execution memory operations occur. Therefore, besides logical assertions, the only statements actually transformed are assignments, memory allocation, deallocation, and code blocks (to account for automatic allocation and deallocation of local variables).

$\llbracket e \rrbracket_t.code = \quad \llbracket t \rrbracket_t.res = e;$

$\llbracket \ast t_1 \rrbracket_t.code = \quad \{$
    $\mathrm{mkdecl}(\llbracket t_1 \rrbracket_t.res)$
    $\llbracket t_1 \rrbracket_t.code$
    $\llbracket t \rrbracket_t.res = \ast\, \llbracket t_1 \rrbracket_t.res;\ \}$

$\llbracket \&t_1 \rrbracket_t.code = \{ \ldots \}$ // similar to $\llbracket \ast t_1 \rrbracket_t$

$\llbracket t_1 \mp t_2 \rrbracket_t.code = \quad \{$
    $\mathrm{mkdecl}(\llbracket t_1 \rrbracket_t.res)$
    $\mathrm{mkdecl}(\llbracket t_2 \rrbracket_t.res)$
    $\llbracket t_1 \rrbracket_t.code$
    $\llbracket t_2 \rrbracket_t.code$
    $\llbracket t \rrbracket_t.res = \llbracket t_1 \rrbracket_t.res \ddagger \llbracket t_2 \rrbracket_t.res;\ \}$

$\llbracket \bar{\mp}\, t_1 \rrbracket_t.code = \quad \{$
    $\mathrm{mkdecl}(\llbracket t_1 \rrbracket_t.res)$

$\llbracket t_1 \rrbracket_t.code$
$\llbracket t \rrbracket_t.res = \dagger\, \llbracket t_1 \rrbracket_t.res\ \}$

$\llbracket \backslash \texttt{base\_address}(t_1) \rrbracket_t.code = \quad \{$
    $\mathrm{mkdecl}(\llbracket t_1 \rrbracket_t.res)$
    $\llbracket t_1 \rrbracket_t.code$
    $\llbracket t \rrbracket_t.res = \texttt{base\_address}(\llbracket t_1 \rrbracket_t.res);\ \}$

$\llbracket \backslash \texttt{offset}(t_1) \rrbracket_t.code = \quad \{$
    $\mathrm{mkdecl}(\llbracket t_1 \rrbracket_t.res)$
    $\llbracket t_1 \rrbracket_t.code$
    $\llbracket t \rrbracket_t.res = \texttt{offset}(\llbracket t_1 \rrbracket_t.res);\ \}$

$\llbracket \backslash \texttt{block\_length}(t_1) \rrbracket_t.code = \quad \{$
    $\mathrm{mkdecl}(\llbracket t_1 \rrbracket_t.res)$
    $\llbracket t_1 \rrbracket_t.code$
    $\llbracket t \rrbracket_t.res = \texttt{block\_length}(\llbracket t_1 \rrbracket_t.res);\ \}$

Fig. 11. Translation of terms, where t denotes the currently translated term for short.

When translating a logical assertion over a predicate p, a block of code is generated, ending with a C-like assertion over a local variable, $\llbracket p \rrbracket_p.res$, that will receive the result of p's translation. Its declaration is generated from its name (and, implicitly, type) using a dedicated function mkdecl. As for the code, $\llbracket p \rrbracket_p.code$, it is inserted just before the final assertion. The execution of such a block therefore follows these steps: first, the control enters the block and $\llbracket p \rrbracket_p.res$ is allocated; then $\llbracket p \rrbracket_p.code$ executes, computing p's truth value and writing the result (0 or 1) into $\llbracket p \rrbracket_p.res$; finally, the assertion is evaluated, halting the program if $\llbracket p \rrbracket_p.res$ is zero (meaning that p is false in the source program), and resuming otherwise; in the latter case, the control exits the block and $\llbracket p \rrbracket_p.res$ is automatically deallocated, returning the memory to its previous state.

4.2   Predicate Translation

The predicate translation is the main component of the program transformation as a whole. Its purpose is to convert a logical predicate into code reflecting the evaluation of this predicate. Figure 10 presents the definition of $\llbracket p \rrbracket_p.code$, inductively defined on the structure of p. Regarding the result variable ($\llbracket p \rrbracket_p.res$), we only require the transformation to generate a *fresh* name for each predicate. The *code* field of the resulting record is expected to be inserted at a program point at which its result variable, the *res* field, has already been declared and allocated with an adequate memory block.

Our translation introduces many intermediate variables (cf. Fig. 10). To minimize the impact of these variables, we introduce them only when needed, and deallocate them as soon as they are no longer used. Therefore, in all but the most simple cases (\true, \false, and $\neg p$), *code* is a block that limits the scope of the intermediate variable(s) *res*.

4.3   Term Translation

The translation function for terms (see Fig. 11) is quite similar to that of predicates, the main difference being that the type of the result variable depends on the translated term, while it is always a Boolean for predicates. As with predicates, the only requirement for generated variables is freshness.

5   Soundness

Preliminary Notation Convention. Statements in the source language evaluate in some *evaluation context* $\widehat{C} = (\widehat{E}, \widehat{M})$, consisting of a variable environment $\widehat{E}$ and an execution memory state $\widehat{M}$. In the destination language, an evaluation context $\mathscr{C} = (E, M, \overline{M})$ has an additional third component: the observation memory $\overline{M}$. By abuse of notation, we also write $\mathscr{C} = (C, \overline{M})$ with $C = (E, M)$. In both languages, statement evaluation only affects memory states, and does not alter environments. Therefore, an evaluation such as $\widehat{C_i} \vDash_s s \Rightarrow \widehat{M_f}$ actually links the initial context $\widehat{C_i} = (\widehat{E_i}, \widehat{M_i})$ to a final context $\widehat{C_f} = (\widehat{E_f}, \widehat{M_f})$, where $\widehat{E_f} = \widehat{E_i}$. For the sake of conciseness, we assume that any memory state $\widehat{M_k}$ at some program point k is implicitly extended to a context $\widehat{C_k}$ by the current environment $\widehat{E_k}$. Reciprocally, any context $\widehat{C_k}$ may implicitly be decomposed into its components $\widehat{E_k}$ and $\widehat{M_k}$. The same holds for the destination language.

5.1   Definitions

Let us elaborate a notion of semantics preservation for our program transformation. Assume a source program s sucessfully evaluates from the initial evaluation context $\widehat{C_i}$: we have $\widehat{C_i} \vDash_s s \Rightarrow \widehat{M_f}$. We want to relate this evaluation of s and that of its associated transformed program $[\![s]\!]_s$. The preservation property states that if the initial evaluation context of the source program $\widehat{C_i}$ and that of the transformed program $\mathscr{C_i}$ are related according to a certain relation $\mathcal{R}$, then evaluating $[\![s]\!]_s$ in $\mathscr{C_i}$ should succeed and terminate in a final context $\mathscr{C_f}$ that is also related to $\widehat{C_f}$ by $\mathcal{R}$. More formally, our transformation soundness theorem states:

$$\forall s, \widehat{C_i}, \mathscr{C_i}, \widehat{C_f}, \begin{cases} \widehat{C_i} \vDash_s s \Rightarrow \widehat{C_f} \\ \widehat{C_i} \; \mathcal{R} \; \mathscr{C_i} \end{cases} \implies \exists \mathscr{C_f}, \begin{cases} \mathscr{C_i} \vDash_s [\![s]\!]_s \Rightarrow M_f, \overline{M_f} \\ \widehat{C_f} \; \mathcal{R} \; \mathscr{C_f} \end{cases}$$

We now have to define an appropriate relation $\mathcal{R}$ between a source context $\widehat{C}$ and an associated destination context $\mathscr{C}$. They have the following differences. First, the content of the destination execution memory M is larger than its source counterpart $\widehat{M}$, because in addition to the memory of the source program, it also stores the intermediate variables introduced by the instrumentation (those generated by predicates and terms translation). M can thus be divided into two distinct regions, the original program memory M^p and the monitor memory M^m, such that no pointer value stored in M^p points to a location in M^m (because the monitored program should not refer to the memory of the monitor). We call this property *separation* and extend it to contexts.

Definition 1 (Context separation). *A context C is separated into two sub-contexts C^p and C^m (denoted $C = C^p \uplus C^m$) if:*

- *E is the disjoint union of maps E^p and E^m;*
- *the set of valid blocks in M is the disjoint union of those of M^p and M^m;*
- *any valid block in M, which is also valid in either M^p or M^m, has the same content in M^p or M^m as in M;*
- *no value in M^p is a pointer to a block in M^m.*

Second, the destination context $\mathscr{C}$ includes an observation memory $\overline{M}$. Assuming context separation, the requirement for $\overline{M}$ is to be an accurate description of the monitored program memory M^p. $\overline{M}$ is then said to *represent* M^p.

Definition 2 (Representation). *An observation memory $\overline{M}$ represents an execution memory M (denoted $M \triangleright \overline{M}$) if:*

$$\begin{cases} \forall \tau, b, \delta, \ M \vDash \tau @ b, \delta \implies \text{is\_valid}(\tau, \overline{M}, b, \delta) = \text{true} \\ \forall \tau, b, \delta, \ \text{load}(\tau, M, b, \delta) = \lfloor v \rfloor \wedge v \neq \text{Undef} \implies \text{is\_initialized}(\tau, \overline{M}, b, \delta) = \text{true} \\ \forall b, \ \text{length}(M, b) = \text{length}(\overline{M}, b) \end{cases}$$

Third, in our memory model, blocks are identifiers. Therefore two memory states (or environments) may have the same content up to block permutation.

Definition 3 (Isomorphism). *Two execution memories M_1 and M_2 are isomorphic (denoted $M_1 \sim M_2$) if there is a permutation σ on the set of blocks such that $\forall \tau, b, \delta, \ \tilde{\sigma}(\text{load}(\tau, M_1, b, \delta)) = \text{load}(\tau, M_2, \sigma(b), \delta)$, where $\tilde{\sigma}$ is the function over values (more precisely over value options) that applies σ to pointers: $\text{Ptr}(b, \delta) \mapsto \text{Ptr}(\sigma(b), \delta)$, and leaves other values unchanged. Environments E_1 and E_2 are isomorphic (denoted $E_1 \sim E_2$) if $x \mapsto b \in E_1 \Leftrightarrow x \mapsto \sigma(b) \in E_2$. Contents C_1 and C_2 are isomorphic (denoted $C_1 \sim C_2$) if $E_1 \sim E_2$ and $M_1 \sim M_2$ with the same permutation σ.*

Definition 4 (Context monitoring). *The monitoring relation $\mathcal{R}$ between a source context $\widehat{C}$ and a destination context $\mathscr{C} = (C, \overline{M})$ is defined as follows: $\widehat{C} \ \mathcal{R} \ \mathscr{C}$ iff $\exists C^p, C^m$ s.t. $C = C^p \uplus C^m$ and $\widehat{C} \sim C^p$ and $M^p \triangleright \overline{M}$.*

5.2 Soundness Theorem

Theorem 1 (Soundness of program transformation). *Let $\widehat{C_i} \vDash_s s \Rightarrow \widehat{C_f}$ be the evaluation of a source program s, from initial context $\widehat{C_i}$ to final context $\widehat{C_f}$, and $\mathscr{C}_i$ a destination context that monitors $\widehat{C_i}$, i.e. $\widehat{C_i} \ \mathcal{R} \ \mathscr{C}_i$. Then $[\![s]\!]_s$ evaluates from $\mathscr{C}_i$ to a final destination context $\mathscr{C}_f$ that monitors $\widehat{C_f}$, that is, $\exists \mathscr{C}_f, \ \mathscr{C}_i \vDash_s [\![s]\!]_s \Rightarrow M_f, \overline{M_f}$ and $\widehat{C_f} \ \mathcal{R} \ \mathscr{C}_f$.*

Proof. We proceed by induction on the evaluation of s. The proof is straightforward for all cases but that of `logical_assert()`, which requires a specific lemma. To give a flavor of the proof, we present the case of assignments. Throughout the proof, we manipulate various execution contexts and their components (execution and observation memories, and environments). In order to help relating them together, we index them according to the intuitive notion of program point: the initial context C_i is also C_0; after execution of an atomic statement, the next one is C_1, etc. We simply write $\widehat{E}$ for $\widehat{E}_i$ (resp., E for E_i) if it does not change.

Case E_ASSIGN. If s is an assignement $e_1 = e_2$; then its translation $[\![s]\!]_s$ is $e_1 = e_2;$ `initialize`$(\&e_1)$; (cf. Fig. 9), and its evaluation (cf. Fig. 5) is:

$$\frac{\widehat{E}, \widehat{M_i} \vDash_e e_2 \Rightarrow v \quad \widehat{E}, \widehat{M_i} \vDash_{lv} e_1 \Rightarrow \widehat{b}, \widehat{\delta} \quad \text{typeof}(e_2) = \tau \quad \text{store}(\tau, \widehat{M_i}, \widehat{b}, \widehat{\delta}, v) = \lfloor \widehat{M_f} \rfloor}{\widehat{E}, \widehat{M_i} \vDash_s e_1 = e_2; \Rightarrow \widehat{M_f}}$$

We want to prove the existence of a destination evaluation context $\mathscr{C}_f$ such that $\mathscr{C}_i \vDash_s e_1 = e_2;$ `initialize`$(\&e_1); \Rightarrow M_f, \overline{M_f}$ and $\widehat{C_f} \; \mathcal{R} \; \mathscr{C}_f$. Let us build an evaluation derivation for $[\![s]\!]_s$ and then prove preservation of $\mathcal{R}$. We want to build, for suitable memory states, a derivation ending by:

$$\frac{\dfrac{E, M_i \vDash_e e_2 \Rightarrow v \quad E, M_i \vDash_{lv} e_1 \Rightarrow b, \delta}{\text{typeof}(e_2) = \tau \quad \text{store}(\tau, M_i, b, \delta, v) = \lfloor M_1 \rfloor} \quad \dfrac{\cdots}{\text{initialize}(\tau, \overline{M_1}, b, \delta) = \lfloor \overline{M_2} \rfloor}}{\mathscr{C}_i \vDash_s e_1 = e_2; \Rightarrow M_1, \overline{M_1} \qquad \mathscr{C}_1 \vDash_s \text{initialize}(\&e_1); \Rightarrow M_2, \overline{M_2}}}{\mathscr{C}_i \vDash_s e_1 = e_2; \text{initialize}(\&e_1); \Rightarrow M_2, \overline{M_2}}$$

where $\overline{M_1} = \overline{M_i}$ and $M_2 = M_1$ remain unchanged (cf. Fig. 5, 8, Sect. 3.2). Thus, in destination context $\mathscr{C}_1 = (E, M_1, \overline{M_1})$ only M_1 is changed w.r.t $\mathscr{C}_i = (E, M_i, \overline{M_i})$, and in context $\mathscr{C}_f = \mathscr{C}_2 = (E, M_2, \overline{M_2})$, only $\overline{M_2}$ is new w.r.t $\mathscr{C}_1$.

Since $\widehat{C_i} \; \mathcal{R} \; \mathscr{C}_i$, C_i may be separated into $C_i^p \uplus C_i^m$, with $\widehat{C_i} \sim C_i^p$. As a consequence e_2 evaluates to the same value in C_i as in $\widehat{C_i}$: $C_i \vDash_e e_2 \Rightarrow v$. Now, let (b, δ) be the result of the left-value evaluation of e_1 in the destination program: $C_i \vDash_{lv} e_1 \Rightarrow b, \delta$. Define $\lfloor M_1 \rfloor = \text{store}(\tau, M_i, b, \delta, v)$; this store operation is valid for M_i, because the corresponding store is valid in the source memory $\widehat{M_i}$, and $\widehat{M_i}$ is isomorphic to M_i^p, which is a subpart of M_i. Then C_1 can be separated as $C_1^p \uplus C_1^m$, with $C_1^m = C_i^m$ (since the only memory operation was performed in the M^p part), and the isomorphism $\widehat{C_i} \sim C_i^p$ was preserved since the same store operation (up to isomorphism) was performed in both contexts. Therefore $\widehat{C_f} \sim C_i^p$. The representation property, however, no longer holds: indeed (b, δ) now contains initialized data, but this was not reported to the observation memory $\overline{M_1} = \overline{M_i}$. Now, if we define $\overline{M_2}$ by $\lfloor \overline{M_2} \rfloor = \text{initialize}(\tau, \overline{M_1}, b, \delta)$, the representation property is restored: $\widehat{C_f} \; \mathcal{R} \; \mathscr{C}_f$.

Case E_LOGICAL_ASSERT. If s is a logical assertion, the evaluation judgement is $\widehat{C_i} \vDash_s$ `logical_assert`$(p); \Rightarrow \widehat{M_f}$, with premise $\widehat{C_i} \vDash_p p \Rightarrow \text{true}$.

The generated code is: $\{\text{mkdecl}\,([\![p]\!]_p.res); [\![p]\!]_p.code; \text{assert}([\![p]\!]_p.res); \}$. Let C_i be an initial destination evaluation context, and C_1 the context after allocation of $[\![p]\!]_p.res$. By applying Lemma 2 we get $\exists C_2$ s.t. $\mathscr{C}_1 \vDash_s [\![p]\!]_p.code \Rightarrow M_2, \overline{M}$ and $C_2 \vDash_e [\![p]\!]_p.res \Rightarrow int(true)$. The evaluation derivation may then be completed by using the rules for C-like assertion and for code block. Preservation of $\mathcal{R}$ follows from Lemma 1. □

Lemma 1 (Preservation of context monitoring by predicate translation). *Let p be a predicate, $\widehat{C}$ a source context, and $\mathscr{C}_i$ and $\mathscr{C}_f$ destination contexts. If $\mathscr{C}_i \vDash_s [\![p]\!]_p \Rightarrow M_f$ and $\widehat{C} \, \mathcal{R} \, C_i$, then $\widehat{C} \, \mathcal{R} \, C_f$.*

Proof (sketch). The code generated by predicate translation does not modify the observation memory $\overline{M_i}$ (it only reads from it). Moreover, since the only assignments performed in the generated code write to result variables, any modification of the execution memory takes place in the *monitoring* part of the execution memory (M^m in the definition of $\mathcal{R}$), leaving the *program* part (M^p) untouched. This ensures preservation of $\mathcal{R}$. □

Lemma 2 (Soundness of predicates translation) . *Let $\widehat{C} \vDash_p p \Rightarrow b$ be the evaluation of a predicate p; let C, C_i and $\overline{M}$ be such that $\widehat{C} \, \mathcal{R} \, (C, \overline{M})$ and $C_i = (E_i, M_i) = alloc\_vars([\![p]\!]_p.res, C)$. Let $\overline{M_i} = \overline{M}$ and $\mathscr{C}_i = (E_i, M_i, \overline{M_i})$. Then $\exists C_f = (E_i, M_f)$ s.t. $\mathscr{C}_i \vDash_s [\![p]\!]_p.code \Rightarrow M_f, \overline{M}$ and $C_f \vDash_e [\![p]\!]_p.res \Rightarrow int(b)$ (where int() encodes Booleans by mapping false on 0 and true on 1).*

Proof. We prove the lemma by induction on p's evaluation. Base cases of the induction correspond to predicates such as validity, initialization, or term comparison; these cases are proved using a lemma expressing the soundness of *terms* translation, which is very similar to Lemma 2 both conceptually and technically. Therefore, we do not prove it here. To give an intuition of the proof on other cases (logical connectives), we present one of the two cases for disjunction.

Case E_OR2. The considered predicate evaluation is $\widehat{C} \vDash_p p_1 \vee p_2 \Rightarrow b$, with assumptions $\widehat{C} \vDash_p p_1 \Rightarrow false$ and $\widehat{C} \vDash_p p_2 \Rightarrow b$. Let us build an evaluation for $[\![p_1 \vee p_2]\!]_p.code$ (defined in Fig. 10). We start from context C_i as defined by the lemma's hypothesis, and build step by step every memory state the generated code is going through. Let $C_1 = alloc\_vars([\![p_1]\!]_p.res, C_i)$. By induction hypothesis on p_1 (instantiating C_i with C_1), there exists C_2 s.t. $\mathscr{C}_1 \vDash_s [\![p_1]\!]_p.code \Rightarrow M_2, \overline{M}$ and $C_2 \vDash_e [\![p_1]\!]_p.res \Rightarrow 0$ (since p_1 evaluates to false).

Now, let $C_5 = alloc\_vars([\![p_2]\!]_p.res, C_2)$. By induction on p_2, there exists $C_5 = (E_5, M_6)$ s.t. $\mathscr{C}_5 \vDash_s [\![p_2]\!]_p.code \Rightarrow M_6, \overline{M}$ and $C_6 \vDash_e [\![p_2]\!]_p.res \Rightarrow int(b)$. Finally, let us define the following memories and associated contexts:

$$M_7 = store(int, M_6, E_6([\![p]\!]_p.res), 0, int(b))$$

$$C_8 = dealloc\_vars([\![p_2]\!]_p.res, C_7) \qquad C_9 = dealloc\_vars([\![p_1]\!]_p.res, C_8)$$

Let us prove that C_9 satisfies the expected properties for the C_f of the proof goal. Using the above definition, we can derive the following derivation for

$[\![p_1 \vee p_2]\!]_p.code$ (in this derivation tree, for lack of space, the res field is abbreviated to r, $code$ to c, and $\overline{M}$—that remains unchanged—is omitted):

$$
\cfrac{
C_1 \vDash_s [\![p_1]\!]_p.c \Rightarrow M_2 \qquad
\cfrac{
\cfrac{
C_2 \vDash_e [\![p_1]\!]_p.r \Rightarrow 0 \qquad
\cfrac{
\cfrac{C_5 \vDash_s [\![p_2]\!]_p.c \Rightarrow M_6 \qquad
\cfrac{
\cfrac{C_6 \vDash_{1v} [\![p]\!]_p.r \Rightarrow E_6([\![p]\!]_p.r),0}{} \qquad
\cfrac{C_6 \vDash_e [\![p_2]\!]_p.r \Rightarrow \mathrm{int}(\mathbf{b})}{C_6 \vDash_s [\![p]\!]_p.r = [\![p_2]\!]_p.r \Rightarrow M_7}
}{C_5 \vDash_s [\![p_2]\!]_p.c;\,[\![p]\!]_p.r = [\![p_2]\!]_p.r \Rightarrow M_7}
}{C_2 \vDash_s else\_block \Rightarrow M_8}
}{C_2 \vDash_s \text{if } (\ldots) \text{ then } \ldots \text{ else } \ldots \Rightarrow M_8}
}{C_1 \vDash_s [\![p_1]\!]_p.c;\,\text{if}\ldots \Rightarrow M_8}
}{C_i \vDash_s [\![p_1 \vee p_2]\!]_p.c \Rightarrow M_9}
$$

All that is left to do now is to prove $C_9 \vDash_e [\![p]\!]_p.res \Rightarrow \mathrm{int}(\mathbf{b})$. This follows from the definitions of M_7, C_8 and C_9: M_7 results from storing $\mathrm{int}(\mathbf{b})$ at location $(E_6([\![p]\!]_p.res),0)$ therefore $C_7 \vDash_e [\![p]\!]_p.res \Rightarrow \mathrm{int}(v)$; since C_8 and C_9 are obtained by deallocating variables other than $[\![p]\!]_p.res$, this evaluation also holds for C_9: $C_9 \vDash_e [\![p]\!]_p.res \Rightarrow \mathrm{int}(\mathbf{b})$. $\qquad\square$

6 Related Work

More and more languages include a notion of contract. Design-by-contract is one of the main features of Eiffel [22], contracts have been introduced in Java through JML [18] in 1999, in Ada 2012 [1], and the C++ standardization committee considered contracts for C++ 20, although this new feature has been finally deferred to a later standard. In Eiffel, assertions are Boolean expressions written in the programming language. In Ada 2012, it is also the case, but the language has been extended with *quantified expressions* to allow bounded universal and existential quantification. These new expressions have been inspired by Spark, a well-defined subset of Ada, extended to express contracts for static and dynamic verification.

Zhang et al. [33] studies verified runtime checking in the context of Spark: the checks to be performed are however not explicitly stated as assertions in the source language, but are implicit (e.g. division by zero). The authors provide a formalization and proofs using the Coq proof assistant [3]. Cheon [6] formalizes runtime assertion checking of JML, but provides no proof of soundess, while Lehner [19] formalizes the semantics of a large subset of JML and proves in Coq an algorithm that checks `assignable` clauses at runtime. Such clauses are memory properties that do not require memory observation. As our work focuses on memory observation, it is related but complementary to these works. Indeed, in the context of Java and Ada, even runtime checks for out-of-bounds accesses are related to arithmetic inequalities. In the case of C, however, as the bounds of an array are not attached to the array itself, out-of-bound access corresponds to an invalid access to the memory, and is therefore handled in ACSL by the predicate \valid. More generally, the formal verification efforts on languages such as Eiffel, Java, Ada and Spark do not consider such properties because the design of the language prevents most memory problems that can arise in the context of C.

As runtime checking is costly, most approaches rely on an optimization phase, based on static analysis. Zhang et al. propose and verify such a phase. It is also the case for our approach and prior work [21]. Such optimizations are thus related to the verification of static analysis [14].

Our contribution targets the C language, the Frama-C framework, the ACSL specification language and the E-ACSL plug-in. In particular we focus on memory properties. In Frama-C, the plug-in RTE [11] generates ACSL assertions for runtime errors, and the E-ACSL plug-in can translate these assertions into C code. As C++ includes C, in the long term, the work presented in this paper could contribute to the verified compilation of a future standard of C++ including contracts. It is interesting to note that a recent language, Rust, that aims at combining the high-efficiency of C with strong guarantees, does not include contracts. As there is an interest in formally verifying that the type system of Rust indeed provides strong guarantees [15], that the Rust language also provides *unsafe* pointers, and there exist Rust libraries to provide rudimentary support to express contracts, our contribution may be interesting in the context of future iterations of Rust.

We aim at extending the proposed approach to consider a larger subset of E-ACSL, such as support of mathematical integers and their translation using a library such as GMP. It makes the correctness of such a library a related topic [24]. One strength of Frama-C is the use of the common ACSL language by all plug-ins. For the verification of RAC, it means reusing existing formalizations of ACSL designed in the context of the verification of deductive verification [10] for our extended source language. Finally, the E-ACSL plug-in currently does not support the translation of axiomatized predicates. A possible *verified* extension of E-ACSL could be based on the work of Tollitte et al. [30].

7   Conclusion

Runtime assertion checking of memory related properties for a mainstream language like C is a complex task involving various program transformation steps with additional recording of memory block metadata in a non-trivial dedicated observation memory model. This work makes a significant step toward a formally proved runtime assertion checker. We have presented a formalization of the underlying program transformation for a representative programming language with dynamic memory allocation and proved the soundness of the resulting verification verdicts. Future work includes an extension of the present proof to a real-life language like C, as well as a formalization and a mechanized proof of the runtime assertion checker in the Coq proof assistant [3].

Acknowledgment. The authors thank the Frama-C team for providing the tool and support, as well as the anonymous reviewers for their helpful comments. The first author was partially funded by a grant of the French Ministry of Defense.

References

1. Ada Reference Manual, 2012 Edition. http://www.ada-auth.org/standards/ada12.html

2. Barnett, M., Fähndrich, M., Leino, K.R.M., Müller, P., Schulte, W., Venter, H.: Specification and verification: the spec# experience. Commun. ACM (2011). https://doi.org/10.1145/1953122.1953145

3. Bertot, Y., Castéran, P.: Interactive Theorem Proving and Program Development. Coq'Art: The Calculus of Inductive Constructions. TTCS. Springer, Heidelberg (2004). https://doi.org/10.1007/978-3-662-07964-5

4. Blazy, S., Leroy, X.: Mechanized semantics for the clight subset of the C language. J. Autom. Reasoning **43**(3), 263–288 (2009). https://doi.org/10.1007/s10817-009-9148-3

5. Bruening, D., Zhao, Q.: Practical memory checking with Dr. Memory. In: Proceedings of the CGO 2011, The 9th International Symposium on Code Generation and Optimization, Chamonix, France, 2–6 April 2011, pp. 213–223. IEEE Computer Society (2011). https://doi.org/10.1109/CGO.2011.5764689

6. Cheon, Y.: A runtime assertion checker for the Java Modeling Language. Ph.D. thesis, Iowa State University (2003)

7. Clarke, L.A., Rosenblum, D.S.: A historical perspective on runtime assertion checking in software development. ACM SIGSOFT Softw. Eng. Not. **31**(3), 25–37 (2006). https://doi.org/10.1145/1127878.1127900

8. Correnson, L., Signoles, J.: Combining analyses for C program verification. In: Formal Methods for Industrial Critical Systems - Proceedings of the 17th International Workshop, FMICS 2012, Paris, France, 27–28 August 2012, pp. 108–130 (2012). https://doi.org/10.1007/978-3-642-32469-7_8

9. Delahaye, M., Kosmatov, N., Signoles, J.: Common specification language for static and dynamic analysis of C programs. In: Proceedings of the 28th Annual ACM Symposium on Applied Computing, SAC 2013, Coimbra, Portugal, 18–22 March 2013, pp. 1230–1235 (2013). https://doi.org/10.1145/2480362.2480593

10. Herms, P.: Certification of a tool chain for deductive program verification. (Certification d'une chaine de vérification déductive de programmes). Ph.D. thesis, University of Paris-Sud, Orsay, France (2013). https://tel.archives-ouvertes.fr/tel-00789543

11. Herrmann, P., Signoles, J.: Annotation generation: Frama-C's RTE plug-in. http://frama-c.com/download/frama-c-rte-manual.pdf

12. ISO/IEC 9899:1999: Programming languages - C (1999)

13. Jakobsson, A., Kosmatov, N., Signoles, J.: Fast as a shadow, expressive as a tree: optimized memory monitoring for C. Sci. Comput. Program. **132**, 226–246 (2016). https://doi.org/10.1016/j.scico.2016.09.003

14. Jourdan, J.H., Laporte, V., Blazy, S., Leroy, X., Pichardie, D.: A formally-verified C static analyzer. SIGPLAN Not. **50**(1), 247–259 (2015). https://doi.org/10.1145/2775051.2676966

15. Jung, R., Jourdan, J.H., Krebbers, R., Dreyer, D.: RustBelt: securing the foundations of the rust programming language. Proc. ACM Program. Lang. **2**(POPL) (2017). https://doi.org/10.1145/3158154

16. Kirchner, F., Kosmatov, N., Prevosto, V., Signoles, J., Yakobowski, B.: Frama-C: a software analysis perspective. Form. Aspects Comput. **27**(3), 573–609 (2015). https://doi.org/10.1007/s00165-014-0326-7

17. Kosmatov, N., Petiot, G., Signoles, J.: An optimized memory monitoring for run-time assertion checking of C programs. In: Legay, A., Bensalem, S. (eds.) RV 2013. LNCS, vol. 8174, pp. 167–182. Springer, Heidelberg (2013). https://doi.org/10.1007/978-3-642-40787-1_10

18. Leavens, G.T., Baker, A.L., Ruby, C.: Preliminary design of JML: a behavioral interface specification language for Java. ACM SIGSOFT Softw. Eng. Not. **31**(3), 1–38 (2006). https://doi.org/10.1145/1127878.1127884

19. Lehner, H.: A formal definition of JML in Coq and its application to runtime assertion checking. Ph.D. thesis, ETH Zurich (2011)

20. Leroy, X., Blazy, S.: Formal verification of a C-like memory model and its uses for verifying program transformations. J. Autom. Reasoning **41**(1), 1–31 (2008). https://doi.org/10.1007/s10817-008-9099-0

21. Ly, D., Kosmatov, N., Loulergue, F., Signoles, J.: Soundness of a dataflow analysis for memory monitoring. In: Workshop on Languages and Tools for Ensuring Cyber-Resilience in Critical Software-Intensive Systems (HILT). ACM (2018)

22. Meyer, B.: Eiffel: The Language. Prentice-Hall, Upper Saddle River (1991)

23. Nethercote, N., Seward, J.: How to shadow every byte of memory used by a program. In: Proceedings of the 3rd International Conference on Virtual Execution Environments, VEE 2007, San Diego, California, USA, 13–15 June 2007, pp. 65–74 (2007). https://doi.org/10.1145/1254810.1254820

24. Rieu-Helft, R., Marché, C., Melquiond, G.: How to get an efficient yet verified arbitrary-precision integer library. In: Paskevich, A., Wies, T. (eds.) VSTTE 2017. LNCS, vol. 10712, pp. 84–101. Springer, Cham (2017). https://doi.org/10.1007/978-3-319-72308-2_6

25. Serebryany, K., Bruening, D., Potapenko, A., Vyukov, D.: AddressSanitizer: a fast address sanity checker. In: 2012 USENIX Annual Technical Conference, Boston, MA, USA, 13–15 June 2012, pp. 309–318 (2012)

26. Seward, J., Nethercote, N.: Using Valgrind to detect undefined value errors with bit-precision. In: USENIX Annual Technical Conference, pp. 17–30. USENIX (2005)

27. Signoles, J.: E-ACSL: executable ANSI/ISO C specification language. http://frama-c.com/download/e-acsl/e-acsl.pdf

28. Signoles, J., Kosmatov, N., Vorobyov, K.: E-ACSL, a runtime verification tool for safety and security of C programs (tool paper). In: RV-CuBES 2017. An International Workshop on Competitions, Usability, Benchmarks, Evaluation, and Standardisation for Runtime Verification Tools, 15 September 2017, Seattle, WA, USA, pp. 164–173 (2017). http://www.easychair.org/publications/paper/t6tV

29. Sullivan, M., Chillarege, R.: A comparison of software defects in database management systems and operating systems. In: Digest of Papers: FTCS-22, The Twenty-Second Annual International Symposium on Fault-Tolerant Computing, Boston, Massachusetts, USA, 8–10 July 1992, pp. 475–484 (1992). https://doi.org/10.1109/FTCS.1992.243586

30. Tollitte, P.-N., Delahaye, D., Dubois, C.: Producing certified functional code from inductive specifications. In: Hawblitzel, C., Miller, D. (eds.) CPP 2012. LNCS, vol. 7679, pp. 76–91. Springer, Heidelberg (2012). https://doi.org/10.1007/978-3-642-35308-6_9

31. Vorobyov, K., Kosmatov, N., Signoles, J.: Detection of security vulnerabilities in C code using runtime verification: an experience report. In: Dubois, C., Wolff, B. (eds.) TAP 2018. LNCS, vol. 10889, pp. 139–156. Springer, Cham (2018). https://doi.org/10.1007/978-3-319-92994-1_8

32. Vorobyov, K., Signoles, J., Kosmatov, N.: Shadow state encoding for efficient monitoring of block-level properties. In: Proceedings of the 2017 ACM SIGPLAN International Symposium on Memory Management, ISMM 2017, Barcelona, Spain, 18 June 2017, pp. 47–58 (2017). https://doi.org/10.1145/3092255.3092269

33. Zhang, Z., Robby, Hatcliff, J., Moy, Y., Courtieu, P.: Focused certification of an industrial compilation and static verification toolchain. In: Cimatti, A., Sirjani, M. (eds.) Software Engineering and Formal Methods. SEFM 2017. LNCS, vol. 10469, pp. 17–34. Springer, Cham (2017). https://doi.org/10.1007/978-3-319-66197-1_2

Testing for Race Conditions
in Distributed Systems via SMT Solving

João Carlos Pereira[1](✉)[ID], Nuno Machado[2][ID], and Jorge Sousa Pinto[1][ID]

[1] HASLab - INESC TEC & U. Minho, Braga, Portugal
joao.c.pereira@inesctec.pt, jsp@di.uminho.pt
[2] Teradata Iberia, Madrid, Spain
nuno.machado@teradata.com

Abstract. Data races, a condition where two memory accesses to the same memory location occur concurrently, have been shown to be a major source of concurrency bugs in distributed systems. Unfortunately, data races are often triggered by non-deterministic event orderings that are hard to detect when testing complex distributed systems.

In this paper, we propose SPIDER, an automated tool for identifying data races in distributed system traces. SPIDER encodes the causal relations between the events in the trace as a symbolic constraint model, which is then fed into an SMT solver to check for the presence of conflicting concurrent accesses. To reduce the constraint solving time, SPIDER employs a pruning technique aimed at removing redundant portions of the trace.

Our experiments with multiple benchmarks show that SPIDER is effective in detecting data races in distributed executions in a practical amount of time, providing evidence of its usefulness as a testing tool.

1 Introduction

Distributed systems are at the core of a wide range of applications nowadays, namely large-scale processing and storage, service synchronization, and cluster management [18]. Unfortunately, their inherent heterogeneity and complexity renders testing and debugging notoriously hard. As a consequence, bugs often surface in production, hampering the availability of services that are used everyday by millions of people which leads to huge economic costs [28,32].

A recent study has shown that, among the different types of distributed system bugs, *data races* are particularly challenging to find and debug, as they are non-deterministic and rarely manifest [18]. A data race consists in two *concurrent* accesses to the same memory location, where at least one access is a write. Such races in distributed systems typically stem from unpredictable message arrivals that violate the order or the atomicity of the protocols [18,20].

Over the last years, there have been multiple efforts to test and debug data races, although prior work has mostly focused on multithreaded programs [7,10,13,19]. Alongside, there has also been an increasing interest in applying

© Springer Nature Switzerland AG 2020
W. Ahrendt and H. Wehrheim (Eds.): TAP 2020, LNCS 12165, pp. 122–140, 2020.
https://doi.org/10.1007/978-3-030-50995-8_7

formal verification techniques to prove correctness properties of distributed protocols, including the absence of race conditions [9,35]. However, these techniques are not yet suitable for mainstream usage because they require writing lengthy correctness proofs, which becomes a daunting task for complex systems [36].

More recently, Liu et al. proposed DCatch [20], a tool to discover distributed concurrency bugs that operates by employing a *happens-before* (HB) analysis on traces captured at runtime. DCatch was effective in finding races in popular applications, such as Apache Cassandra and ZooKeeper, even when monitoring correct executions. To keep the trace analysis tractable, DCatch relies on static analysis and hints provided manually by the programmer to capture solely events that lead to explicit failures. Despite that, its approach scales poorly, as the experimental results in the paper revealed that DCatch consumes GBs of memory for processing traces with a few MBs.

In this paper, we make the observation that distributed protocols typically involve inter-node communication steps that occur repeatedly along the execution (e.g. the leader election protocol in Zookeeper or the node heartbeats in Cassandra). Such redundant patterns, although useful to accurately understand the behavior of the system, not only produce large event traces that are prohibitively expensive to process, but also typically do not contribute to the occurrence of new data races. We thus believe that removing redundant events from traces can improve the performance and scalability of distributed system testing solutions without compromising their accuracy.

This paper proposes SPIDER, an automated approach to detect data races in distributed systems using redundancy pruning and symbolic constraint solving. Given a trace of a distributed system under test, SPIDER starts by performing a trace analysis aimed at eliminating events that appear recurrently in the execution and whose absence does not lead to any missed races. To this end, we leverage prior work on redundancy pruning for single-machine multithreaded applications [11] and extend it to message-passing systems.

After trimming the trace, SPIDER builds a causality model by encoding the HB relationships between events into a system of constraints over logical order variables. Finally, SPIDER resorts to an off-the-shelf SMT solver to compute the pairs of conflicting events that can run concurrently and, thus, form a data race.

Prior work has shown that SMT constraint solving can be successfully applied to reproduce [12], expose [24], and isolate [23,31] concurrency bugs in multithreaded programs. Alongside, SMT solving has also been employed to detect message races in models of distributed systems that are partially synchronous [33] or written as BPEL processes [5]. However, to the best of our knowledge, this is the first application of SMT solvers for race detection in arbitrarily large traces of distributed executions captured when testing unmodified source code.

We conducted an experimental evaluation of SPIDER using multiple benchmarks with distributed data races. Our results show that SPIDER is effective in detecting the bugs and that our redundancy pruning algorithm dramatically reduces the size of the traces (especially for distributed protocols based on rounds of message exchanges), which is paramount to scale our constraint solving approach. In fact, our redundancy pruning strategy was able to remove between 22% and 48% of the total amount of events in our experiments (Sect. 4.3).

In summary, this paper makes the following contributions.

- We present an algorithm, which draws on prior work [11], to eliminate redundant events from distributed system traces without hampering the race detection accuracy.
- We propose SPIDER, a tool that leverages redundancy pruning and SMT constraint solving for finding data races in distributed systems.
- We assess the performance and effectiveness of SPIDER on several benchmarks and show that our tool is capable of finding distributed races in a practical amount of time, even for executions with thousands of events.

The rest of the paper is organized as follows. Section 2 discusses some background concepts relevant to this work. Section 3 presents SPIDER and details both its architecture and *modus operandi*. Section 4 describes the experimental evaluation of SPIDER. Section 5 overviews the related work. Finally, Sect. 6 concludes the paper by summarizing its main findings.

2   Background

This section discusses some background aspects relevant to this paper, namely the types of data races in distributed systems and Satisfiability Modulo Theories.

2.1   Data Races in Distributed Systems

In general, a data race occurs when two accesses compete for the same resource in a non-synchronized fashion and at least one is modifying the resource. Since there is no causal relationship enforced between the two accesses, their ordering can vary across executions, which in some cases leads to failures.

Addressing data races in multithreaded applications has been the subject of extensive research over the years [7,10,13,19]. Unfortunately, data races in distributed systems are much more challenging than their single-machine counterparts. A distributed system comprises multiple nodes that interact with each other by exchanging messages, therefore concurrency occurs not only at the thread level but also at the node level and in a much larger scale. As message handlers often change the node's local state and trigger additional actions (e.g. sending a new message to another node), the timing in which messages are delivered and processed plays a decisive role in the correct execution of distributed protocols. In fact, most concurrency bugs in real-world distributed systems stem from the untimely delivery of messages [20]. Since those problematic execution interleavings are typically rare, they go unnoticed during testing and only surface in production with serious consequences.

According to the TaxDC study [18], distributed data races can be classified into two categories based on their message timing conditions:

– **Order violation:** An order violation occurs when the correct execution of a protocol in a node N requires that two events e_1 and e_2 run in a determined order (say, e_1 should execute before e_2) but the program code wrongly permits an execution interleaving in which e_2 occurs before e_1, thus causing an error. At one node, order violations can occur due to races between: i) two message arrivals, ii) a message arrival and a message sending, and iii) a message arrival and a local computation. In turn, across multiple nodes, they are caused by races between two message arrivals at different nodes.

– **Atomicity violation:** An atomicity violation occurs when the correct execution of a protocol in a node N requires that a critical region of events, denoted as $e_1, e_2, ..., e_n$, executes atomically but the program code wrongly permits an execution interleaving in which an external event x executes in-between e_1 and e_n, thus causing an error. The error would not manifest if x happens either before or after the critical region.

At one node, atomicity violations can occur due to data races between a message arrival and an atomic local computation, whereas across multiple nodes they stem from races between a message arrival and an atomic global computation.

Figure 2 illustrates several of the aforementioned scenarios of order and atomicity violations, which were implemented as micro-benchmarks for the experimental evaluation conducted in this paper.

We now discuss SMT constraint solving, which is at the heart of our approach to detect distributed data races.

2.2 Satisfiability Modulo Theories

Satisfiability Modulo Theories (SMT) is the decision problem of determining whether a first-order logical formula is satisfiable with respect to a *background theory*. A background theory provides interpretations for function and predicate symbols. For example, the theory of integers T_Z provides interpretations for the symbols 0, 1, $+$, $-$ and $\leq$. It is possible to devise theories to reason about varied kinds of objects, from real numbers to data structures such as arrays [30].

The SMT problem can be seen as a generalization of the SAT [3] problem where, in the place of propositional boolean variables, formulas may have predicates over non-binary variables (i.e. binary-valued functions of non-binary variables) whose interpretations are given by a background theory. As an example, consider the following two formulas:

$$x + y \leq z \wedge z \leq x - y \tag{1}$$

$$x \leq 0 \wedge 1 \leq x \tag{2}$$

Assuming the T_Z theory (also called *Presburger arithmetic*), formula (1) is satisfiable, for example with the assignment $\{x = 1, y = -1, z = 1\}$. In turn, formula (2) is *unsatisfiable* because there is no assignment of variables that evaluates the formula to *true*.

Programs which take as input a set of first-order formulas written in the context of a background theory and determine the satisfiability of the set are called *SMT solvers*. Modern SMT solvers, like Z3 [25], are already capable of solving formulations with thousand of constraints in a timely manner. Nevertheless, there is extensive ongoing research aimed at further improving their performance and features. SMT solvers have been employed in a wide range of applications, from program synthesis [6] to testing and debugging [10,12,23,24,31], as seen on this paper.

3   SPIDER

This section details SPIDER, a scalable approach to detect data races in distributed systems via SMT solving. We start by providing an overview of the solution, then describe the redundancy pruning algorithm and the happens-before SMT constraint model.

3.1   Overview

SPIDER assumes the existence of a trace with events captured from the execution of a distributed system either during testing or in production. We assume that traces contain the following events of interest, already considered in previous work [21,26]:

- **Intra-node thread events:** *fork*, *join*, *start* and *end* events which respectively represent the spawn of a new thread in a node, the termination of a thread, and the start and end of a thread's execution;
- **Inter-node communication events:** events *send* or *receive* representing respectively the sending and receiving of a message through sockets;
- **Intra-node events:** *read* or *write* accesses to shared variables, as well as *lock* and *unlock* events;
- **Message handling region delimiters:** events signaling the beginning and the end of a message handler.

Given an execution trace, SPIDER operates in three steps (see Fig. 1):

1. **Redundancy Pruning:** SPIDER employs a trace analysis to identify patterns of shared-memory accesses and message exchanges that appear replicated in the trace. These events, once removed, do not affect the causal dependencies of the remaining ones. In other words, these events are not relevant to the occurrence of new races and, therefore, can be safely excluded from the trace in order to reduce the size of the search space.
2. **HB Model Generation:** The pruned trace is then used to generate an SMT model that represents the events' logical clocks as symbolic variables and encodes the causality dependencies as constraints over those variables. This way, SPIDER is able to search for races over the entire set of possible logical time orderings of events, regardless of the execution recorded at runtime.

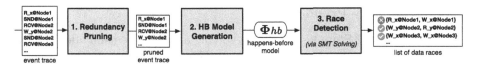

Fig. 1. Execution flow of SPIDER.

3. **Race Detection:** Once the HB model is generated, SPIDER produces a list of potential *data race candidates*. For each candidate, SPIDER then resorts to an off-the-shelf SMT solver to check whether the two accesses can have the same logical clock, meaning they execute concurrently and thus form an actual race. The list of valid data races is output at the end of the verification procedure.

The next sections describe each step in more detail, starting with a definition of the system model and its terminology.

3.2 System Model

For the purposes of this paper, a distributed system is modeled as a set of *nodes*, with at least one *thread* running at each node. Different threads communicate through message sending, with no further assumptions on message losses and network delays. Each thread can be viewed as a sequence of *events* of different types as defined in Sect. 3.1.

SPIDER is able to model multiple distributed execution orderings from the same event trace by leveraging the *Happens-Before (HB)* $\prec_{hb}$ relationship between events. This relationship states that, for two events e_1 and e_2 in the trace, if $e_1 \prec_{hb} e_2$ then event e_1 occurs before event e_2 at runtime [16]. In other words, the $\prec_{hb}$ relation encodes event causal dependencies in a *strict partial order*, which means that it has the following properties: *i) irreflexivity* – no event can happen before itself; *ii) transitivity* – if an event a happens before an event b and b happens before another event c, then a happens before c; *iii) asymmetry* – no event a can simultaneously happen before and after another event b.

The HB relation is commonly captured by means of *logical clocks* (also known as *Lamport clocks*) [16], which are integer values that indicate the logical time in which events occur in the execution. If an event e_1 happens-before an event e_2, then their respective logical clocks $C(e_1)$ and $C(e_2)$ will reflect that dependency: $e_1 \prec_{hb} e_2 \rightarrow C(e_1) < C(e_2)$.

SPIDER casts the problem of assigning logical clocks to events as an SMT constraint solving problem. However, since the time necessary to solve an SMT formulation increases proportionally to its number of constraints, it is of paramount importance to reduce them as much as possible in order to obtain a solution in a practical amount of time. In the next section, we describe how SPIDER employs redundancy pruning to achieve this goal.

3.3 Redundancy Pruning

The performance of SPIDER's constraint solving approach is mainly determined by the number of events present in the trace. Thus, by reducing the trace length, one is able to decrease the time necessary to discover data races. Alas, blindly removing events can affect the causality originally present in the execution and lead to both false negatives and false positives during race detection [11].

To address this issue, we leverage the ReX algorithm proposed by Huang et al. [11], which allows eliminating redundancy in multithreaded traces. In this context, a memory access is deemed *redundant* if its removal from the trace does not hamper the soundness or precision of race detectors.

ReX identifies redundant events using the concept of *concurrential-subsume equivalence*. Let e_i and e_j be two memory accesses made by a thread t, then e_i concurrentially-subsumes e_j when the following three conditions hold:

  i) *Lexical Equivalence:* e_i and e_j originate from the same program instruction and have the same access type (i.e., both are reads or both are writes);
 ii) *Memory Equivalence:* e_i and e_j access the same dynamic memory location;
iii) *HB-subsume:* for every event e_k such that $t_{e_k} \neq t_{e_i} \wedge t_{e_k} \neq t_{e_j}$: $e_k \prec_{hb} e_i \rightarrow e_k \prec_{hb} e_j$ and $e_i \prec_{hb} e_k \rightarrow e_j \prec_{hb} e_k$.

According to this concept, an event is considered redundant if the trace contains one concurrential-subsuming event from the same thread or two concurrential-subsuming events from different threads. ReX's redundancy pruning algorithm thus consists of checking, for each event in the trace, whether it is concurrential-subsumed by other events already in the trace and, if so, the event is eliminated.

To improve the efficiency of the analysis (especially for assessing condition *iii*), ReX computes the *concurrency context* for each thread while processing the trace in a stream-based fashion. The concurrency context of a thread consists in the sequence of *send* and *unlock* events observed up to a certain point. Since these events are the ones generating inter-thread HB dependencies, one can easily check whether condition *iii*) holds for e_i and e_j simply by comparing their threads' concurrency context. If the concurrency contexts match, then e_j is concurrential-subsumed by e_i, otherwise, it is not. We defer further details on the ReX algorithm to the original paper by Huang et al. [11].

Inspired by this work, we have implemented a redundancy pruning strategy that improves the performance of SPIDER's data race detection approach while maintaining its accuracy. Our strategy consists in a sequence of two passes over the traces that filter redundant events.

First, we apply a version of the ReX algorithm adapted to our system's model, namely by augmenting the concurrency context with *fork* events.[1] After this pass, the trace will be left with all but redundant *read* and *write* events.

---

[1] The original ReX algorithm does not take into consideration the existence of *fork* and *join* events signaling the creation and joining of threads.

We then perform a second pass on the trace designed to filter out *redundant message handlers* and *redundant threads*. These two terms can be defined by generalizing the redundancy criterion for a block of events: a block β of contiguous events occurring in the same thread is redundant if the removal of every event in β from the trace does not change the number of unique races detected. This means that, in order to be redundant, β must exhibit the following properties:

i) it does not contain non-redundant *read* or *write* events[2];
ii) it does not contain *send* or *receive* events;
iii) it does not contain *fork* events that spawn non-redundant child threads;
iv) all locks acquired in the block are released within its boundaries.

Based on the definition of redundant block, we can now define a *redundant message handler* as a redundant block that starts (resp. ends) with an event signaling the beginning (resp. the end) of a message handler. Alongside, a *redundant thread* is defined as a redundant block comprising all events of a thread.

Note that the second pass does not remove any memory access nor does it modify the HB relation between non-redundant events. As such, the number of unique data races computed by an HB-based race detector after applying the two filters will not differ from those obtained using the full original trace.

3.4 Happens-Before Model Generation

After pruning the trace, SPIDER builds the HB model, denoted Φ_{hb}, by *i)* representing each event's logical clock as a symbolic integer variable and *ii)* encoding their causal dependencies $\prec_{hb}$ as constraints over those symbolic variables. Considering the types of the events, the Φ_{hb} model can be defined as a conjunction of following sub-formulae:

- **Program Order:** Let E_1 and E_2 be the logical clocks of two events e_1 and e_2 occurring in the same thread context (meaning that either e_1 and e_2 are outside of any message handler or both are inside the same handler). If e_1 appears before e_2 in the trace, then: $E_1 < E_2$.
- **Thread Synchronization:** assuming that $Fork_t$, $Start_t$, End_t, and $Join_t$ represent, respectively, the logical clocks of the creation, beginning, end, and join operations of a thread t, then:

$$Fork_t < Start_t \qquad (3)$$

$$End_t < Join_t \qquad (4)$$

$$Start_t < End_t \qquad (5)$$

- **Message Exchange:** let Snd_{m,l_1} and Rcv_{m,l_2} represent the logical clocks of the events of sending a message m on location l_1 and receiving m on location l_2, respectively. Then:

---

[2] Note that the second pass is performed after ReX, so any memory access existing in the block is guaranteed to be non-redundant. Thus, condition *i)* is automatically satisfied when block β does not contain any memory accesses.

$$Snd_{m,l_1} < Rcv_{m,l_2} \tag{6}$$

Simply put, a message can only be received if it was previously sent.

– **Message Handling:** let $Rcv_{m,l}$ denote the event logical clock for receiving m on location l, and let H_Begin_m and H_End_m represent, respectively, the logical clocks signaling the beginning and the end of m's message handler. Then:

$$Rcv_{m,l} = H\_Begin_m \tag{7}$$
$$H\_Begin_m < H\_End_m \tag{8}$$

Assuming that the handler is the region of the program responsible for processing the message, the first constraint states that a message m cannot be processed before it was received, as m's handler can only begin when m arrives. Moreover, the constraint also guarantees that no other message m' can be processed in-between $Rcv_{m,l}$ and H_Begin_m.

The second constraint ensures that the event signaling the beginning of an handler occurs before the event signaling its end.

– **Mutual Exclusion:** let $Lock_{t,v,l_1}$ and $Unlock_{t,v,l_2}$ represent, respectively, the logical clocks of the lock acquisition and release operations by thread t on a synchronization variable v at locations l_1 and l_2. Then:

$$Lock_{t,v,l_1} < Unlock_{t,v,l_2} \tag{9}$$

Moreover, when different threads compete to execute the same critical region, we need additional constraints to ensure mutual exclusion, i.e., that only one thread at a time accesses the variables encompassed by the lock.

Let P denote the set of locking pairs on a synchronization variable and let (L, U) and (L', U') be any two different locking pairs in P. The constraint encoding the mutual exclusion between locking pairs is as follows:

$$\forall_{(L,U),(L',U')\in P} :\ U < L' \ \lor \ U' < L \tag{10}$$

Solving the constraint model thus consists in assigning an integer value to each symbolic variable (i.e. to each logical clock), such that all constraints are satisfied. In other words, by solving the model, SPIDER is able to obtain a *feasible execution interleaving*, in which events are guaranteed to be ordered according to their happens-before relations.

3.5   Race Detection via SMT Solving

The last step of SPIDER's approach consists in using an SMT solver to identify race conditions. Let (e_1, e_2) represent a pair of *conflicting accesses* (i.e., read-write events to the same variable on the same node, with at least one write), and let E_1 and E_2 be the respective logical clocks of e_1 and e_2. The pair (e_1, e_2) is considered a data race iff it verifies the following *race* property:

$$race(e_1, e_2) \equiv \Phi_{hb} \wedge (E_1 = E_2) \tag{11}$$

The data race property Φ_{race} requires that the logical clocks E_1 and E_2 to have identical values while satisfying all other constraints in Φ_{hb}, which can only occur when the events e_1 and e_2 are not causally ordered. In other words, e_1 and e_2 form a data race because they do not have a happens-before relationship.

SPIDER resorts to an SMT solver to check whether Eq. 11 holds for each *candidate pair* (e_1, e_2). If the solver returns *satisfiable*, then (e_1, e_2) is considered an actual data race. Conversely, if the formula is *unsatisfiable*, then e_1 and e_2 cannot execute concurrently, hence (e_1, e_2) is not reported as a race.

After validating all candidate pairs of conflicting accesses, SPIDER outputs the list with the data races detected in the execution trace. It should be noted that the checking procedure is *embarrassingly parallel*, as each pair can be checked independently from the others.

Handling Intra-thread Data Races. Contrary to shared-memory programs on a single machine, in which data races can only occur in the presence of multiple threads, distributed systems can suffer from race conditions in a single thread. This scenario happens when there is an order violation due to a race between the arrival of two messages processed by the same thread, where at least one of the message handlers changes the node's state (see Fig. 2b for an example).

SPIDER addresses these type of data races in a two-fold fashion. First, it identifies message races in each thread. This is done by applying Eq. 11 to pairs of send events. Let m_1 and m_2 be two different messages processed by thread t and let Snd_{m_1} and Snd_{m_2} be the logical clocks of their sending events. If $race(Snd_{m_1}, Snd_{m_2})$ is satisfiable, then both messages are racing.

Second, SPIDER detects conflicting accesses in the message handlers by computing the intersection of their read-write sets. Let rw_1 and rw_2 be two events belonging to the handlers of m_1 and m_2, respectively, that access the same variable and at least one is to write. If m_1 and m_2 are racing, then (rw_1, rw_2) form a intra-thread data race.

4 Evaluation

To assess the benefits and limitations of SPIDER, we conducted an experimental evaluation focused on answering the following four questions:

- How effective is SPIDER in finding data races in distributed executions? (Sect. 4.2)
- How does the SPIDER's efficiency vary with the size of the execution trace? (Sect. 4.3)
- How does redundancy pruning affect SPIDER's effectiveness and efficiency? (Sect. 4.3)
- Is SPIDER sound and precise? (Sect. 4.4).

Our prototype of SPIDER was implemented in Java in around 1.9K lines of code and is publicly available at https://github.com/jcp19/SPIDER.

In the experiments, we used testing framework Minha [21] to collect the execution traces, and the SMT solver Z3 (version 4.4.1) to solve the constraints. We assumed a timeout of 2 h for constraint solving, after which the Z3 process was killed. All the experiments were ran on commodity hardware equipped with an Intel Core i7-8550U CPU and 16 GB of RAM.

The next sections describe the benchmarks used to evaluate SPIDER and discuss the results obtained.

4.1 Benchmarks

We used the following test cases to evaluate SPIDER's race detection approach.

TaxDC Micro-benchmarks. We designed five micro-benchmarks that were inspired by real-world races on popular distributed systems, namely HBase [2] and Hadoop MapReduce [1], as described in the TaxDC database [18]. These micro-benchmarks contain different types of data races (see Sect. 2) and are

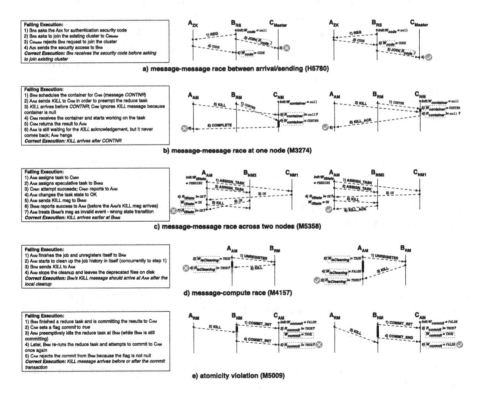

Fig. 2. Overview of the TaxDC micro-benchmarks with distributed data races. Boxes on the left describe the steps of the failing executions, as well as how the bugs are prevented. Message diagrams containing, respectively, the failing and correct executions are depicted on the right of the figure. Data races detected by SPIDER are represented by red dashed boxes. (Color figure online)

publicly available [22], therefore we believe they can be useful for the community to evaluate similar testing tools in the future.

Figure 2 depicts the distributed data races considered in our micro-benchmarks. Following TaxDC's notation, in Fig. 2, each race condition is associated with a label that indicates the real-world bug on which the test case is inspired: the starting letter indicates the system (H stands for HBase, whereas M stands for MapReduce) and the number denotes the issue identifier (e.g. $H5780$ represents the issue 5780 in HBase's issue tracking system). In turn, the node subscript indicates the system component present in the original buggy scenario: ZK stands for ZooKeeper, RS for region server, $Master$ for master node, AM for application master, RM for resource manager, and NM for node manager.

Since the purpose of these benchmarks is to allow evaluating SPIDER's ability to automatically detect different types of distributed data races rather than mimicking real-world workloads and code complexity, we developed them focusing solely on the aspects that contribute to the occurrence of the bug. As such, we represent local state queries and updates respectively as reads and writes on shared variables, and confine the behavior of each node to its message handlers.

a) **Message-message race between arrival/sending (H5780).** B_{RS} attempts to join the cluster by sending C_{Master} a JOIN message. However, since it does so before receiving the security-key message from A_{ZK}, the value null is sent to C_{Master}, thus causing an error.

b) **Message-message race at one node (M3724).** B_{RM} schedules a container for C_{NM} to work on a reduce task by sending the message $CONTNR$. Concurrently, A_{AM} sends a $KILL$ message to C_{NM} in order to preempt the reduce task. Since the two messages race with each other, the $KILL$ message can arrive before $CONTNR$ and be ignored by C_{NM} because no container exists yet (i.e. container = null). This untimely message arrival will cause C_{NM} to later reply to A_{AM} with a task-completion message, instead of the expected ACK.

c) **Message-message race across two nodes (M5358).** A_{AM} assigns a task to C_{NM1} along with a backup speculative task to B_{NM2}. When receiving the success confirmation from C_{NM1}, A_{AM} changes the state of the task to succeeded (tState = OK) and sends a $KILL$ message to B_{NM2}. However, if B_{NM2} manages to finish the task and also send the confirmation message OK to A_{AM} prior to receiving the $KILL$ signal, A_{AM} will consider B_{NM2}'s message as a wrong state transition and throw an exception.

d) **Message-compute race (M4157).** In the original bug, after finishing the task, A_{AM} unregisters itself to B_{RM} and starts removing its local temporary files. Concurrently to the local cleanup, B_{RM} sends a $KILL$ message to A_{AM} for stopping its execution. As a consequence, A_{AM} does not finish removing all files, which might cause storage space issues in the future.

This error is illustrated in our benchmark by means of a flag isCleaning in A_{AM}. In particular, A_{AM} spawns a worker thread to perform the local cleanup. This thread sets flag isCleaning to true (resp. true) at the beginning (resp. end) of the cleaning task. If A_{AM} receives B_{RM}'s *KILL* before its working thread completes the cleanup, an error will occur.

e) ***Atomicity violation (M5009).*** After finishing a reduce task, B_{NM} starts committing the results to C_{AM} (which sets the flag commit to true). Simultaneously, A_{RM} sends a *KILL* message to B_{NM}, thus preempting the task without resetting the commit states on C_{AM}. As a result, when later B_{NM} reruns the task and attempts to initiate a new commit transaction, C_{AM} fails due to a double-commit exception. The error does not manifest if the *KILL* message arrives either before or after the transaction.

Peer Sampling Service. To assess how SPIDER's constraint solving time varies with the increase in the number of events in the execution, we used the implementation of a popular peer sampling service (PSS), named Cyclon [34], already used by prior work [21]. The goal of a PSS is to provide a gossip-based application with a churn-tolerant logical overlay for message dissemination.

Briefly, the Cyclon protocol operates as follows. For each node of the system, Cyclon maintains a *view*, which is a set of references to other nodes in the network associated with a timestamp. To ensure that this view remains consistent with the nodes alive at each moment, Cyclon performs periodic *shuffle cycles*, in which a node A sends a subset of randomly sampled peers to another node B, and receives a random subset of B's entries in return. Upon receiving a shuffle response, A replaces the oldest entries in its view by those received from B.

As noted by Machado et al. [21], the atomicity of the shuffle operation is not guaranteed by the original description of the Cyclon. This scenario happens when a node A requests a shuffle to a node B and, before receiving the response from B, A receives a shuffle request from another node C. As a result, the state of A's view upon receiving the references from B will not be the expected, as it was already updated with the entries sent by C. In the long term, this atomicity violation may generate corrupted views and break the connectivity of the dissemination overlay provided by Cyclon.

We picked the Cyclon PSS to evaluate SPIDER due to the possibility of obtaining arbitrarily large traces simply by changing the number of nodes and cycles used by the protocol. Moreover, we note that Cyclon is an *adversarial example* for race detection, as the message race scenario described above might not manifest in every the execution of the protocol and, when it does, the nodes involved and the cycles in which the violation occurs might vary across test runs.

4.2   Effectiveness

Table 1 reports the results of running SPIDER over traces captured from the benchmarks' execution. The experiments show that SPIDER successfully found all the pairs of racing instructions that caused the concurrency bugs. In particular, for test case H5780, SPIDER detects that there is a data race between the read of and the write to variable *code*, in steps 2 and 4. For M3724, SPIDER finds the data race on variable container. For M5358, SPIDER is able to detect that the state of variable tState can be concurrently modified by the message handlers of

Table 1. Race detection results without redundancy pruning. Column "Actual Races (Unique)" reports the number of data race candidate pairs that were confirmed by the SMT solver (the value within parenthesis indicates the amount of data races with unique code locations). Benchmarks whose names are of the form $Cyclon\text{-}X N\text{-}Y C$ indicate that the trace was obtained from runs of the protocol with X nodes and Y cycles. "-" means that SPIDER did not output any results due to timeout.

Benchmark	Trace size	#Trace events	#Constraints	#Race candidates	#Actual races (unique)	Solving time
h5780	3 KB	15	12	3	1 (1)	<1 s
m3274	3 KB	18	14	1	1 (1)	<1 s
m5358	5 KB	27	19	2	2 (2)	<1 s
m4157	2 KB	12	11	4	2 (2)	<1 s
m5009	4 KB	19	14	2	2 (2)	<1 s
Cyclon-5N-5C	74 KB	420	488	325	121 (1)	<1 s
Cyclon-5N-10C	145 KB	820	1464	1150	481 (1)	1.8 s
Cyclon-5N-100C	1433 KB	8020	104505	101500	49835 (1)	1 h 43 m
Cyclon-10N-5C	147 KB	840	976	650	243 (1)	<1 s
Cyclon-10N-10C	290 KB	1640	2920	2300	969 (1)	7.8 s
Cyclon-10N-100C	2869 KB	16040	6031	203000	-	Timeout
Cyclon-100N-5C	1486 KB	8401	9800	6500	2394 (1)	2 min 53 s
Cyclon-100N-10C	2934 KB	16401	29298	23000	9651 (1)	1 h 03 min
Cyclon-100N-100C	29076 KB	160400	60301	2030000	-	Timeout

C_{NM1} and B_{NM2}. For M4157, SPIDER correctly signals the flag set in the worker thread and the flag check in the message handler as a data race. Alongside, for M5009, SPIDER warns that the write to flag commit on step 2 and the read of the same variable on step 5 are not causally ordered (because they occur on two independent message handlers) and thus form a data race.

Finally, for Cyclon test cases, SPIDER is also effective in discovering problematic data races in the different execution scenarios. We note, however, that all of the races actually refer to the same unique pair of instructions in the source code. The reason why SPIDER reports them individually is that they correspond to events on different nodes and at different cycles. As shown in previous work [11], not all data race candidates with lexical equivalence are true data races.

4.3 Efficiency

We assessed the efficiency of SPIDER's data race detection technique by measuring its time and space overhead, respectively in terms of constraint solving time and trace sizes. To this end, we executed SPIDER with multiple configurations of Cyclon, varying the number of nodes in the system and the number of cycles of the protocol between the values $\{5, 10, 100\}$. The different configurations show how the constraint solving approach scales with the increase in the number of events in the execution and, consequently, the constraints in the

Table 2. Race detection results with redundancy pruning.

Benchmark	#Redundant events	#Constraints	#Candidate data races	#Actual races (unique)	Solving time (speed up)
Cyclon-5N-5C	122 (29%)	196	62	27 (1)	<1 s
Cyclon-5N-10C	296 (36%)	339	99	45 (1)	<1 s
Cyclon-5N-100C	3875 (48%)	2179	135	65 (1)	8.0 s (↓ 777.5x)
Cyclon-10N-5C	207 (24%)	446	173	78 (1)	<1 s
Cyclon-10N-10C	520 (32%)	838	348	149 (1)	<1 s (↓ 7.8x)
Cyclon-10N-100C	7466 (47%)	5180	1028	509 (1)	4 min 44 s
Cyclon-100N-5C	1980 (24%)	4437	1668	753 (1)	30.3 s (↓ 5.7x)
Cyclon-100N-10C	3719 (22%)	11893	6615	3134 (1)	22 min 25 s (↓ 2.8x)
Cyclon-100N-100C	47800 (30%)	47601	350202	-	Timeout

model. Table 1 reports the results of our experiments. The columns of the table indicate, respectively, the benchmark name, the size of the trace, the number of events in the trace, the number of constraints in the SMT model, the number of candidate data race pairs (i.e. the number of pairs of events with conflicting memory accesses in the trace), the number of confirmed pairs of events which contain data races, and the time the SMT solver took to check all candidate pairs.

The results show that, as expected, the constraint solving time increases with the number of events in the trace. From our experiments, it also became clear that the traces contain a large portion of redundant events, varying between 22% and 48% of the total number of events. Table 2 summarizes our observations. The columns of the table indicate, respectively, the benchmark that was run, the number of redundant events and its percentage of the total trace, the number of constraints in the generated SMT model after removing redundant events, the number of candidate data race pairs, the number of confirmed pairs of instructions which contain data races, and the time the SMT solver took to check all candidate pairs. Table 2 shows that removing redundant events before looking for data races can lead to big speedups in the time that the analysis takes. Despite this fact, there's still a *timeout* when SPIDER runs with the largest benchmark (Cyclon-100N-100C). We believe that this problem can be mitigated in future versions of SPIDER by optimizing the number of queries that are performed: instead of determining wether the events are concurrent for all pairs of candidates, we can analyse only the pairs whose corresponding code locations haven't yet been shown to produce concurrent events. Finally, we observe that even though the elimination of redundancy causes a decrease in the number of data race candidate pairs that were confirmed by the SMT solver, the number of data races with unique code locations remains unchanged and thus, no race was missed by removing redundant events.

4.4   Discussion About the Soundness and Precision of the Approach

In this section, we discuss why the results of data race analysis using SPIDER are to be trusted. First, we observe that SPIDER is *sound* in the sense that, given any trace, SPIDER is always able to find all pairs of instructions which lead to data races present in the trace. The analysis performed by SPIDER always terminates because, for each trace, there is a finite number of data race candidates, and the SMT constraints used to encode the causality model, and to find which pairs of instructions are concurrent, are encoded in *Quantifier-Free Integer Difference Logic (QF_IDFL)*, a decidable fragment of first-order logic.

Furthermore, we claim, without giving a formal proof, that redundant events are indeed of no importance for data race detection. As such, the redundancy pruning algorithm does not affect the soundness of Spider.

Assuming that the tracing mechanism captures all relevant synchronization events, no false positives will be reported by SPIDER, i.e. SPIDER will only report pairs of instructions if they can indeed produce non-synchronized (and thus, concurrent) memory accesses. Given that the redundancy pruning algorithm does not modify the HB relation between non-redundant events, it cannot lead to false positives being introduced in the results. As such, the elimination of redundant events does not affect the precision of the results.

It is important to stress that SPIDER should be used with traces captured during executions which exercise as much code as possible from the traced program, since SPIDER can only detect a race between two instructions if there are events in the trace pertaining to both instructions. Alternatively, SPIDER can be used with multiple traces to achieve a considerable coverage of the code of the traced program.

5   Related Work

SMT constraint solving has been successfully employed in the past to test and debug concurrent programs. For instance, CLAP [12] uses SMT solving to replay failing interleavings, MCR [10] and Cortex [24] to uncover latent concurrency bugs, and Symbiosis [23,31] to isolate their root cause.

Prior research efforts have also shown that SMT constraint solving can be useful to find races in distributed systems. However, contrary to SPIDER, these solutions assume that the system is either partially synchronous [33] or modeled as BPEL processes [5].

Like SPIDER, DCatch [20] also aims at detecting distributed concurrency bugs based on an HB model. This work abstracts the causality of events into HB rules and builds a graph representing the timing relationships of several distributed concurrency and communication mechanisms. However, DCatch does not attempt to remove redundant portions of the state space, thus incurring unnecessary slowdowns during the analysis of the trace.

Another approach for testing distributed systems is model checking. Model checkers, such as MaceMC [14], Demeter [8], MoDist [37], dBug [29] and SAMC

[17], systematically explore different execution orderings by permuting message arrivals and injecting node crashes and timeouts. Despite being effective in discovering failures, this approach falls short for large distributed systems due to the exponential increase of the state space [17].

The verification of the correctness of distributed systems can also be achieved through formal methods, typically through soundness proofs based on the notion of *inductive invariant* [9,27]. Coq [4] and TLA+ [15] are frameworks that have been used to build formal models of distributed systems and prove their correctness. Verdi [35] is another verification framework based on Coq, that supports automatic transformation of soundness proofs to assume different fault network models. Verification techniques are useful to prove the absence of errors in executions. Alas, they require a thorough formal model of the system, which may be time-consuming to write and significantly longer than the implementation code.

6   Conclusion

In this paper, we propose SPIDER, a tool that relies on SMT constraint solving to detect data races in execution traces captured during the testing of distributed systems. To reduce the time necessary to solve the constraints and scale to executions with thousands of events, SPIDER employs a redundancy pruning step aimed at eliminating portions of the trace that are not relevant to the occurrence of new races.

Our experiments with multiple benchmarks show that SPIDER is capable of discovering different types of distributed data races in a timely fashion and that our redundancy pruning algorithm is effective at reducing the size of the trace with no consequences to the accuracy of our tool.

Acknowledgements. This work is financed by the ERDF - European Regional Development Fund through the North Portugal Regional Operational Programme - NORTE2020 Programme and by National Funds through the Portuguese funding agency, FCT - Fundação para a Ciência e a Tecnologia within project NORTE-01-0145-FEDER-028550-PTDC/EEI-COM/28550/2017.

References

1. Apache Hadoop. http://hadoop.apache.org
2. Apache HBase. http://hbase.apache.org
3. Cook, S.A.: The complexity of theorem-proving procedures. In: STOC 1971. ACM (1971)
4. The Coq proof assistant. https://coq.inria.fr/
5. Elwakil, M., Yang, Z., Wang, L., Chen, Q.: Message race detection for web services by an SMT-based analysis. In: Xie, B., Branke, J., Sadjadi, S.M., Zhang, D., Zhou, X. (eds.) ATC 2010. LNCS, vol. 6407, pp. 182–194. Springer, Heidelberg (2010). https://doi.org/10.1007/978-3-642-16576-4_13
6. Feng, Y., Martins, R., Bastani, O., Dillig, I.: Program synthesis using conflict-driven learning. In: Proceedings of the 39th ACM SIGPLAN Conference on Programming Language Design and Implementation, PLDI 2018. ACM (2018)

7. Flanagan, C., Freund, S.N.: FastTrack: efficient and precise dynamic race detection. In: PLDI 2009 (2009)
8. Guo, H., Wu, M., Zhou, L., Hu, G., Yang, J., Zhang, L.: Practical software model checking via dynamic interface reduction. In: SOSP 2011 (2011)
9. Hawblitzel, C., et al.: IronFleet: proving practical distributed systems correct. In: SOSP 2015. ACM (2015)
10. Huang, J.: Stateless model checking concurrent programs with maximal causality reduction. In: PLDI 2015. ACM (2015)
11. Huang, J., Rajagopalan, A.K.: What's the optimal performance of precise dynamic race detection? - a redundancy perspective. In: ECOOP (2017)
12. Huang, J., Zhang, C., Dolby, J.: CLAP: recording local executions to reproduce concurrency failures. In: PLDI 2013. ACM (2013)
13. Kasikci, B., Zamfir, C., Candea, G.: Data races vs. data race bugs: telling the difference with portend. In: ASPLOS 2012. ACM (2012)
14. Killian, C., Anderson, J.W., Jhala, R., Vahdat, A.: Life, death, and the critical transition: finding liveness bugs in systems code. In: NSDI 2007. USENIX Association (2007)
15. Lamport, L.: The TLA+ home page. https://lamport.azurewebsites.net/tla/tla.html. Accessed 10 Oct 2019
16. Lamport, L.: Time, clocks, and the ordering of events in a distributed system. Commun. ACM **21**(7), 558–565 (1978)
17. Leesatapornwongsa, T., Hao, M., Joshi, P., Lukman, J.F., Gunawi, H.S.: SAMC: semantic-aware model checking for fast discovery of deep bugs in cloud systems. In: OSDI 2014. USENIX Association (2014)
18. Leesatapornwongsa, T., Lukman, J.F., Lu, S., Gunawi, H.S.: TaxDC: a taxonomy of non-deterministic concurrency bugs in datacenter distributed systems. In: ASPLOS 2016. ACM (2016)
19. Li, G., Lu, S., Musuvathi, M., Nath, S., Padhye, R.: Efficient scalable thread-safety-violation detection: finding thousands of concurrency bugs during testing. In: SOSP 2019. ACM (2019)
20. Liu, H., et al.: DCatch: automatically detecting distributed concurrency bugs in cloud systems. SIGOPS Oper. Syst. Rev. **51**(2), 677–691 (2017)
21. Machado, N., Maia, F., Neves, F., Coelho, F., Pereira, J.: Minha: large-scale distributed systems testing made practical. In: OPODIS 2019. Leibniz International Proceedings in Informatics (LIPIcs) (2019)
22. Machado, N.: TaxDC Micro-benchmarks Repository (2018). https://github.com/jcp19/micro-benchmarks
23. Machado, N., Lucia, B., Rodrigues, L.: Concurrency debugging with differential schedule projections. In: PLDI 2015. ACM (2015)
24. Machado, N., Lucia, B., Rodrigues, L.: Production-guided concurrency debugging. In: PPoPP 2016. ACM (2016)
25. de Moura, L., Bjørner, N.: Z3: an efficient SMT solver. In: Ramakrishnan, C.R., Rehof, J. (eds.) TACAS 2008. LNCS, vol. 4963, pp. 337–340. Springer, Heidelberg (2008). https://doi.org/10.1007/978-3-540-78800-3_24
26. Neves, F., Machado, N., Pereira, J.: Falcon: a practical log-based analysis tool for distributed systems. In: DSN 2018 (2018)
27. Padon, O., McMillan, K.L., Panda, A., Sagiv, M., Shoham, S.: Ivy: safety verification by interactive generalization. SIGPLAN Not. **51**(6), 614–630 (2016). https://doi.org/10.1145/2980983.2908118

28. Popper, N.: The stock market bell rings, computers fail, wall street cringes (2015). https://www.nytimes.com/2015/07/09/business/dealbook/new-york-stock-exchange-suspends-trading.html. Accessed 06 Aug 2019
29. Simsa, J., Bryant, R., Gibson, G.: DBug: Systematic evaluation of distributed systems. In: Proceedings of the 5th International Conference on Systems Software Verification, SSV 2010, p. 3. USENIX Association, Berkeley (2010)
30. SMT-LIB: Logics. http://smtlib.cs.uiowa.edu/logics.shtml
31. Terra-Neves, M., Machado, N., Lynce, I., Manquinho, V.: Concurrency debugging with MaxSMT. In: AAAI 2019. AAAI Press (2019)
32. Summary of the Amazon EC2 and Amazon RDS Service Disruption in the US East Region (2011). https://aws.amazon.com/message/65648/. Accessed 03 Mar 2019
33. Tekken Valapil, V., Yingchareonthawornchai, S., Kulkarni, S., Torng, E., Demirbas, M.: Monitoring partially synchronous distributed systems using SMT solvers. In: Lahiri, S., Reger, G. (eds.) RV 2017. LNCS, vol. 10548, pp. 277–293. Springer, Cham (2017). https://doi.org/10.1007/978-3-319-67531-2_17
34. Voulgaris, S., Gavidia, D., van Steen, M.: CYCLON: inexpensive membership management for unstructured P2P overlays. J. Netw. Syst. Manag. **13**(2), 197–217 (2005)
35. Wilcox, J.R., et al.: Verdi: A framework for implementing and formally verifying distributed systems. In: PLDI 2015. ACM (2015)
36. Woos, D., Wilcox, J.R., Anton, S., Tatlock, Z., Ernst, M.D., Anderson, T.: Planning for change in a formal verification of the Raft consensus protocol. In: CPP 2016. ACM (2016)
37. Yang, J., et al.: MODIST: transparent model checking of unmodified distributed systems. In: NSDI 2009. USENIX Association (2009)

Tool Demonstration Papers

SASA: A SimulAtor of Self-stabilizing Algorithms

Karine Altisen, Stéphane Devismes,

and Erwan Jahier[✉]

Univ. Grenoble Alpes, CNRS, Grenoble INP, VERIMAG,
Grenoble 38000, France
{Karine.Altisen,Stephane.Devismes,
Erwan.Jahier}@univ-grenoble-alpes.fr

Abstract. In this paper, we present SASA, an open-source SimulAtor of Self-stabilizing Algorithms. Self-stabilization defines the ability of a distributed algorithm to recover after transient failures. SASA is implemented as a faithful representation of the atomic-state model. This model is the most commonly used in the self-stabilizing area to prove both the correct operation and complexity bounds of self-stabilizing algorithms.

SASA encompasses all features necessary to debug, test, and analyze self-stabilizing algorithms. All these facilities are programmable to enable users to accommodate to their particular needs. For example, asynchrony is modeled by programmable stochastic daemons playing the role of input sequence generators. Algorithm's properties can be checked using formal test oracles.

The design of SASA relies as much as possible on existing tools: OCAML, DOT, and tools developed in the *Synchrone Group* of the VERIMAG laboratory.

Keywords: Simulation · Debugging · Reactive programs · Synchronous languages · Distributed computing · Self-stabilization · Atomic-state model

1 Introduction

Starting from an arbitrary configuration, a self-stabilizing algorithm [8] makes a distributed system eventually reach a so-called *legitimate* configuration from which every possible execution suffix satisfies the intended specification. Self-stabilization is defined in the reference book of Dolev [9] as a conjunction of two properties: *convergence*, which requires every execution of the algorithm to eventually reach a legitimate configuration; and *correctness*, which requires every execution starting from a legitimate configuration to satisfy the specification. Since an arbitrary configuration may be the

This study was partially supported by the French ANR projects ANR-16-CE40-0023 (DESCARTES) and ANR-16 CE25-0009-03 (ESTATE).

W. Ahrendt and H. Wehrheim (Eds.): TAP 2020, LNCS 12165, pp. 143–154, 2020.
https://doi.org/10.1007/978-3-030-50995-8_8

result of transient faults,[1] self-stabilization is considered as a general approach for tolerating such faults in a distributed system.

The definition of self-stabilization does not directly refer to the possibility of (transient) faults. Consequently, proving or simulating a self-stabilizing system does not involve any failure pattern. Actually, this is mainly due to the fact that, in contrast with most of existing fault tolerance (*a.k.a.*, robust) proposals, self-stabilization is a non-masking approach: it does try to hide effects of faults, but to repair the system after faults. As a result, only the consequences of faults, modeled by the arbitrary initial configuration, are treated. Hence, the actual convergence of the system is guaranteed only if there is a sufficiently large time window without any fault, which is the case when faults are transient.

Self-stabilizing algorithms are mainly compared according to their *stabilization time*, *i.e.*, the maximum time, starting from an arbitrary configuration, before reaching a legitimate configuration. By definition, the stabilization time is impacted by worst case scenarios which are unlikely in practice. So, in many cases, the average-case time complexity may be a more accurate measure of performance assuming a probabilistic model. However, the arbitrary initialization, the asynchronism, the maybe arbitrary network topology, and the algorithm design itself often make the probabilistic analysis intractable. In contrast, another popular approach consists in empirically evaluating the average-case time complexity via simulations. A simulation tool is also of prime interest since it allows testing to find flaws early in the design process.

Contribution. We provide to the self-stabilizing community an open-source, versatile, lightweight (in terms of memory footprint), and efficient (in terms of simulation time) simulator, called SASA,[2] to help the design and evaluate average performances of self-stabilizing distributed algorithms written in the *atomic-state model* (ASM). The ASM is a locally shared memory model in which each process can directly read the local states of its neighbors in the network. This computational model is the most commonly used in the self-stabilizing area.[3]

The SASA programming interface is simple, yet rich enough to allow a direct encoding of any distributed algorithm described in the ASM. All important concepts used in this model are available: simulation can be run and evaluated in moves, atomic steps, and rounds; the three main time units used in the ASM. Classical execution schedulers, *a.k.a.* daemons, are available: the central, locally central, distributed, and synchronous daemons. All levels of anonymity can be modeled, such as fully anonymous, rooted, or identified. Finally, distributed algorithms can be either uniform (all nodes execute the same local algorithm), or non-uniform.

SASA can perform batch simulations that use test oracles to check expected properties. For example, one can check that the stabilization time in rounds is upper bounded by a given function. SASA can also be run in an interactive mode, to ease algorithms debugging. During the simulator development, a constant guideline has been to take,

---

[1] A transient fault occurs at an unpredictable time, but does not result in a permanent hardware damage. Moreover, as opposed to intermittent faults, the frequency of transient faults is considered to be low.

[2] http://www-verimag.imag.fr/DIST-TOOLS/SYNCHRONE/sasa.

[3] To the best of our knowledge, this model is exclusively used in the self-stabilizing area.

as much as possible, advantage of existing tools. In particular, SASA heavily relies on the Synchrone Reactive Toolbox [19] and benefits from its supporting tools, *e.g.*, for testing using formal oracles and debugging. Another guideline has been to make all SASA's facilities easily configurable and programmable so that users can define specific features tailored for their particular needs.

Related Work. Only few simulators dedicated to self-stabilization in locally shared memory models, such as the ASM, have been proposed [11,15,21]. Overall, they all have limited capabilities and features, and are not extensible since not programmable. Using these simulators, only few pre-defined properties, such as convergence, can be checked on the fly.

In more detail, Flatebo and Datta [11] propose a simulator of the ASM to evaluate leader election, mutual exclusion, and ℓ-exclusion algorithms on restricted topologies, mainly rings. This simulator is not available today. It proposes limited facilities including classical daemons and evaluation of stabilization time in moves only.

Müllner *et al.* [21] present a simulator (written in Erlang) of the register model, a computational model which is close to the ASM. This simulator does not allow to evaluate stabilization time. Actually, it focuses on three fault tolerance measures, initially devoted to masking fault-tolerant systems (namely, reliability, instantaneous availability, and limiting availability [24]) to evaluate them on self-stabilizing systems. However, these measures are still uncommon today in analyses of self-stabilizing algorithms. Moreover, this simulator is heavy in terms of memory footprint. As an illustrative example, it simulates the same spanning tree constructions as we do: while they need up to 1 gigabits of memory for simulating a 256-node random network, we only need up to 235 megabits for executing the same algorithms in the same settings.

The simulator (written in Java) proposed by Har-Tal [15] allows to run self-stabilizing algorithms in the register model on small networks (around 10 nodes). It only proposes a small amount of facilities, *i.e.*, the execution scheduling is either synchronous, or controlled step by step by the user. Only the legitimacy of the current configuration can be tested. Finally, it provides neither batch mode, nor debugging tools.

Roadmap. Section 2 is a digest of the ASM. SASA is presented in Sect. 3. We give experimental results in Sect. 4; an artifact to reproduce these results is available in appendix. We conclude in Sect. 5 with future work.

2   An Example: Asynchronous Unison in the Atomic-State Model

We present the atomic-state model (ASM) using the *asynchronous unison* algorithm of [7] as a running example: a clock synchronization problem which requires the difference between clocks of every two neighbors to be at most one increment at each instant.

Algorithm 1. Asynchronous Unison, local algorithm for each node p

---

Constant Input: $\mathcal{N}_p$, the set of p's neighbors

Variable: $p.c \in \{0, ..., K-1\}$, where $K > n^2$, and n is the number of nodes

Predicate: $behind(a, b) = ((b.c - a.c) \bmod K) \leq n$

Actions:

$I(p) :: \forall q \in \mathcal{N}_p, behind(p, q)$ $\qquad\qquad\qquad\qquad\qquad \hookrightarrow p.c \leftarrow (p.c + 1) \bmod K$

$R(p) :: p.c \neq 0 \wedge (\exists q \in \mathcal{N}_p, \neg behind(p, q) \wedge \neg behind(q, p)) \hookrightarrow p.c \leftarrow 0$

Distributed Algorithms. A distributed algorithm consists of a collection of local algorithms, one per node. The local algorithm of each node p (see Algorithm 1) is made of a finite set of *variables* and a finite set of *actions* (written as guarded commands) to update them.

Some of the variables, like $\mathcal{N}_p$ in Algorithm 1, may be constant inputs in which case their values are predefined. Actually, here, $\mathcal{N}_p$ represents the local view of the network topology at each node p: $\mathcal{N}_p$ is the set of p's neighbors in the network. Algorithm 1 assumes the network is connected and bidirectional, so $q \in \mathcal{N}_p$ if and only if $p \in \mathcal{N}_q$. Then, each node holds a single writable variable, noted $p.c$ and called its local *clock*. Each clock $p.c$ is actually an integer with range 0 to $K-1$, where $K > n^2$ is a parameter common to all nodes, and n denotes the number of nodes. Communication exchanges are carried out by read and write operations on variables: a node can read its variables and those of its neighbors, but can write only to its own variables. For example, in Algorithm 1, each node p can read the value of $p.c$ and that of $q.c$, for every $q \in \mathcal{N}_p$, but can only write to $p.c$. The *state* of a node is defined by the values of its variables. A *configuration* is a vector consisting of the states of each node.

Each action is of the following form: $\langle label \rangle :: \langle guard \rangle \hookrightarrow \langle statement \rangle$. *Labels* are only used to identify actions. A *guard* is a Boolean predicate involving the variables of the node and those of its neighbors. The *statement* is a sequence of assignments on the node's variables. An action can be executed only if its guard evaluates to *true*, in which case, the action is said to be *enabled*. By extension, a node is enabled if at least one of its actions is enabled. In Algorithm 1, we have two (locally mutually exclusive) actions per node p, $I(p)$ and $R(p)$.

Steps and Executions. Nodes run their local algorithm by *atomically* executing actions. Asynchronism is modeled by a *nondeterministic* adversary called *daemon*. Precisely, an execution is a sequence of configurations, where the system moves from a configuration to another as follows. Assume the current configuration is γ. If no node is enabled in γ, the execution is done and γ is said to be *terminal*. Otherwise, the daemon *activates* a non-empty subset S of nodes that are enabled in γ; then every node in S atomically executes one of its action enabled in γ, leading the system to a new configuration γ', and so on. The transition from γ to γ' is called a *step*. Usual daemons include: (1) the *synchronous* daemon which activates every enabled node at each step, (2) the *central* daemon which activates exactly one enabled node at each step, (3) the *locally central* daemon which never activates two neighbors at the same step, and (4) the *distributed* daemon which activates at least one, maybe more, node at each step.

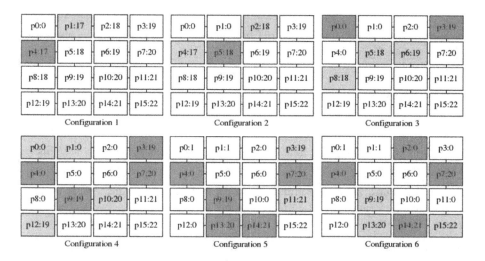

Fig. 1. Five steps of Algorithm 1 for $K = 257$ on a 16-node grid (from SASA). "$pi : j$" means that $pi.c = j$. Enabled nodes are in orange and green. Moreover, orange nodes are activated within the next step. (Color figure online)

Self-stabilization of Algorithm 1. Let p be any node. When the clock of p is at most n increments behind the clock values of all its neighbors, p is enabled to increment its clock modulo K by Action $I(p)$; see, e.g., node $p4$ in Configuration 5 of Fig. 1. In contrast, if the clock of p is not equal to 0 and p has a neighbor q such that $p.c$ is more than n increments behind $q.c$ and $q.c$ more than n increments behind $p.c$, then p should reset its clock to 0 using Action $R(p)$; see, e.g., node $p1$ in Configuration 1. The legitimate configurations of Algorithm 1 are those where for any two neighbors p and q, we have $p.c \in \{(q.c - 1) \bmod K, q.c, (q.c + 1) \bmod K\}$. Algorithm 1 is a self-stabilizing algorithm under the distributed daemon in the sense that starting from an arbitrary configuration, every asynchronous execution of Algorithm 1 eventually reaches a legitimate configuration from which every possible execution suffix satisfies the following specification: (1) in each configuration, the difference between clocks of every two neighbors is at most one (*Safety*); and (2) each clock is incremented infinitely often (*Liveness*).

Time Complexity Units. Three main units are used for counting time: *steps, moves,* and *rounds*. Steps simply refer to atomic steps of the execution. A node *moves* when it executes an action in a step. Hence, several moves may occur in a step. Rounds capture the execution time according to the speed of the slowest node. The first round of an execution e is the minimal prefix e' of e during which every node that is enabled in the first configuration of e either executes an action or becomes disabled (due to some neighbor actions) at least once. The second round of e starts from the last configuration of e', and so on.

These notions are illustrated by Fig. 1. The second step (from Configuration 2 to 3) contains two moves (by $p2$ and $p4$). The first round ends in Configuration 3. Indeed, there are two enabled nodes, $p1$ and $p4$ in Configuration 1. Node $p1$ moves in the first step, however in Configuration 2, the round is not done since $p4$ has neither moved nor become disabled. The first round terminates after $p4$ has moved in the second step. Consequently, the second round starts in Configuration 3. This latter actually terminates in Configuration 6.

3   The SASA Simulator

3.1   SASA Features

This Section surveys the SASA main features. More information is available online as SASA tutorials [16].

Batch Simulations. They are useful to perform simulation campaigns, *e.g.*, to evaluate the average-case complexity of an algorithm on wide families of networks, including random graphs. They can also be used to study the influence on some parameters.

Interactive Graphical Simulations. It is possible to run a simulation step by step, or round by round, forward or backward, while visualizing the network as well as the enabled and activated nodes; see snapshots in Fig. 1. New commands can be also programmed so that users can navigate through the simulation according to their specific needs.

Predefined and Custom Daemons. The daemon, which parameterizes the simulation, can be configured. First, SASA provides several *predefined daemons*, including the synchronous, central, locally central, or distributed daemon; for such daemons, non-determinism is resolved uniformly at random. But, the user can also build its own *custom daemon*: this is useful to experiment new activation heuristics, or explore worst cases. Indeed, the daemon can be interactively controlled using a graphical widget: at each step, the user selects the nodes to be activated among the enabled ones. The daemon can also be programmed; such a program can take advantage of the simulation history to guide the simulation into particular directions.

Test Oracles. Expected (safety) properties of algorithms can be formalized and used as test oracles. Typically, they involve the number of steps, moves, or rounds that is necessary to reach a (user-defined) legitimate configuration. In order to define such properties, one has access to node state values and activation status [16]. Properties are checked on the fly at every simulation step.

3.2   The Core of SASA

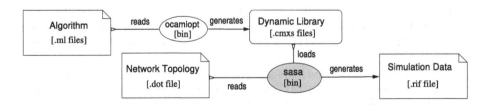

Fig. 2. The SASA Core simulator architecture

The core of SASA is a stand-alone simulator; see Fig. 2. The user has to define both a network and a self-stabilizing algorithm following the API given in Sect. 3.3. The algorithm is written as an OCAML program: the interface has been designed in such a way that the OCAML program implementing the algorithm is as close as possible to guarded commands, the usual way to write algorithms in the ASM. The network topology is specified using the DOT language [12] for which many support exists such as visualization tools and graph editors. The OCAML algorithm is compiled into a dynamic library which is used, together with the DOT network file, by SASA to generate simulation data. A simulation data file contains an execution trace made of the sequence of configurations. That trace also contains the enabled and activated action history. Such traces can be visualized using chronograms viewers.

3.3   The SASA Algorithm Programming Interface

SASA algorithms are defined using a simple programming interface specified in the 37 lines OCAML file, algo.mli, which is presented below.

Local States. Node states are defined by the polymorphic type 'st which can represent any data the designer needs, *e.g.*, integers, arrays, or structures. Nodes can access their neighbor states using the abstract type 'st neighbor (the "'st" part means that the type neighbor is parameterized by the type 'st). The access to neighboring states is made by Function state which takes a neighbor as input and returns its state; see Listing 1.1.

```
type 'st neighbor
val state: 'st neighbor -> 'st
```

Listing 1.1. Access to neighbors' states

Algorithms. To define an instance of the local algorithm of each node, SASA requires:

1. a list of action names;
2. an enable function, which encodes the guards of the algorithm;
3. a step function, that triggers an enabled action;
4. a state initialization function, used if no initial configuration is provided in the DOT file. Indeed, even if self-stabilization does not require it, initialization is mandatory to begin the simulation. For example, pseudo-random functions can be used to obtain an arbitrary initial configuration.

```
type action   = string
type 'st enable_fun = 'st -> 'st neighbor list -> action list
type 'st step_fun = 'st -> 'st neighbor list -> action -> 'st
type 'st state_init_fun = int -> 'st
```

Listing 1.2. The step, enable, and initialization function types

The enable function takes the current state of the node and the list of its neighbors as arguments. It returns a list of enabled actions. The step function takes the same arguments plus the action to activate, and returns an updated state. The initial configuration can be set using an initialization function that takes as argument the node's number of neighbors.

Topological Information. Algorithms usually depend on parameters relative to the network topology. For example, Algorithm 1 uses the number n of nodes. SASA provides access to those parameters through various functions that the algorithms can use.

```
val card: unit -> int
val diameter: unit -> int
val min_degree : unit -> int
val max_degree: unit -> int
val is_connected : unit -> bool
```

Listing 1.3. Some of the topological parameters provided by the API

Example. Listing 1.4 shows the implementation of Algorithm 1 in SASA: notice that we obtain a faithful direct translation of Algorithm 1.

```
open Algo
let n = Algo.card()
let k = n * n + 1
let (init_state: int state_init_fun) = fun _ -> (Random.int k)
let modulo x n = (* for it to return positive values *)
  if x < 0 then n+x mod n else x mod n
let behind pc qc = (modulo (qc-pc) k) <= n
let (enable_f: int enable_fun) = fun c nl ->
    if List.for_all (fun q -> behind c (state q)) nl
    then ["I(p)"] else
    if List.exists (fun q -> not (behind c (state q)) &&
                             not (behind (state q) c)) nl
        && c <> 0
    then ["R(p)"] else []
let (step_f: int step_fun) = fun c nl a ->
  match a with
  | "I(p)" -> modulo (c + 1) k
  | "R(p)" -> 0
  | _ -> assert false
let actions = Some ["I(p)"; "R(p)"]
```

Listing 1.4. Implementation of Algorithm 1

3.4   Connection to the Synchrone Reactive Toolbox

In SASA, a simulation is made of steps executed in a loop. Each step consists of two successive stages. The first stage is made of the atomic and synchronous execution of all activated nodes (1-a), followed by the evaluation of which nodes are enabled in the next step (1-b).[4] At the second stage, a daemon non-deterministically chooses among the enabled nodes which ones should be activated at the next step (2). Overall, this can be viewed as a *reactive* program (Stage (1)) that runs in closed-loop with its environment (Stage (2)), where the outputs (resp. the inputs) of the program are the inputs (resp. the outputs) of its environment.

Thus, we could enlarge the functionalities offered by SASA by connecting our simulator to the *Synchrone Reactive Toolbox* [19], which targets the development and validation of reactive programs. The LUTIN language [23], which was designed to model stochastic reactive systems, is used to program daemons that take the feedback-loop into account. The synchronous language LUSTRE [14] is used to formalize the expected properties. Indeed, this language is well-suited for the definition of such properties, as they involve the logical time history of node states. Such Lustre formalizations are used as oracles to automate the test decision [18]. Finally, RDBG [17], a programmable debugger for reactive programs, provides the ability to perform interactive simulations, visualize the network, and implement user tailored features.

4   Experimental Results

To validate the tool, we have implemented and tested classical algorithms using various assumptions on the daemon and topology. Below, we give our methodology and some results.

Algorithms Under Test. We have implemented the following self-stabilizing algorithms: a token circulation for rooted unidirectional rings assuming a distributed daemon (DTR [8]); a breadth first search spanning tree construction for rooted networks assuming a distributed daemon (BFS [2]); a depth first search spanning tree construction for rooted networks assuming a distributed daemon (DFS [6]); a coloring algorithm for anonymous networks assuming a locally central daemon (COL [13]); a synchronous unison for anonymous networks assuming a synchronous daemon (SYN [3]); and Algorithm 1 (ASY [7]). All these algorithms can be found in the SASA gitlab repository (see footnote 2).

Methodology. For each algorithm of the above list, we have written a direct implementation of the original guarded-command algorithm. Such implementations include the running assumptions, *e.g.*, the topology and daemon. Then, we have used the interactive graphical feature of SASA through the debugger RDBG to test and debug them on well-chosen small corner-case topologies. Finally, we have implemented test oracles to check known properties of these algorithms, including correctness from (resp. convergence to) a legitimate configuration, as well as bounds on their stabilization time in moves, steps, and rounds, when available. Testing all those properties is a way to check the implementation of the algorithms. But, as these properties are well-known results, this is, above all, a mean to check whether the implementation of SASA fits the computational model and its semantics.

---

[4] At the first step, the simulation loop starts in (1-b).

Performances. The results, given in Table 1, have been obtained on an Intel(R) Xeon(R) Gold 6 138 CPU at 2.00 GHz with 50 GB of RAM. We are interested in comparing the performances of the simulator on the above algorithms, according to different topologies. Note that every algorithm assumes an arbitrary topology, except **DTR** which requires a ring network. Hence we perform measurements on every algorithm, except **DTR**. We have ran simulations on several kinds of topologies: two square grids, noted grid.dot and biggrid.dot, of 100 nodes (180 links) and 10 000 nodes (19 800 links), respectively; as well as two random graphs, noted ER.dot and bigER.dot, built using the Erdös-Rényi model [10] with 256 nodes (9 811 links, average degree 76) and 2 000 nodes (600 253 links, average degree 600), respectively. Every simulation, launched automatically, lasts up to 10 000 steps, except for the two big graphs (biggrid.dot and bigER.dot). For these latter, we have only performed 10 steps. For fair evaluation, we provide the execution time elapsed per step (Time/Step). Note that the DFS algorithm has been implemented using two different data structures to encode the local states, namely lists and arrays. This leads to different performances; see **DFS-l** for list implementation and **DFS-a** for array implementation.

Table 1. Performance evaluation of SASA on the benchmark algorithms. Time elapsing is measured in user + system time in seconds or milliseconds, and has been divided by the number of simulation steps. Memory consumption is given in MegaBytes, and has been obtained using the "Maximum resident set size" given by the GNU time utility.

	grid.dot		ER.dot		biggrid.dot		bigER.dot	
	Time/step	Memory	Time/step	Memory	Time/step	Memory	Time/step	Memory
BFS	0.6 ms	10 MB	12 ms	22 MB	2 s	59 MB	2 s	922 MB
DFS-l	0.8 ms	11 MB	66 ms	31 MB	3 s	67 MB	14 s	953 MB
DFS-a	0.6 ms	12 MB	70 ms	112 MB	8 s	7464 MB	64 s	30808 MB
COL	0 ms	10 MB	12 ms	21 MB	18 s	59 MB	7 s	941 MB
SYN	0.4 ms	11 MB	12 ms	31 MB	826 s	898 MB	12 s	1019 MB
ASY	0.1 ms	10 MB	5 ms	31 MB	0 s	67 MB	2 s	953 MB

The results in Table 1 show that SASA can handle dense networks of huge size. Hence, it allows to measure the evolution of time complexity of algorithms using a wide size variety of networks. Note that every simulation has been performed without data file (.rif, see Fig. 2) generation. Indeed, for large networks, this would produce huge files and the simulator would use most of its time writing the data file. For example, a 10 000 steps simulation of **DFS-a** on bigER.dot generates 2 GB of data and takes several days (instead of 15 min). Indeed, 100 millions values are generated at each step. For such examples, being able to generate inputs and check oracles on the fly is a real advantage.

5   Conclusion and Future Work

This article presents an open-source SimulAtor of Self-stabilizing Algorithms, called SASA. Its programming interface is simple, yet rich enough to allow a direct encoding of any distributed algorithm written in the atomic-state model, the most commonly used model in the self-stabilizing area.

In order to limit the engineering effort, SASA relies on existing tools such as, the OCAML programming environment to define the algorithms, DOT to define the networks, and the Synchrone Reactive Toolbox [19] to carry out formal testing and interactive simulations.

In the spirit of TLA+ [20], an interesting future work consists in connecting SASA to tools enabling formal verification of self-stabilizing algorithms. By connecting SASA to model-checkers [5,22], the expected properties specified as LUSTRE oracles could be verified on some particular networks. This would imply to provide a LUSTRE version of the OCAML API to encode algorithms.

Furthermore, SASA could be connected to the PADEC framework [1], which provides libraries to develop mechanically checked proofs of self-stabilizing algorithms using the Coq proof assistant [4]. Since Coq is able to perform automatic OCAML program extraction, we should be able to simulate the certified algorithms using the same source. During the certification process, it could be useful to perform simulations in order to guide the formalization into Coq theorems, or find flaws (*e.g.*, into technical lemmas) early in the proof elaboration.

A   Artifact

We have set up a zenodo entry that contains the necessary materials to reproduce the results given in this article: https://doi.org/10.5281/zenodo.3753012. This entry contains:

- a zip file containing an artifact based on the (public) TAP 2020 Virtual Machine (https://doi.org/10.5281/zenodo.3751283). It is the artefact that has been validated by the TAP 2020 evaluation committee.
- a zip file made out of a public git repository containing the same set of scripts; the differences are that it is much smaller, and that the top-level script uses docker to replay the experiments. The entry also contains a link to this git repository.
- a zip file containing the raw data produced by the experiment scripts via a Gitlab CI pipeline of the git repository.

In more details, the artefact contains instructions to install the necessary tools, to replay the interactive session described in Sect. 2 of the present paper, and to automatically generate the data contained in Table 1 of Sect. 4. The objective of this artifact is only to let one reproduce the results. If you want to learn more about the tool-set, we advice the reader to look at the documentation and tutorials online [16].

References

1. Altisen, K., Corbineau, P., Devismes, S.: A framework for certified self-stabilization. Log. Methods Comput. Sci. **13**(4) (2017)
2. Altisen, K., Devismes, S., Dubois, S., Petit, F.: Introduction to Distributed Self-Stabilizing Algorithms. Synthesis Lectures on Distributed Computing Theory. Morgan & Claypool Publishers, New York (2019)

3. Arora, A., Dolev, S., Gouda, M.G.: Maintaining digital clocks in step. Parallel Process. Lett. **1**, 11–18 (1991)
4. Bertot, Y., Castéran, P.: Interactive Theorem Proving and Program Development - Coq'Art: The Calculus of Inductive Constructions. TTCS. Springer, Heidelberg (2004). https://doi.org/10.1007/978-3-662-07964-5
5. Champion, A., Mebsout, A., Sticksel, C., Tinelli, C.: The KIND 2 model checker. In: Chaudhuri, S., Farzan, A. (eds.) CAV 2016. LNCS, vol. 9780, pp. 510–517. Springer, Cham (2016). https://doi.org/10.1007/978-3-319-41540-6_29
6. Collin, Z., Dolev, S.: Self-stabilizing depth-first search. Inf. Process. Lett. **49**(6), 297–301 (1994)
7. Couvreur, J.-M., Francez, N., Gouda, M.G.: Asynchronous unison (extended abstract). In: Proceedings of the 12th International Conference on Distributed Computing Systems, pp. 486–493 (1992)
8. Dijkstra, E.W.: Self-stabilizing systems in spite of distributed control. Commun. ACM **17**(11), 643–644 (1974)
9. Dolev, S.: Self-Stabilization. MIT Press, Cambridge (2000)
10. Erdös, P., Rényi, A.: On random graphs I. Publ. Math. Debrecen. **6**, 290 (1959)
11. Flatebo, M., Datta, A.K.: Simulation of self-stabilizing algorithms in distributed systems. In: Proceedings of the 25th Annual Simulation Symposium, pp. 32–41. IEEE Computer Society (1992)
12. Gansner, E.R., North, S.C.: An open graph visualization system and its applications to software engineering. Softw. Pract. Exp. **30**(11), 1203–1233 (2000)
13. Gradinariu, M., Tixeuil, S.: Self-stabilizing vertex coloration and arbitrary graphs. In: Butelle, F. (ed.) Proceedings of the 4th International Conference on Principles of Distributed Systems (OPODIS). Studia Informatica Universalis, pp. 55–70 (2000)
14. Halbwachs, N., Caspi, P., Raymond, P., Pilaud, D.: The synchronous data flow programming language Lustre. Proc. IEEE **79**(9), 1305–1320 (1991)
15. Har-Tal, O.: A simulator for self-stabilizing distributed algorithms (2000). https://www.cs.bgu.ac.il/~projects/projects/odedha/html/. Distributed Computing Group at ETH Zurich
16. Jahier, E.: Verimag tools tutorials: tutorials related to SASA. https://verimag.gricad-pages.univ-grenoble-alpes.fr/vtt/tags/sasa/
17. Jahier, E.: RDBG: a reactive programs extensible debugger. In: International Workshop on Software and Compilers for Embedded Systems (2016)
18. Jahier, E., Halbwachs, N., Raymond, P.: Engineering functional requirements of reactive systems using synchronous languages. In: International Symposium on Industrial Embedded Systems (2013)
19. Jahier, E., Raymond, P.: The synchrone reactive tool box. http://www-verimag.imag.fr/DIST-TOOLS/SYNCHRONE/reactive-toolbox
20. Lamport, L.: Specifying Systems: The TLA+ Language and Tools for Hardware and Software Engineers. Addison-Wesley Longman Publishing Co. Inc., Boston (2002)
21. Müllner, N., Dhama, A., Theel, O.E.: Derivation of fault tolerance measures of self-stabilizing algorithms by simulation. In: Proceedings of the 41st Annual Simulation Symposium, pp. 183–192. IEEE Computer Society (2008)
22. Ratel, C., Halbwachs, N., Raymond, P.: Programming and verifying critical systems by means of the synchronous data-flow programming language LUSTRE. In: ACM-SIGSOFT 1991 Conference on Software for Critical Systems, New Orleans, December 1991
23. Raymond, P., Roux, Y., Jahier, E.: Lutin: a language for specifying and executing reactive scenarios. EURASIP J. Embed. Syst. **2008**, 1–11 (2008)
24. Trivedi, K.S.: Probability and Statistics with Reliability, Queuing and Computer Science Applications, 2nd edn. Wiley, Hoboken (2002)

A Graphical Toolkit for the Validation of Requirements for Detect and Avoid Systems

Paolo Masci[1]($\boxtimes$) and César A. Muñoz[2]

[1] National Institute of Aerospace, Hampton, VA, USA
paolo.masci@nianet.org
[2] NASA Langley Research Center, Hampton, VA, USA
cesar.a.munoz@nasa.gov

Abstract. Detect and Avoid (DAA) systems are safety enhancement software applications that provide situational awareness and maneuvering guidance to aid aircraft pilots in avoiding and remaining well clear from other aircraft in the airspace. This paper presents a graphical toolkit, called DAA-Displays, designed to facilitate the assessment of compliance of DAA software implementations to formally specified functional and operational requirements. The toolkit integrates simulation and prototyping technologies allowing designers, domain experts, and pilots to compare the behavior of a DAA implementation against its formal specification. The toolkit has been used to validate an actual software implementation of DAA for unmanned aircraft systems against a standard reference algorithm that has been formally verified.

Keywords: Validation · Verification · Requirements · Detect and Avoid · Formal methods

1 Introduction

Aircraft pilots operating under visual flight rules, including pilots of remotely operated vehicles, have the legal responsibility to see and avoid other aircraft in the airspace [17,18]. In the case of manned aircraft operations, the ability to remain well-clear and see and avoid other aircraft depends upon the perception and judgement of the human pilot. In the absence of an on-board pilot, there is a need for an objective definition of the notion of well-clear that is appropriate for Unmanned Aircraft Systems (UAS). This need has motivated the development of a Detect and Avoid (DAA) capability for UAS that provides situational awareness and maneuver guidance to UAS operators, to aid them in avoiding and remaining well-clear of other aircraft in the airspace [3].

Research by first author was supported by the National Aeronautics and Space Administration under NASA/NIA Cooperative Agreement NNL09AA00A.

W. Ahrendt and H. Wehrheim (Eds.): TAP 2020, LNCS 12165, pp. 155–166, 2020.
https://doi.org/10.1007/978-3-030-50995-8_9

The RTCA[1] standard document DO-365 [15] specifies the minimum operational and functional DAA requirements for large UAS, e.g., those that fly in Class A airspace. DAIDALUS (Detect and Avoid Alerting Logic for Unmanned Systems) [11,13] is an open source software library[2] that implements the functional requirements specified in DO-365. The core algorithms in DAIDALUS, including detection, alerting, and maneuver guidance logics, are formally verified in the Prototype Verification System (PVS) [14]. Similar standardization efforts are currently under way for small UAS. In the case of general aviation, the DAA in the Cockpit (DANTi) concept [1,2] developed at NASA leverages advancements in DAA technologies for UAS as a safety enhancing capability for pilots flying under visual flight rules and who are not receiving Air Traffic Control radar services. The DAIDALUS library can be configured to support DAA capabilities for all those operational cases, i.e., small to large UAS and general aviation aircraft.

DAA systems use aircraft state information, e.g., position and velocity 3-D vectors, to predict a loss of well-clear between the primary vehicle, known as the *ownship*, and traffic aircraft, known as *intruders*. In case of a predicted loss of well-clear between the ownship and an intruder aircraft, an alert level is generated. The alert level is an indication of the severity of the predicted loss assuming the ownship and the intruder do not maneuver. Depending on the alert level maneuver guidance is provided to the ownship to avoid the intruders. Maneuver guidance has the form of *bands*, i.e., ranges of heading, horizontal speed, vertical speed, and altitude maneuvers that are predicted to be conflict free. The determination of the well-clear status is based on a mathematical formula that uses distance and time separation thresholds. The actual values of these thresholds depend on the operational case. For instance, in DO-365, the minimum separation is 4000 ft horizontally and 450 ft vertically. Furthermore, there is a time component that accounts for encounters with a high closure rate. That time component, which is an approximation of the time to closest point of approach, is 35 s. These thresholds define a volume in space and time, called *well-clear volume*, that has the shape of a cylinder elongated in the direction of the relative velocity between the ownship and the intruder [10]. The thresholds for small UAS are smaller and the definition does not include a time component. For general aviation, the thresholds are slightly larger than for UAS.

In addition to minimum operational and functional requirements, DO-365 provides a set of test vectors intended to facilitate the validation of DAA implementations against these requirements. DAA developers may use DAIDALUS, the reference implementation, to *validate* their DAA implementations against the test vectors. If the two systems provide the same outputs for all test vectors, then confidence is gained in the functional correctness of the implementation. While this validation approach based on systematic comparison with a reference specification is conceptually simple, it poses some key challenges. One main hurdle originates from round-off errors in machine arithmetic. In fact, DAA implemen-

---

[1] RTCA was formerly known as Radio Technical Commission for Aeronautics.

[2] https://shemesh.larc.nasa.gov/fm/DAIDALUS.

tations, including those developed for DAIDALUS, use floating-point arithmetic. The verified algorithms used in DAIDALUS, on the other hand, are specified in PVS, and use real arithmetic. When numeric computations are used in control flows, round-off errors introduced by floating-point arithmetic may alter the logic of a real-valued algorithm.

A precise characterization of all possible differences produced by round-off errors is not trivial (see, for example, [16]). In the case of DAA functions, round-off errors can introduce delays in the time when a maneuver guidance is provided, or even change the alert level. The net result is that validation approaches based on simple comparison of numerical values are often *inconclusive*, in the sense that numerical differences between the output of a DAA implementation and that of the reference specification do not necessarily flag problems in the implementation. It is also true that, depending on the considered scenario, small numerical differences may flag actual implementation problems.

To assess compliance with the reference specification, a more empirical method can be adopted in addition to numerical comparisons. The method addresses the following question: *"If domain experts look at the maneuver guidances and alert levels provided by both the DAA implementation and the reference specification, would they judge the information provided by the two systems to be the same?"* The work presented in this paper introduces a toolkit, DAA-Displays, that can be used to answer such an empirical question.

Contribution. This paper introduces a toolkit, DAA-Displays, for the validation of DAA implementations. The toolkit can be used by software developers to validate a DAA implementation against a reference specification. It can also be used by domain experts that design and develop DAA requirements for operational concepts, to validate DAA requirements. The toolkit is freely available on GitHub[3] under the NASA Open Source License Agreement.

2 DAA-Displays

DAA-Displays is a graphical toolkit for the design and analysis of DAA implementations and requirements. The toolkit provides three main functionalities:

1. **Rapid prototyping** of cockpit displays with DAA functions;
2. **Split-view simulations** for the validation of DAA implementations against reference specifications;
3. **3D simulations** of flight scenarios with aircraft using DAA functions.

2.1 Rapid Prototyping

The rapid prototyping functionalities allow formal methods experts to create realistic simulations suitable to discuss DAA algorithms with a multi-disciplinary team of developers. This feature is particularly useful when executable formal

---

[3] https://github.com/nasa/daa-displays.

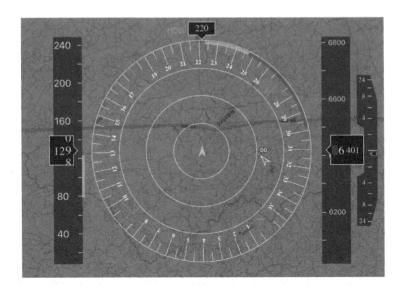

Fig. 1. DAA cockpit display. (Color figure online)

specifications of DAA functional requirements are available. In this case, DAA-Displays enables the visualization of the behavior of the formal specifications on concrete flight scenarios. This way, team members who may not be familiar with formal methods can get a better understanding of the type of alerting and maneuver guidance provided by a DAA logic.

An example prototype used for this purpose is in Fig. 1. This prototype was created with the DAA-Displays toolkit to discuss different DAA configurations with domain experts and pilots. The prototype reproduces the look and feel of a real cockpit display. It includes the following elements:

– An *interactive map* showing the position and heading of the ownship in the airspace (the blue chevron at the center of the map) as well as the position and heading of traffic aircraft (the other chevrons in the map) relative to the ownship. Color-coded chevrons are used to denote alert levels. These colors are specified in standard documents. For example, in DO-365, a yellow chevron denotes a *corrective* alert level between the ownship and the aircraft. The color red denotes a *warning* alert level. Labels next to the chevrons show the relative altitude of the aircraft with respect to the ownship in hundreds of feet, e.g., 00 indicates co-altitude.

– A *compass* over the map indicates the heading of the ownship. Heading maneuver guidance is displayed on the compass. For example, the yellow and red bands shown on the compass in Fig. 1 indicate that the current heading, 220°, is conflict free, but a small change to the right will potentially create a conflict with the traffic aircraft. Similar to alert levels, these bands are color-coded, where yellow denotes a corrective maneuver and red denotes a warning maneuver. According to DAA requirements, bands and alert colors should correspond in the sense that if a traffic aircraft is represented by a chevron of a certain color, there should be a band, in the current trajectory of the aircraft, of the same or higher level, e.g., warning is higher than corrective. In Fig. 1, if the ownship maneuvers to the right, e.g., 230°, the traffic aircraft becomes yellow. If the ownship maneuvers to 260°, the traffic aircraft becomes red.

- *Tape indicators* at the two sides of the display provide information for airspeed (indicator on the left) in knots, altitude in feet (large indicator on the right), and vertical speed (small indicator on the right) in feet per minute of the ownship. Maneuver guidance involving change of airspeed, altitude, and vertical speed are represented by colored bands over these indicators. For example, the yellow band shown in Fig. 1 for the airspeed indicator states that airspeeds in the range 80 to 120 knots would create a potential conflict with the traffic aircraft.

The display elements described above are available in the toolkit in the form of a library of widgets. Additional details on the full set of widgets available in the library are provided in the tool documentation.[4]

2.2 Split-View Simulations

Split-view simulations can be used to visually and systematically compare the output of two DAA logics on the same encounter. The outputs can be from different implementations and executable formal models, or from the same implementation/formal model but with different configuration parameters.

An example split-view simulation used for this purpose is shown in Fig. 2. The view includes the following elements:

- *Cockpit displays* show alert levels and maneuver guidance by two DAA implementations for a given encounter and selected configurations at a given moment in time.
- *Spectrogram plots* show alert levels and maneuver guidance as they vary with time; the x-axis in each plot represents time and the y-axis indicates alert levels and maneuver guidance ranges.

The cockpit displays include information about the flight scenarios but focus on single time instants. Spectrogram plots, on the other hand, focus on the temporal behavior of the DAA logics, and give insights on the evolution of alert levels and maneuver guidance over time for a given encounter. For example, with reference to Fig. 2, visual inspection of the plot diagrams allows one to confirm that the two DAA implementations under analysis generate maneuver guidance that, judged by a domain expert, are "sufficiently similar," even though the numerical values produced by the two implementations are slightly different in all time instants (as highlighted by the yellow markers at the bottom of the plots).

By inspecting the plot diagrams in Fig. 2, one can also notice a delay in changing a red alert to a yellow alert at about 75 s. The relevance of these kinds

---

[4] http://shemesh.larc.nasa.gov/fm/DAA-Displays.

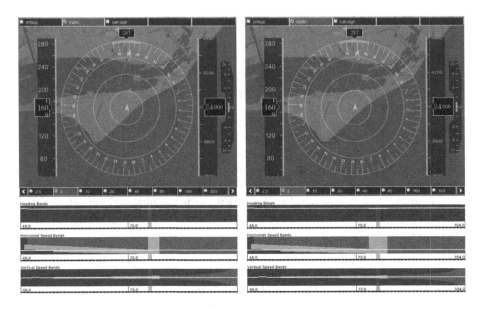

Fig. 2. Example split-view simulation created with DAA-Displays. (Color figure online)

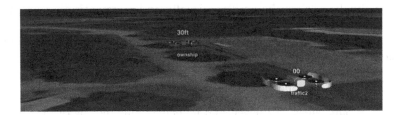

Fig. 3. Example 3D simulation created with DAA-Displays.

of differences may need careful assessment, and typically involves engaging with pilots or DAA designers. This assessment can be carried out with this same split view simulation, as the cockpit displays embedded in the view show the flight scenario in a form that can be understood by both pilots and DAA designers. The simulation is interactive, therefore one can easily jump to specific time instants, and play back fragments of the scenario that are deemed important for the assessment.

2.3   3D Simulations

The 3D simulation capability of the toolkit moves the focus of the analysis from a cockpit-centric view to a scenario-centric view that includes the wider airspace around the ownship. The viewport can be adjusted by tilting, panning, and zooming the view. This capability can be used by developers to gain a better

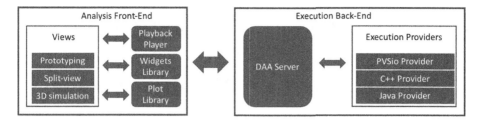

Fig. 4. Architecture of the DAA-displays toolkit.

understanding of spatial information on the trajectories followed by the ownship and traffic aircraft in a given scenario. This is useful, e.g., when assessing DAA algorithms with computer-generated flight scenarios, as this view provides a tangible idea of what the scenario is about.

An example 3D simulation realized to examine a computer-generated flight scenario is showed in Fig. 3. It includes two drones flying over a terrain. The ownship is flying at an altitude of 30 feet. The other drone is following the ownship. The two drones are at the same altitude.

3   Architecture

The architecture of the toolkit is shown in Fig. 4. Three main *views* are used to present the functionalities of the toolkit to developers. Underneath, a number of components are used to implement the functionalities of the views. These components can be customized and reused to create new views. A client-server architecture is used to create a separation of concerns between visual components necessary for interactive analysis of DAA functions, and functional components necessary for the execution of DAA specifications and implementations.

Analysis Front-End. The analysis front-end constitutes the client side of the architecture. It builds on Web technologies, as this makes it easier to deploy on different platforms, including tablets and mobile devices. The front-end element is implemented in TypeScript, a strict superset of JavaScript annotated with type information. This element includes three main reusable components:

- A *playback player* providing interactive controls for navigating simulation scenarios (e.g., jump to specific time instants and playback of scenarios);
- A *widgets library* containing a series of interactive display elements that can be used to assemble realistic cockpit display simulations;
- A *plot library* providing functionalities for creating interactive plots suitable for rendering alerts and maneuver guidance computed by a DAA implementation over time.

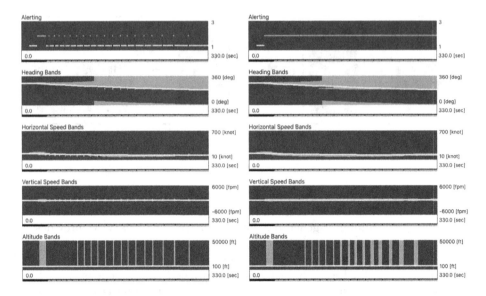

Fig. 5. Spectrogram plots for the analysis of alert flickering.

Execution Back-End. The execution back-end includes two main components:

- A *DAA Server* implementing communication mechanisms necessary to exchange simulation events and data with the analysis front-end;
- An array of *Execution Providers* designed to connect the DAA Server to the native execution environments necessary for the evaluation of DAA specifications and implementations. Each provider implements a standard interface that enables the communication between a given execution environment and the DAA Server. It also incorporates functions for automatic testing of properties that should always be true during the execution of DAA specifications and implementations.

4   Use Cases

The toolkit is currently used to support the development of NASA's DANTi concept [1,2] and the development of operational and functional requirements for large UAS in landing and departing operations. These latter requirements are being defined by RTCA Special Committee 228 and will be included in the upcoming revision of DO-365. Example analyses and findings are discussed in the remainder of this section.

Alert Flickering. A number of parameters can be used to configure when and how alerting and maneuver guidance are computed in DAIDALUS. The toolkit was used to gather additional insights on corner cases identified for certain configurations. An example corner case relates to *alert flickering*, i.e., situations where an alert level intermittently changes from one second to the next. This unintended behavior has been detected in certain scenarios for specific configurations.

Split-view simulations proved useful for the identification of these problems and for the development of possible solutions. In particular, spectrogram plots helped with the identification of flickering in alert levels and spikes in maneuver guidance. An example split-view simulation carried out to evaluate a DAA algorithm providing a possible solution to alert flickering is given in Fig. 5. The simulation shows alerts and bands computed by the original algorithm (diagrams on the left-hand side of the figure) against those computed by a new algorithm that uses hysteresis (diagrams on the right side). As it can be seen in the *Alerting* plot (first plot from the top), alerts are not toggling in the new algorithm. This solution, however, does not mitigate all problems. In fact, altitude bands are still toggling—this can be easily seen from the spikes in the altitude bands plot at the bottom of Fig. 5.

Quick identification of these kinds of shortcomings at the early stage of design of new algorithms is key to speed up development. The sheer use of simulation and visualization technologies was sufficient to identify this issue on the spot. It can be argued that this behavior would have been eventually discovered with formal proofs. However, in this particular case, flickering is caused by small numerical errors in the computation of alerts and maneuver guidance. These kinds of errors are difficult to find and fix in a formal setting, as they often require floating point round-off error analysis.

DANTi Display. The prototyping capabilities of the toolkit are currently being used to support the development of a cockpit display for the DANTi concept. Different prototypes have been developed in rapid succession to explore display layouts and functionalities.

The initial DANTi prototype is shown in Fig. 1. The new version introduces new visual elements on the display for changing the zoom level of the map (buttons at the bottom of the display) and for selecting the level of details shown for traffic information (buttons at the top of the display). Future versions, currently under development, include rendering of virtual regions in the airspace (geofences) as well as aircraft trajectories. All these prototypes can be deployed on portable electronic flight bags that can be carried by pilots and can be employed for user evaluations, e.g., to perform acceptability studies where pilots are asked to assess the utility of the display in enhancing their see-and-avoid capabilities.

Since the prototypes created with DAA-Displays can be driven by formal specifications this opens the possibility to the use of formal models directly in user evaluations, removing the burden of creating implementations that mimic the formal specifications.

5   Related Work

PVSio-web [9] is a formal methods framework for modeling and analysis of interactive systems. That framework has been extensively used for the analysis of medical devices [8]. The toolkit presented in this work builds on experiences with developing and using that framework. The main design aspect inherited from PVSio-web is the architecture for linking interactive prototypes to executable formal specifications. New design concepts are introduced in DAA-Displays that are not present in PVSio-web such as split-view simulation components, a widgets library of cockpit display elements, and 3D visualization capabilities. SCADE Displays [7] is a prototyping tool for cockpit displays. The tool can be used to create cockpit display prototypes suitable to visualize maneuver recommendations. However, mechanisms are not provided for linking the prototype to formal specifications. SCR [6] is a toolset for the analysis of software requirements. Prototyping functionalities are supported, and the prototypes can be linked to executable formal models. However, SCR does not support split-view simulations facilitating systematic comparison of different implementations. PVSioChecker [5] and MINERVA [12] are formal methods tools for comparative analysis of PVS specifications and software code. These tools, however, focus on checking *numerical differences* between the output produced by the implementation and the specification. As argued in this paper, this comparison method is often inconclusive because of round-off errors.

Related to DAA algorithms, a comparative analysis between DAIDALUS and ACAS-Xu, another well-known DAA algorithm for UAS, is presented in [4]. In that work, plot diagrams similar to those used in DAA-Displays are employed to present the results of the analysis. The development of analysis tools was, however, not the main focus of their work. While some tools may have been developed, they are not publicly available.

6 Conclusion

A toolkit, called DAA-Displays, has been presented that enables a systematic comparison between DAA software implementations and reference specifications. Because of round-off errors introduced in software implementations, such comparison cannot usually be done by checking numerical differences. The toolkit provides specialized front-end views that enable comparison by simple visual inspection of plot diagrams and interactive display prototypes. Future aspects that will be incorporated into the toolkit include integration with hardware-in-the-loop simulation tools for coupling simulations with hardware modules.

References

1. Carreño, V., Consiglio, M., Muñoz, C.: Analysis and preliminary results of a concept for detect and avoid in the cockpit. In: Proceedings of the 38th Digital Avionics Systems Conference (DASC 2019), San Diego, CA, US (September 2019)
2. Chamberlain, J.P., Consiglio, M.C., Muñoz, C.: DANTi: detect and avoid in the cockpit. In: 17th AIAA Aviation Technology, Integration, and Operations Conference, p. 4491 (2017). https://doi.org/10.2514/6.2017-4491

3. Cook, S.P., Brooks, D., Cole, R., Hackenberg, D., Raska, V.: Defining well clear for unmanned aircraft systems. In: Proceedings of the 2015 AIAA Infotech @ Aerospace Conference. No. AIAA-2015-0481, Kissimmee, Florida (January 2015). https://doi.org/10.2514/6.2015-0481

4. Davies, J.T., Wu, M.G.: Comparative analysis of ACAS-Xu and DAIDALUS detect-and-avoid systems. Tech. rep. (2018). https://ntrs.nasa.gov/search.jsp?R=20180001564

5. Dutle, A.M., Muñoz, C.A., Narkawicz, A.J., Butler, R.W.: Software validation via model animation. In: Blanchette, J.C., Kosmatov, N. (eds.) TAP 2015. LNCS, vol. 9154, pp. 92–108. Springer, Cham (2015). https://doi.org/10.1007/978-3-319-21215-9_6

6. Heitmeyer, C., Kirby, J., Labaw, B., Bharadwaj, R.: SCR: a toolset for specifying and analyzing software requirements. In: Hu, A.J., Vardi, M.Y. (eds.) CAV 1998. LNCS, vol. 1427, pp. 526–531. Springer, Heidelberg (1998). https://doi.org/10.1007/BFb0028775

7. Le Sergent, T.: SCADE: a comprehensive framework for critical system and software engineering. In: Ober, I., Ober, I. (eds.) SDL 2011. LNCS, vol. 7083, pp. 2–3. Springer, Heidelberg (2011). https://doi.org/10.1007/978-3-642-25264-8_2

8. Masci, P., Oladimeji, P., Curzon, P., Thimbleby, H.: Using PVSio-web to demonstrate software issues in medical user interfaces. In: Huhn, M., Williams, L. (eds.) FHIES/SEHC - 2014. LNCS, vol. 9062, pp. 214–221. Springer, Cham (2017). https://doi.org/10.1007/978-3-319-63194-3_14

9. Masci, P., Oladimeji, P., Zhang, Y., Jones, P., Curzon, P., Thimbleby, H.: PVSio-web 2.0: joining PVS to HCI. In: Kroening, D., Păsăreanu, C.S. (eds.) CAV 2015. LNCS, vol. 9206, pp. 470–478. Springer, Cham (2015). https://doi.org/10.1007/978-3-319-21690-4_30

10. Muñoz, C., Narkawicz, A., Chamberlain, J., Consiglio, M., Upchurch, J.: A family of well-clear boundary models for the integration of UAS in the NAS. In: Proceedings of the 14th AIAA Aviation Technology, Integration, and Operations (ATIO) Conference. No. AIAA-2014-2412, Georgia, Atlanta, USA (June 2014). https://doi.org/10.2514/6.2014-2412

11. Muñoz, C., Narkawicz, A., Hagen, G., Upchurch, J., Dutle, A., Consiglio, M.: DAIDALUS: detect and avoid alerting logic for unmanned systems. In: Proceedings of the 34th Digital Avionics Systems Conference (DASC 2015), Prague, Czech Republic (September 2015). https://doi.org/10.1109/DASC.2015.7311421

12. Narkawicz, A., Muñoz, C., Dutle, A.: The MINERVA software development process. In: Shankar, N., Dutertre, B. (eds.) Automated Formal Methods, vol. 5, pp. 93–108. Kalpa Publications in Computing. EasyChair (2018)

13. Narkawicz, A., Muñoz, C., Dutle, A.: Sensor uncertainty mitigation and dynamic well clear volumes in DAIDALUS. In: Proceedings of the 37th Digital Avionics Systems Conference (DASC 2018), London, England, UK (September 2018)

14. Owre, S., Rushby, J.M., Shankar, N.: PVS: a prototype verification system. In: Kapur, D. (ed.) CADE 1992. LNCS, vol. 607, pp. 748–752. Springer, Heidelberg (1992). https://doi.org/10.1007/3-540-55602-8_217

15. RTCA SC-1228: RTCA-DO-365, Minimum Operational Performance Standards for Detect and Avoid (DAA) Systems (May 2017)

16. Titolo, L., Muñoz, C.A., Feliú, M.A., Moscato, M.M.: Eliminating unstable tests in floating-point programs. In: Mesnard, F., Stuckey, P.J. (eds.) LOPSTR 2018. LNCS, vol. 11408, pp. 169–183. Springer, Cham (2019). https://doi.org/10.1007/978-3-030-13838-7_10

17. US Code of Federal Regulations: Title 14 Aeronautics and Space; Part 91 General operating and fight rules; Section 111 (1967)
18. US Code of Federal Regulations: Title 14 Aeronautics and Space; Part 91 General operating and fight rules; Section 113 (1967)

Short Paper

ScAmPER: Generating Test Suites to Maximise Code Coverage in Interactive Fiction Games

Martin Mariusz Lester[✉] iD

University of Reading, Reading, UK
m.lester@reading.ac.uk

Abstract. We present ScAmPER, a tool that generates test suites that maximise coverage for a class of interactive fiction computer games from the early 1980s. These games customise a base game engine with scripts written in a simple language. The tool uses a heuristic-guided search to evaluate whether these lines of code can in fact be executed during gameplay and, if so, outputs a sequence of game inputs that achieves this. Equivalently, the tool can be seen as attempting to generate a set of test cases that maximises coverage of the scripted code. The tool also generates a visualisation of the search process.

Keywords: Reachability · Coverage · Explicit state · Interactive fiction

1 Introduction

A common complaint concerning tools in automated verification is that they are inadequate for handling the complex software of today, written in modern programming languages. What about the software of yesterday?

Interactive fiction or *text adventure* games are a genre of computer game that peaked in popularity in the 1980s, although a small but active community continues to create and play new games. The games take the form of a textual dialogue between a player, who gives commands, and the computer, which executes the commands and describes their effect in a game world.

These games are conceptually easy to understand, but making progress within them often involves a mixture of high-level planning (such as deciding in which order to solve in-game puzzles) and low-level execution (such as moving objects to specific locations). For this reason, they present an appealing case study for the application of automated verification tools.

An occasional complaint concerning research in automated verification is that tools are sometimes benchmarked either against large, inaccessible, incomprehensible pieces of commercial software, or against unrealistic toy examples that have been chosen to showcase the strengths of a tool. Using older software as a benchmark addresses some of these concerns, as while it is still covered by

© Springer Nature Switzerland AG 2020
W. Ahrendt and H. Wehrheim (Eds.): TAP 2020, LNCS 12165, pp. 169–179, 2020.
https://doi.org/10.1007/978-3-030-50995-8_10

copyright, it is often freely available and small enough to be comprehensible, yet still realistic.

In terms of implementation detail, two aspects of interactive fiction games make them relevant to modern software. Firstly, the structure of an interpreter loop, which is used to execute scripted actions in many games, is commonly used in software that features scripting. Secondly, the pattern of repeatedly reading user input and responding by updating internal state or occasionally triggering events is also used in GUI applications and some control software.

We investigated whether tools from automated verification and formal methods could be used to explore, test and solve interactive fiction games, considering specifically the Scott Adams Grand Adventures (SAGA) series. When we discovered that they were unsuccessful, we wrote a specialised tool to tackle this problem.

Our tool, ScAmPER (Scott Adams exPlicitly Evaluating Reachability), is an explicit-state on-the-fly model checker that uses a heuristic-guided search to determine whether certain lines of script code within these games are reachable. When it finds· that they are, it outputs a sequence of game inputs to witness this. Equivalently, this sequence of game inputs is a test for the reached line of script code. Taken together, these tests form a suite that aims to maximise both branch coverage and modified condition/decision coverage (MC/DC) of the script code. In addition, the tool generates a visualisation of the search process. The tool is available online [3,9].

Appendix A gives some background on SAGA games. Section 2 outlines our initial attempts to analyse them with existing tools. Section 3 demonstrates how our tool works, describes how it works and evaluates its performance. We consider related work on interactive fiction games and more generally in Sect. 4, concluding with lessons learned and suggestions for future work in Sect. 5.

2   Preliminary Investigation

We thought it was plausible to use automated tools on interactive fiction games for two reasons. Firstly, measured by number of player actions, solutions to interactive fiction games are often relatively short. A game might be solvable with a hundred commands or under, compared with thousands of joystick inputs for an arcade game. This limits the depth of search tree that must be considered, although the range of possible commands means the branching factor may be large. Secondly, many interactive fiction games published by the same company consisted of a generic interpreter and a game-specific data file. Many of these interpreters have now been rewritten in C, allowing the games to be played on modern computers. This meant we could use off-the-shelf tools for C programs.

We initially attempted to use off-the-shelf tools for C programs to determine reachability of scripted events within a game. Bounding loops with constants allowed bounded model checkers such as CBMC to unroll them. We replaced the input of commands with a nondeterministic choice of a sequence of verb/noun pairs and tested reachability by adding an assertion that a line of script would not be executed. Then, a counterexample trace would give the inputs necessary to reach the assertion. However, neither of the tools we tested could produce plays of the game longer than a single command. We concluded that this was because a single command involved executing every line of script, each of which executed the script interpreter, meaning that the unrolled straight-line code could be tens of thousands of lines per game command.

We also tried using the fuzzing tool American Fuzzy Lop (AFL). While its genetic algorithms generated plays of reasonable length, most of the commands in them did not progress through the game. Movement commands or commands to pick up or drop objects usually fail if their sequence is changed, so combining two interesting plays is unlikely to produce an interesting new play. AFL instruments the code it is fuzzing to identify when it has found a new path of execution. However, in an interpreter loop, almost all executions will pass through the same lines of source code, just with different data, making this technique ineffective.

3 ScAmPER

Usage. ScAmPER takes as input the database that defines a game. It uses a heuristic search to find sequences of commands that reach *novel* states. *Novel* states are those in which, for the first time during play, the player enters a room, triggers execution of a line of script (*action*), or sees a message. States where the conditions in the guard of an action take on a new permutation of truth values, thereby increasing MC/DC coverage, are also novel. The tool outputs the commands needed to reach these novel states and a visualisation of the search process. ScAmPER stops when it has explored an initial pre-defined number of states *and* has not recently encountered any novel states. It prints statistics showing what percentage of rooms, actions and messages it could reach, as well as MC/DC coverage.

Figure 1 shows a still from a visualisation, which is rendered using GraphViz's `dot` and animated using `gifsicle`. The main part of the image shows the game map, with rooms that have been reached filled in. The two grids show the IDs of

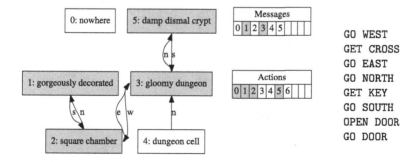

Fig. 1. Left: Still image from visualisation of Tutorial 4 of Scott Adams Compiler [14]. Right: A sample test input trace generated by ScAmPER to trigger action 4.

Game	Rooms reached	Messages shown	Actions reached	MC/DC	Time (s)	Mem (MB)
1	88 % / 34	80 % / 77	75 % / 170	76 %	209	431
2	77 % / 27	75 % / 90	66 % / 178	64 %	25	37
3	54 % / 24	65 % / 82	54 % / 162	64 %	18	32
4	92 % / 26	80 % / 100	83 % / 190	83 %	96	105
5	86 % / 23	89 % / 89	84 % / 220	78 %	39	51

Fig. 2. Benchmarks of ScAmPER on 5 SAGA games. For more benchmarks, see Fig. 5 in Appendix A.

the game's scripted actions and messages. Again, those that have been reached are filled in. Next to the still is an example of a sequence of input commands needed to trigger a scripted action.

Benchmarks. We tested ScAmPER on the first 5 original SAGA games [1]. Results are shown in Fig. 2. By various metrics, coverage is typically 60–90%. Timings are for an Intel Core i7-7500U at 2.70 GHz with 16 GB of RAM.

Architecture. Figure 3 shows the architecture of ScAmPER. In order to ensure that it accurately models the behaviour of a game, it makes heavy use of the existing ScottFree interpreter [2]. The first component of ScAmPER is a modified version of the interpreter that, rather than running a game, loads its database, then dumps it as a series of variable definitions in a C header file. The second component, which actually performs the search, links against a modified version of the interpreter that includes the header file, effectively hard-coding the game's database.

The second modified version of the interpreter is heavily optimised for use in the search. All startup code and any code handling message display has been removed. Code to get user input and parse it has also been removed. Instead, a

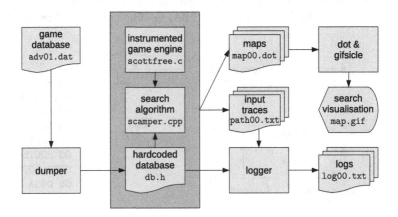

Fig. 3. The architecture of ScAmPER.

"next state" function has been added that takes as arguments the game state and the numeric IDs of a verb and a noun; these are passed directly to the code that evaluates the user's commands. In order to support this, the game's mutable data has been separated from its immutable data and bundled in a single, fixed-size C struct. As the game's database is hard-coded, variables referring to the sizes of arrays of rooms, items and so on have been replaced with defined constants, enabling more optimisation by the compiler.

Search Algorithm. Before the search starts, the tool uses a simple static analysis to determine all possible commands accepted by the game. A few commands are hard-coded into the game engine. These are navigation commands ("GO X", for any direction X) and commands to pick up or drop an item ("GET X" or "DROP X", for any movable item X). The possible directions are hardcoded into the game engine and the movable items are marked with a flag in the game database, so these are easy to determine. All other valid commands are handled by scripted actions. These are also easy to determine, as the verb/noun combination that triggers an action must be stored in a specific field in the game database.

The search algorithm itself is relatively straightforward. A game tree is initialised with a node containing the starting state of the game. On each iteration of the search, a state is picked (according to heuristics) to expand as follows. Firstly, a breadth-first search using navigation commands finds all rooms accessible using "GO X" only. From each of these rooms, the search tries: picking up or dropping any item ("GET X" or "DROP X"); and any combination of verb and noun that is listed as a trigger in the game's scripts. This is sufficient to solve a large number of in-game puzzles, many of which involve taking an item to a certain location and entering a specific command.

Rather than attempting to determine in advance whether these commands will be fruitful, ScAmPER simply tries them all, as that is likely to be faster. Most of the commands will fail with an error, for example if the command was "GO NORTH", but there was no exit to the north, or the command was "GET KEY", but the key was not in the player's current room. In order to detect this, the interpreter has been instrumented with a flag that is set when a command fails. If a command fails, the resulting state is discarded. Otherwise, it is added to the game tree. If the command triggered a previously unseen message or unexecuted line of script, this is recorded. Again, the interpreter is instrumented with flags to detect this. The goal of this expansion strategy is to find all currently accessible scripted actions, without wasting time moving back and forth aimlessly between locations in the game's map.

The interpreter is also instrumented to evaluate and record the value of all conditions in the guards of scripted actions after every move. This is necessary in order to determine MC/DC coverage, as if any condition in a guard is false, the subsequent conditions would not normally be evaluated.

Explored states are stored in a hash table for easy lookup. If a duplicate state is ever encountered, it is immediately discarded. This cuts out many pointless

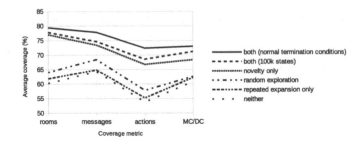

Fig. 4. Average coverage over first 5 SAGA games with different search heuristics.

sequences of commands, such as returning to the room from which the player just came, or dropping an object and immediately picking it up again.

A small number of scripted actions occur with random probability. For the sake of reproducibility, we decided to use a simplified random number generator and store its state as part of the game state. However, we ignore it when hashing states or comparing them for equality in order to avoid filling the game tree with many copies of the same state that differ only by random number generator state. Similarly, we also ignore the state of the counter that records how much longer a light source will last for. These simplifications aside, the search process is complete, in the sense that it will eventually explore all possible states of a game, although in practice this only happens within reasonable time/memory limits for extremely small examples.

ScAmPER uses two main heuristics to pick the node to expand. Firstly, novel states (as described above) are preferred. Secondly, new states encountered during expansion are themselves immediately expanded, as are those encountered during this second round of expansion; this ensures that paths from any state chosen for expansion are explored to a reasonable depth. The rationale is that games usually feature a number of dependent puzzles. Completion of one puzzle grants access to a new item or location, or sets a flag, which enables other puzzles to be completed. In order to complete the later puzzles (and execute their associated lines of script), the search must focus on states where the earlier puzzles have already been solved; these are more likely to be the novel states and deeper in the game tree.

We evaluated both heuristics on the first 5 SAGA games, stopping the search after 100,000 states had been explored. Our results are shown in Fig. 4. Both heuristics improved coverage, but novelty was far more significant. For comparison, we also evaluated a search strategy that randomly picks a state to explore and tries all available commands when it does so. This performed acceptably and was comparable to our expansion strategy without the novelty heuristic.

4   Related Work

Machine Learning for Playing Video Games. The successful application of machine learning to playing old Atari video games [10,11] has captured the interest of both researchers and the general public. There are several key differences in the problem we chose to tackle. Firstly, in many interactive fiction games, there is no equivalent of the player's score for assessing the success or progress. Secondly, we allow tools to access the internal state and code of the program we are analysing. Thirdly, the tree of game states has a higher degree of branching (as there are more possible actions at any point), but successful or interesting paths are shorter while potentially more intricate.

Narasimhan and others [12] investigated the use of deep learning to solve interactive fiction using only the text output of the game. Its success was limited in games without a score to guide play.

Model Checking for Solving Interactive Fiction Games. The idea of applying model-checking to interactive fiction was first investigated by Pickett, Verbrugge and Martineau [13]. They introduced the NFG (Narrative Flow Graph), a formalism based on Petri nets, and the higher-level PNFG (Programmable Narrative Flow Graph). They manually encoded some existing games as PNFGs, used a compiler to translate those into NFGs, then used the model-checker NuSMV to attempt to find solutions. They also discussed other properties of such games that one might check, such as the player being unable to reach a state in which the game had not been lost, yet was no longer winnable. Verbrugge and Zhang later addressed the problem of scalability using a heuristic search [15], which was able to solve several NFGs that were infeasibly large for NuSMV.

Our main criticisms of this work concern the choice to re-encode the games as PNFGs. Firstly, the manual translation of games into PNFGs might not be entirely accurate. Looking at the C code for the script interpreter in ScottFree, the behaviour of some scripted events is quite subtle, and it is likely that a manual translation would not capture all the details correctly. Secondly, it is often the case that expressing a problem in a different format makes it easier for automated tools to solve, as it reveals the high-level structure of the problem. If the translation is done manually, the translator may have introduced this structure, and it is not clear that it could be derived automatically.

Automated Test Case Generation. A key problem with automated test generation is generating tests that cover difficult-to-reach parts of a system, in particular when tests are generated randomly. Testar [16], a tool for automated generation of GUI test cases, addresses this using Q-learning. The tool identifies possible actions in a GUI application using its accessibility API. It runs the program being tested and uses instrumented versions of GUI libraries to gather information about the state of GUI widgets; it uses this to determine whether an action caused the application to enter a new state. Q-learning is used to tune the frequency with which different GUI actions are taken in order to maximise the chances of reaching a new state. In contrast, as ScAmPER has access to the internal state of the game and is not limited to constructing whole paths of execution, tuning the frequency with which different actions are taken is less important. All actions from a state of interest can be taken with ease. Nonetheless, this approach could lead to better heuristics for choosing which state to expand.

Fuchs presents a tool [5] for generating test cases for Web applications written in Java. These applications provide a user interface to a database, which is built by combining and customising ready-made components. In that regard, they are somewhat similar to SAGA games. The tool constructs tests using simulated interactions with the application, making use of the compiled application code. Their tool is augmented with a symbolic execution engine.

Julliand and others [8] consider test generation for abstracted event systems. Their approach, called concrete exploration, is based on models written in B, but applicable to other settings. The games we consider could be viewed as event systems, with the obvious abstraction being to group concrete game states in which the player is in the same room; the scripted actions in a game would correspond to guarded actions in the event system. Their work proposes a strategy for covering the abstract transitions of a system by trying to extend existing concrete paths to cover new abstract transitions.

5   Future Work and Conclusions

Despite their relative simplicity, SAGA games were extremely popular and ported to at least 10 different home computer systems. After source code for two games and their interpreter were published in magazines in 1980, the style of the interpreter was copied by other developers. This led to the creation of game authoring packages such as The Quill and Graphic Adventure Creator. Combined, over 500 games were published using these packages. We are highly confident that our techniques are applicable to these engines too, but we leave that for future work. We suspect that adapting our work to more complex and dynamic game engines, such as Infocom's Z-Machine, would prove much more difficult.

Old computer and video games present an appealing challenge for program analysis and automated verification, with relevance to current problems, such as GUI test case generation. Explicit state methods have proven to be successful in model-checkers such as SPIN [7] and FDR [6]. ScAmPER shows once again that explicit state methods can beat symbolic methods when the "next state" function of a system is complex, but can be evaluated cheaply.

One blind spot of ScAmPER is that it only finds when an action can be executed; it never proves that it cannot. Our tool could be improved with better heuristics, by using techniques from model-checking such as CEGAR, or by using symbolic execution to gather constraints and help to guide the search. But we are more interested in how to encode the problem so that it can be handled better by existing tools, or in finding improvements for those tools.

Off-the-shelf verification tools cannot yet handle games from 40 years ago without help, and even then they struggle. ScAmPER shows that a custom tool can tackle these examples. It is unsurprising that a specialised tool should outperform a generic tool on a particular problem. However, it is not clear whether a clever generic tool or a stupid specialised tool, such as ours, is likely to perform better. Our work provides one datapoint to suggest that, for the moment, a stupid specialised tool is better. We hope that it will motivate future developments in verification tools and that its performance on SAGA games will provide a benchmark for others to beat.

A   Scott Adams Grand Adventures

In an interactive fiction game, the computer displays a textual description of the player's location. The player types a command, such as "GO NORTH", "GET KEY" or "OPEN DOOR". The computer parses the command, evaluates its effect on the game world, and displays a textual description of any outcomes. The process repeats until the player wins (for example, by defeating a monster or finding a treasure) or loses (often by dying).

The most popular of the generic interactive fiction interpreters was Infocom's Z-Machine. However, its flexibility, which allows games to include their own customised command parsers, makes it a difficult target for automated analysis. Instead, we decided to tackle an earlier and simpler format, namely Scott Adams Grand Adventures (SAGA) and the corresponding open-source interpreter ScotFree [2]. This format supports only very limited scripting, which makes the behaviour of the games far less dynamic.

Games consist of a fixed number of rooms and objects (usually 20–40 each). Commands consist of one or two words (a verb and a noun), which are taken from a fixed list. The player can move between rooms and pick up and drop objects; this is hard-coded into the engine. A limited scripting system allows the behaviour of each game to be customised. Scripts allow the player to trigger special events by entering certain rooms or typing certain commands, provided a guard consisting of a conjunction (AND) of conditions is satisfied. Examples of conditions that can be checked include the location of a certain object or the value of a finite number of flags and bounded counters. Examples of events include moving objects, moving the player, displaying messages and adjusting the values of flags and counters (Fig. 5).

Figure 6 shows pseudocode illustrating the structure of the game engine and some possible scripted events. Despite the relatively simple structure of the

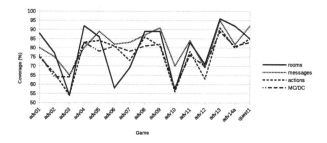

Fig. 5. Coverage achieved by ScAmPER with different metrics on SAGA games.

```
// Game engine
while (not game_over) {
    print(current_room.description());
    execute_automatic_scripts();
    (verb, noun) = parse_player_input();
    if (scripted_action(verb, noun)) {
        execute_scripted_action(verb, noun);
    }
    else if (verb == "go") {
        current_room = current_room.exit[noun];
    }
    else if (verb == "get" and items[noun].location == current_room) {
        items[noun].location = carried;
    }
    else if (verb == "drop" and items[noun].location == carried) {
        items[noun].location = current_room;
    }
}

// Example scripted actions
// Action 0:
if (verb == "score") {
    print_score();
}
// Action 1:
else if (verb == "inventory") {
    print_inventory();
}
// Action 2:
else if (verb == "open" and noun == "door" and items["locked door"].location == current_room and
    items["key"].location != carried and items["key"].location != current_room) {
    print("It's locked.");
// Action 3:
else if (verb == "open" and noun == "door" and items["locked door"].location == current_room) {
    swap(items["locked door"].location, items["open door"].location);
}
// Action 4:
else if (verb == "go" and noun == "door" and items["open door"].location == current_room) {
    current_room = rooms["cell"];
}

// Example automatic scripts
// Action 5:
if (items["vampire"].location == current_room and items["cross"].location != carried) {
    print("Vampire bites me! I'm dead!");
    exit();
}
// Action 6:
if (items["vampire"].location == current_room and items["cross"].location == carried) {
    print("Vampire cowers away from the cross!");
}
```

Fig. 6. Pseudocode for the structure of the game engine and some scripted events. Scripted events are taken from Tutorial 4 of Mike Taylor's Scott Adams Compiler [14]. The functions invoked by actions 0 and 1, which display the player's score and inventory (list of items carried), are built into the game engine.

engine, the open source implementation ScottFree is around 1,500 lines of C, of which around 600 implement an interpreter for the scripting language. Scripts can check around 20 different kinds of condition and trigger around 40 different kinds of event. The state space of a game is finite but too large to enumerate. Its size is dominated by the potential for any movable object to be in any room, ranging from roughly 2^{40} combinations in adventure 11 to 2^{114} in adventure 9.

References

1. Adams, S.: Scott adams grand adventures. http://www.msadams.com/downloads. htm
2. Cox, A.: Scottfree interpreter. https://www.ifarchive.org/indexes/if-archiveXscott-adamsXinterpretersXscottfree.html
3. Dietsch, D., Jakobs, M.C.: Tap 2020 virtual machine, April 2020. https://doi.org/ 10.5281/zenodo.3751284
4. Dubois, C., Wolff, B. (eds.): TAP 2018. LNCS, vol. 10889. Springer, Cham (2018). https://doi.org/10.1007/978-3-319-92994-1
5. Fuchs, A.: Automated test case generation for Java EE based web applications. In: Dubois and Wolff [4], pp. 167–176. https://doi.org/10.1007/978-3-319-92994-1_10
6. Gibson-Robinson, T., Armstrong, P., Boulgakov, A., Roscoe, A.W.: FDR3—a modern refinement checker for CSP. In: Ábrahám, E., Havelund, K. (eds.) TACAS 2014. LNCS, vol. 8413, pp. 187–201. Springer, Heidelberg (2014). https://doi.org/ 10.1007/978-3-642-54862-8_13
7. Holzmann, G.J.: The SPIN Model Checker - Primer and Reference Manual. Addison-Wesley, Boston (2004)
8. Julliand, J., Kouchnarenko, O., Masson, P., Voiron, G.: Under-approximation generation driven by relevance predicates and variants. In: Dubois and Wolff [4], pp. 63–82. https://doi.org/10.1007/978-3-319-92994-1_4
9. Lester, M.M.: ScAmPER: Scott Adams exPlicitly Evaluating Reachability, March 2020. https://doi.org/10.5281/zenodo.3724977
10. Mnih, V., et al.: Playing atari with deep reinforcement learning. CoRR abs/1312.5602 (2013). http://arxiv.org/abs/1312.5602
11. Mnih, V., et al.: Human-level control through deep reinforcement learning. Nature **518**(7540), 529 (2015)
12. Narasimhan, K., Kulkarni, T.D., Barzilay, R.: Language understanding for text-based games using deep reinforcement learning. In: Proceedings of the 2015 Conference on Empirical Methods in Natural Language Processing, EMNLP 2015, Lisbon, Portugal, 17–21 September 2015, pp. 1–11 (2015). http://aclweb.org/anthology/ D/D15/D15-1001.pdf
13. Pickett, C.J., Verbrugge, C., Martineau, F.: NFG: a language and runtime system for structured computer narratives. In: Proceedings of the 1st Annual North American Game-On Conference (GameOn'NA 2005), pp. 23–32 (2005)
14. Taylor, M.: Scott adams compiler (sac). http://www.miketaylor.org.uk/tech/ advent/sac/
15. Verbrugge, C., Zhang, P.: Analyzing computer game narratives. In: Yang, H.S., Malaka, R., Hoshino, J., Han, J.H. (eds.) ICEC 2010. LNCS, vol. 6243, pp. 224–231. Springer, Heidelberg (2010). https://doi.org/10.1007/978-3-642-15399-0_21
16. Vos, T.E.J., Kruse, P.M., Condori-Fernández, N., Bauersfeld, S., Wegener, J.: TESTAR: tool support for test automation at the user interface level. IJISMD **6**(3), 46–83 (2015). https://doi.org/10.4018/IJISMD.2015070103

Author Index